HARD QUESTIONS

HARD QUESTIONS

Facing the Problems of Life

John Kekes

OXFORD
UNIVERSITY PRESS

OXFORD
UNIVERSITY PRESS

Oxford University Press is a department of the University of Oxford. It furthers
the University's objective of excellence in research, scholarship, and education
by publishing worldwide. Oxford is a registered trade mark of Oxford University
Press in the UK and certain other countries.

Published in the United States of America by Oxford University Press
198 Madison Avenue, New York, NY 10016, United States of America.

Library of Congress Cataloging-in-Publication Data
Names: Kekes, John, author.
Title: Hard questions : facing the problems of life / John Kekes.
Description: New York, NY : Oxford University Press, [2019] |
Includes bibliographical references and index.
Identifiers: LCCN 2018026322 (print) | LCCN 2018040088 (ebook) |
ISBN 9780190919993 (updf) | ISBN 9780190920005 (epub) |
ISBN 9780190920012 (online content) | ISBN 9780190919986 (cloth : alk. paper)
Subjects: LCSH: Conduct of life. | Life.
Classification: LCC BJ1521 (ebook) | LCC BJ1521 .K38 2019 (print) |
DDC 170—dc23
LC record available at https://lccn.loc.gov/2018026322

1 3 5 7 9 8 6 4 2

Printed by LSC Communications, United States of America

for J.Y.K.

CONTENTS

ACKNOWLEDGMENTS

I gratefully acknowledge the comments and suggestions of two anonymous readers commissioned by Oxford University Press. Lucy Randall and Hannah Doyle, both editors at Oxford, were exceptionally helpful in making the manuscript into a book. I am grateful for their good advice, efficiency, and ready availability during the process of transforming the manuscript into a book, and for their understanding and sympathy for the aim of this book to reach reflective people who are interested in the hard questions I discuss.

Ann Hartle, Paul Hollander, Jean Kekes, and Leo Zaibert have read and helpfully commented on chapters of the book. The book is the better for it. They took time away from their own work to help me do mine. I am grateful for their help.

In each chapter of the book I draw on anthropological, historical, or literary works that reconstruct the struggles of people with the hard questions I discuss. I acknowledge these works at the appropriate places. But I express here my appreciation for the wonderful imaginative work done by the authors who made vivid how people very from different us, who lived in contexts very different from ours, faced the hard questions we also face. We can learn from their experiments in living how we can conduct our own experiments better as we face the hard questions in our context. It is for this that we should be grateful to them.

I dedicate this book to my wife, Jean Y. Kekes, in gratitude for everything in years past, present, and with luck, in years to come.

A NOTE TO THE READER

The hard questions I discuss in this book are connected, in one way or another, with how we have reason to live now in our present conditions. The questions are hard because they arise from our nature and conditions. If we struggle with giving reasonable answers to them, we realize that we have to make difficult choices between conflicting possibilities we have reason to value. This book is intended as a contribution to a deeper understanding of the hard questions and of the reasons for and against possible answers to them. Such understanding is a matter of interest to all of us who stand back from time to time and reflect on the hard questions we face, the difficult choices we have to make, and the answers we give.

This kind of reflection is philosophical. I have deliberately chosen, for better or worse, not to write a book about other books, and certainly not about specialist journal articles. I have of course read and learned from the works of others, but I have decided not to engage in detailed discussions of what is called "the literature." I have done so in other books. In this one, the discussion ranges far beyond the usual philosophical approach to hard questions. In each chapter, I compare and examine the reasons for and against answers to hard questions drawn from anthropology, history, and literature.

I have tried to make what I have to say of interest both to philosophers and to reflective non-specialist readers, including advanced students. I do my best to write plainly, avoid technicalities, and address the questions directly. But, as philosophers have always done, I am centrally concerned with giving reasons for the answers I give. I hope that it is possible to write in a way that bridges the increasingly deeper gap between technical philosophy and reflective non-philosophers.

Chapter 1

Introduction

THE HARD QUESTIONS

The hard questions I discuss are:

Is there an absolute value that overrides all other considerations?
Must we conform?
Do we owe what our country asks of us?
Must justice be done at all costs?
How should we respond to evil?
Should we forgive wrong actions?
Does shame make life better or worse?
Is it always good to be true to who we are?
Do good intentions justify bad actions?
Are moral values the highest of all values?

Each chapter focuses on one of these questions. It considers why the question is hard, why reasonable answers to it vary with personal and social circumstances, why the answers routinely conflict, and why the balance of reasons in a particular context nevertheless favors a particular answer.

There are reasonable answers to these hard questions, but they are particular and vary from context to context. They depend on the experiences that have formed us; on our often conflicting beliefs, emotions, and desires; and on the varied and changing personal and social circumstances in the context in which we face the questions and seek the answers. These are some of the reasons why reasonable answers to the hard questions cannot be general.

Another reason is that our evaluations of possible answers also conflict in a particularly acute way. We evaluate the conflicting possibilities from the point of view of how we rightly or wrongly think we should live. The conflicts between such evaluations go deep because we regard each as important for living as we think we should. But they conflict, and we are forced to choose between them. Whichever we choose, we forgo the ones we did not choose. Yet those are also important for living as we think we should. Answering a hard question therefore involves giving up something that is important to us. And that is hard to do.

The "we" who face the hard questions can be understood in either an impersonal or a personal sense. In the impersonal one, "we" refers to all human beings, as in we must breathe. But not all of us face all the hard questions, and even the particular ones we do face differ greatly in details and circumstances. In the personal sense, "we" are those who face a particular hard question in particular circumstances. In the rest of the book I will always use "we" in the personal sense and consider hard questions as they arise for us personally in our particular circumstances, not as general problems.

PERSONAL ATTITUDES AND THE EVALUATIVE FRAMEWORK

When we struggle to find reasonable answers to hard questions, we are guided by a more or less conscious and articulate personal attitude to how we think we should live. This attitude is formed of our beliefs, emotions, and desires. But our beliefs may be based on prejudice, ignorance, or childhood fairy tales; emotions are often excessive, deficient, or misdirected; and desires are not just natural and life-enhancing motives for action but also an unruly jumble of unrealistic, incompatible, and foolish drives. It is not easy to avoid such mistakes because ultimately we can rely only on our other, possibly also mistaken beliefs, emotions, and desires—since we can rely on nothing else. This remains so even if we follow the example or advice of others, because our decision to follow someone's example or accept someone's advice also depends on our possibly mistaken beliefs, emotions, and desires.

It adds to our uncertainty that our beliefs, emotions, and desires may not only be mistaken but also conflicting, as we all know from personal experience. We may believe one thing and feel and desire another. We may be proud, jealous, envious, or compassionate and yet suspect that our emotions are unreliable guides to making important and difficult decisions. And we often desire to have or do something and yet feel ashamed or guilty about it, or we believe that it would be dangerous to act on it. The beliefs, emotions, and desires that make our personal attitude what it is often conflict. And when they do, we do not know which we should act on.

Another reason why it is difficult to find reasonable answers to hard questions is that even if, unlikely as that is, our beliefs, emotions, and desires neither conflict nor are mistaken, and we can rely on them for reasonable answers to hard questions, nevertheless they are reasonable only in a particular context at a particular time. They cannot be generalized to other contexts, persons, and times, because they change, and, if we are reasonable, our personal attitude should change in response to them. Even if at one time we are clear about what the reasonable answers to hard questions are, as time passes we have new experiences, grow in breadth and depth of understanding, become more thoughtful, acquire new preferences, reflect on our successes and failures, and change, abandon, or reevaluate the importance we attribute to the beliefs, emotions, and desires that have led us earlier to respond to hard questions as we have done.

Our personal attitude to career, children, comfort, death, friendship, illness, marriage, money, responsibility, security, sex, and work tend to change with the passage of time. We are often ambivalent, confused, indecisive, unconfident, and tempted by the attractions of conflicting answers, reasons, and actions. We need some way of overcoming these uncertainties and to go beyond the often debilitating inward search for a way of reaching clarity. And that makes it natural for us to turn from the personal toward the various moral, political, religious, and other evaluations readily available, indeed pressing on us, in the social context in which we live.

The various customary evaluations of the possibilities of life form the evaluative framework in a particular context at a particular time. Some of the evaluations are aesthetic, economic, legal, medical, moral, personal, political, and religious, but there are also others. I will concentrate only on moral, personal, political, and religious evaluations.

Just as our beliefs, emotions, and desires may conflict and be mistaken, so may be the prevailing evaluations. They may be dogmatic, impoverished, or unrealistic. They may fail to take into account relevant facts of history, psychology, or technology be overly optimistic or pessimistic; permeated by sentimentalism, cynicism, or nostalgia for a past that has never existed; aim at anachronistic or Utopian ideals or at the lowest common denominator that discourages those who aim higher. And each evaluation is routinely criticized for neglecting the others.

The result is that both our often conflicting and mistaken personal attitudes and the particular evaluations of our evaluative framework may motivate us to act in conflicting ways. And that adds to our uncertainty. We depend on our beliefs, emotions, and desires to decide which of the particular moral, personal, political, and religious evaluations in our context we should follow. And, reciprocally, we depend on these evaluations to evaluate our beliefs, emotions, and desires. We try in this way to correct the mistakes and resolve the conflicts between our beliefs, emotions, and desires, on the one hand, and between the prevailing moral, personal, political, and religious evaluations, on the other.

I am not suggesting that we are all incapacitated by mistakes and conflicts. Most of us live the life we have as well as we can, but some do it well and others not so well. All in all, however, most of us are more or less dissatisfied with our life, as we think about it from time to time. We usually know better than others that our life could be better than it is, even if we do not know how to make it better. We do not know it because we are uncertain both about the reliability of our beliefs, emotions, and desires that form our personal attitude and about the moral, personal, political, and religious evaluations of the prevailing evaluative framework in our context.

CONFLICTS

The sources of our uncertainties are these conflicting evaluations of what we rightly or wrongly take to be the available possibilities of how we might live. When we face hard questions, we are compelled to evaluate these conflicting possibilities from the point of view of whether they aid or hinder us in living as we think we should. Such conflicts are within us. We are conflicted about how we should think we should live.

One response to such conflicts is to live with them. Many of us do this. Our evaluations are episodic, not parts of a lifelong policy. We may just evaluate as well as we can what seems best to us in the circumstances in which we find ourselves. This is a possible way of living in view of the constant and unpredictable changes in the prevailing conditions, in our varied and growing experiences, in the more important encounters we have with others, and in our overall evaluations of how well or badly we think our life is unfolding.

There is much to be said both for and against this way of living. In the chapters that follow, I will again and again return to its advantages and disadvantages. Here I mention only that one reason for it is its flexibility in responding to changing circumstances. And one reason against it is that those who follow it have no firm personal attitude to how they should live. They list as the wind blows, their lives have no clear direction, and they have no steady guide to how they should respond to their conflicts. For the moment, I leave it at that.

However we evaluate the reasons for and against living this way, the usual reaction to these conflicts is to regard them as obstacles that have to be overcome in one way or another. This is not my view. I think that the conflicts are not just obstacles but also catalysts that prompt us to seek greater clarity than we have about what is more and what is less important for us in our life. And that in turn may lead us to examine more closely the beliefs, emotions, and desires we have formed in the course of life. If we want to avoid misdirecting our life, it is important to become critical of our beliefs, emotions, desires, reasons, and evaluations, and to think again and perhaps better about how we should live. If the hard questions and the conflicts lead us to do that, then we should welcome them. They are like alarm clocks that wake us up from a slumber into which we lull ourselves to escape from the difficult business of living.

I do not think that the unexamined life is not worth living. Letting sleeping dogs lie may be reasonable. A close scrutiny of our inner life may reveal aspects of it that would be dangerous to dwell on. And it is offensive to suppose that the unexamined lives of unreflective people who are wholeheartedly engaged in worthwhile activities may not be eminently worth living. Socrates's ill-advised words have become an overused cliché.

My view is rather that if we are dissatisfied with our life, we can try to make it better by thinking about the causes of our dissatisfactions. If we do that, we may find that we are dissatisfied because we face hard questions and are uncertain about how we should resolve conflicts between our evaluations of the possible answers. And then we may realize that however we resolve the conflicts we lose something we value and do not want to lose. If we are led by the hard questions and conflicts to think about the sources of our dissatisfaction, then, contrary to initial impressions, it is good to face the questions and to have the conflicts.

THE APPROACH

The approach of the book is distinctive, at once practical, context-dependent, comparative, and markedly different from other contemporary works. It is *practical* because it is concerned with what we personally should do as we face hard questions. It does not aim to construct a universally applicable theory about what any reasonable person should do. It is *context-dependent* because what we should do to answer a hard questions depends on our personal and social circumstances. Reasonable answers are particular ones that particular persons can reasonably arrive at in particular contexts. The approach is also *comparative* because it is concerned with understanding and learning from the good or bad reasons that have led others in very different contexts to give their answers to the same hard questions we face. The comparisons are drawn from anthropology, history, and literature. By critical examination of the reasons that have rightly or wrongly guided others in other contexts, we can improve the reasons that guide us in our efforts to formulate reasonable answers to the hard questions we face. The chapters that follow aim to show how this can be done.

The distinction between theoretical and practical approaches is central to the aims of the book. The theoretical approach aims to understand the nature of the world. The practical approach aims to evaluate how we should live. The two approaches are connected because we live in the world, and we have to have some understanding of it to evaluate reasonably how we should live in it. But the two approaches also differ. The theoretical approach aims to understand the nature of the world independently of how it affects us. The practical approach aims to evaluate the relevant facts from the point of view of how they affect us.

The contemporary theoretical approach has become hardly distinguishable from a synoptic view formed of the various sciences. It is characterized by the growth of knowledge, and it is one of the great human achievements. But it neither is nor meant to be evaluative. The practical approach of this book is essentially evaluative. It takes the form of moral, personal, political, religious, and other evaluations. The approach cuts across the customary disciplinary boundaries in order to compare and evaluate the reasons that have led others to answer the hard questions as they did with the reasons that may lead us in our efforts to find reasonable answers.

What is relevant to this approach depends on whether the evaluations in question help or hinder our efforts to live as we think we should. These evaluations form our personal attitude, but they need not be self-centered. They may be deeply concerned with other-directed moral, political, or religious considerations. If we are fortunate enough to live in a civilized society and are at least moderately intelligent, educated, and have escaped indoctrination, then we can decide what importance we attribute to the often-conflicting evaluations that have influenced us.

Although our evaluations presuppose descriptions of the relevant facts, they go far beyond them and consider whether they aid or hinder us in living as we think we should. We may be wrong to think that we should live in that particular way and wrong to suppose that some facts affect us favorably or unfavorably. How satisfied we are with our lives partly depends on whether our evaluations are reasonable. Even then, however, we may be dissatisfied because adverse circumstances may prevent us from living according to our reasonable evaluations.

The approach I follow involves accepting and welcoming the variety of conflicting moral, personal, political, religious, and other evaluations. Their conflicts make it difficult for us to know how we should respond to a hard question we face. The hardness of the questions, the frequency of conflicts, and the variety of evaluations are, then, inseparable. Part of the reason why hard questions are hard and conflicts frequent follows from the variety of evaluations.

One implication of this approach is the rejection of the assumption that there is an absolute value that should always override any other value that conflicts with it. This assumption has been held by all those who think that there is a highest value—for instance duty, equality, happiness, human rights, justice, liberty, and so on—that overrides whatever value conflicts with it; or who think that there is a supreme principle—the Golden Rule, the categorical imperative, the common good, God's law, and the like.

I do not think that an absolute value has been found, although many have been proposed throughout the millennia. I cannot prove that it could not be found in the future. What I can and will do is to show that there often are strong reasons that favor giving priority to some evaluation that conflicts with whatever is supposed to be required by a putative highest value or supreme principle. Of course I do not deny that in some circumstances a moral, personal, political, or religious evaluation should override conflicting evaluations.

What I deny is that there is any value conformity to which is *always* in *all* conflicts *the* absolute requirement of reason. In the chapters that follow, I will again and again return to the various forms in which the conflict between my approach and the search for an absolute value recurs.

The futility of the search for an absolute value follows from the variety of conflicting evaluations. The reasonable answers we might give to hard questions unavoidably depend on the context and the person for whom a hard question arises. Is it in a time of war or peace? in a stable society or one in turmoil? in the midst of prosperity or scarcity? in democracy or dictatorship? is it motivated by a reasonable personal attitude? is the person facing the question a man or a woman, young or old, healthy or ill, rich or poor, happy or unhappy? There are always answers, some more and others less reasonable. But all reasonable answers must take into account the concrete details of the particular circumstances that vary with contexts and persons. Of course, this also needs to be shown, not just asserted as I do here. I will do my best to show it by means of comparisons between those who face particular hard questions in particular circumstances.

COMPARISONS

I now come to a crucial feature of this approach. It involves the comparison between two people drawn from quite different anthropological, historical, or literary contexts. They faced the same hard question but answered it differently. Both had and considered reasons for and against the answer they gave, so neither was unreasonable, even though he or she may have been mistaken. In each of the following chapters, I show that their answers were different because they had different reasons for them, or because they evaluated the same reasons differently. On the basis of comparisons between the reasons they had and the evaluations they made, or the ones they could or should have had or made, I conclude that their reasons and evaluations were different because they were particular, context-dependent, and varied with their social and personal circumstances. And I conclude as well that the same is true of us in our context as we face and struggle with answering the same hard question as they did.

One crucial implication of these comparisons is that in trying to answer hard questions we have no need of an absolute value that holds whatever the personal and social circumstances are because our reasons and evaluations are particular and context dependent. But if we do without an absolute value, we are not doomed to giving arbitrary answers to hard questions. Better and worse reasons for and against conflicting answers can be and often are given, and the evaluations of reasons can also be more or less reasonable.

I take this to show that the search for an absolute value that determines what reasons are good or bad is misguided. Nor is there a reason to assume that answers to hard questions are ultimately arbitrary. There is an alternative, and in each of the following chapters I try to show by way of comparisons what the reasonable answer is to the hard question considered in that chapter.

The case-based approach, although not the one that involves comparisons, is a familiar feature of the jurisprudence of common law, and of some law and business schools that prepare future judges, lawyers, and executives for reasonable decision making. Their approach is to start with understanding the complexities of the case at hand, rather than trying to impose on it a preexisting rule, principle, or theory. They regard cases as primary, and stress that reasonable decision making can come only after the particular and context-dependent complexities of the case have been understood. In this respect, I strongly agree with this approach, but the comparative approach I follow goes beyond it in two ways.

One is that the simple case-based approach is not comparative. The other is that in simple case-based approaches the reasons and evaluations that are thought to be relevant are drawn from the context of contemporary prosperous, democratic Western societies. And that leaves unexamined and unanswered the crucial question of whether the supposedly relevant reasons and evaluations are reliable. The simple case-based approach takes for granted a shared agreement about the reasons and evaluations, but comparative approach does not. The latter is essentially concerned with probing the reliability of the reasons and evaluations on the basis of which people in the compared cases answered the hard questions they faced.

I stress that the comparative approach in the following chapters is much more than a source of examples. It shows how answers to hard questions and reasons for and against them can be reasonably evaluated. It shows as well that reasonable evaluations must be context-dependent and particular. The people in these cases were sometimes unaware of all the relevant reasons, nor did they examine all the evaluations they should have. From understanding how well or badly they answered the hard questions in their context we can learn how we can be more reasonable in the answers we give to the same hard questions in our context.

The comparative approach aims to show that although we and others live in very different circumstances, we share the human condition in which we must face hard questions. We are often motivated by conflicting reasons and evaluations because the contexts in which we live, the personal attitudes and the possibilities we have, and the evaluative framework of our society are very different.

Another aim of the comparative approach is to show how wide the range of the variety of evaluations is, of the ways of answering hard questions, and of possible responses to conflicts in the very different contexts and circumstances in which human lives are lived. This helps us understand what made the compared people's reasons good or bad, and better or worse. By understanding them, we may learn to enlarge our view of the possibilities of life and thereby overcome the insularity of how we think about the great variety of the reasons and evaluations that guide how we might live.

I hope that readers will find the unfamiliar evaluations discussed in the following chapters intrinsically interesting, regardless of whether they agree with what I say about them. I have found them fascinating and was endlessly provoked to think about them. They show how others at other times and places—but like us in being thinking, feeling, desiring fellow humans—have struggled with the same hard questions as we do. They have conducted their own experiments in living, as we do ours. However different we are, we are alike in sharing the human predicament of having to face and find reasonable answers to the hard questions.

The hard questions I consider in the following chapters are connected, in one way or another, with how we have reason to live in our present circumstances. Discussing them is not an academic exercise, but a matter of interest to all of us who do not just try to live as well as we can in the circumstances in which we find ourselves, but also to stand back from time to time, think about the reasons and evaluations that guide how we think we should live and about the hard questions we face and the answers we might give to them. By means of such reflection, we may arrive at a deeper understanding of the hardness of the questions and the difficulty of the conflicts we face. If the comparative approach enables us to do that, it has proven its importance.

THE BOOK

This book is not about other books and certainly not about journal articles. It is not a historical account of what others have written about the hard questions. It is an attempt to think about the important questions of everyday life. It does not offer universal answers that reason requires everyone to accept and follow. It is a direct and concrete attempt to answer the hard questions we personally face, given the particular individuals we are, as we live in the context of our segment of contemporary Western societies. The book is essentially concerned with finding reasonable answers to the hard questions and with explaining why the answers I propose are more reasonable than alternatives to them.

The conviction that has motivated me in writing the kind of book this is has been expressed by William James:[1]

> if he be a true philosopher he must see that there is nothing final in any given equilibrium of human ideals, but that, as our present laws and customs have fought and conquered other past ones, so they will in their turn be overthrown. . . . . And although a man always risks much when he breaks away from established rules . . . yet the philosopher must allow that it is at all times open to anyone to make an experiment, provided he fear not to stake his life and character upon the throw. . . . Pent upon any system of moral rules are innumerable persons whom it weighs upon, and goods which it represses. . . . These experiments are to be judged not a priori, but by actually finding, after the fact of their making. . . . what can any superficial theorist's judgment be worth in a world where every one of hundreds of ideals has its special champion.

---

1. William James, "The Moral Philosopher and the Moral Life" in *William James: Writings 1878–1899*, ed. Bruce Kuklick (New York: Library of America, 1891/1992), 611–612.

Is There an Absolute Value that Overrides All Other Considerations?

THE QUESTION

Values are one thing, evaluations another. Beauty, courage, democracy, fame, friendship, health, kindness, power, wealth, and wisdom are rightly or wrongly thought to have value. Whether they really have it does not depend on our evaluations. Evaluations only express our favorable or unfavorable attitude toward values. If all goes well, values and our evaluations of them coincide. All, however, may not go well. What we take to be a value may not be and our evaluations may conflict or be based on self-deception, ignorance, lack of imagination, or excessive optimism or pessimism.

It is widely assumed by moral, political, and religious thinkers that there is an absolute value, although they disagree about what it is. If there were one, it would be the most important of all the values there are. We should be unconditionally committed to be guided by it because, if we were reasonable, which we are often not, we would not accept any consideration as sufficient for acting contrary to the absolute value. We could, of course, value many other things, but we could not reasonably value any of them more than the absolute value.

If, however, there were no absolute value, then all values would be conditional. That is, they would depend on the prevailing conditions, and if the conditions change, then the values would also change. Some values will be more important than others in some conditions, but no value would be always, everywhere, in all conditions more important than any other value.

The hard question I ask in this chapter is: Is there an absolute value? In other words, is there some value that reason requires everyone, always, everywhere, in all conditions to value more than any other value that may conflict with it?

ELEAZAR: OLD AND YOUNG

I begin with considering Eleazar, who thought that God's law was the absolute value. He evaluated everything on the basis of whether it conformed to or deviated from it. We read in the *Apocrypha*, 2 *Maccabees* 6 that

> Eleazar, one of the scribes in high position, a man now advanced in age and of noble presence, was being forced to open his mouth to eat swine's flesh. But he, welcoming death with honor rather than life with pollution went up to the rack of his own accord, spitting out the flesh, as men ought to go who have courage to refuse things that it is not right to taste, even for the natural love of life (18) .... [He said] By manfully giving up my life now, I will show myself worthy of my old age and leave to the young a noble example of how to die a good death willingly and nobly for the revered and holy laws (27).

He gave up his life rather than violate what he thought was God's law. But it was not just his life he gave up. He commanded his seven beloved sons to do likewise, and they did. Moreover, they all did so while accepting the most excruciating torture described in gruesome detail in the text. And they did this rather than break a dietary law of God.

If we think about the choice they had made, we may wonder whether there is anything we would choose to die for, even without torture, if we had to make the awful choice between it and life. If the answer is no, then we value human life, especially our own, more than anything else. If the answer is yes, then whatever it is would be what we think has greater or higher value than life. It may be a beloved person, a cause, honor, justice, a clear conscience, revenge, or our country. For Eleazar, it was God's law. He thought that it was the absolute value and it should override all other values that may conflict with it, including human life.

Many of us in effect agree with Eleazar, if not about God's law, but about human life not having absolute value. We testify by our action that we deny it. This may be surprising since its absolute value is enshrined in many renowned documents, such as the Declaration of Independence, the Bill of Rights, and the UN Declaration of Human Rights. But much of what we do is contrary to these documents. There are recognized legal, moral, political, and religious justifications and excuses for taking a human life. Many millions are killed in wars. If soldiers, police officers, firefighters, bomb disposal experts, and others risk and lose their life in the line of duty, they are admired for what they did. We reject as absurd the belief that the life of terrorists, enemy soldiers, and mass murderers has absolute value.

We of course value life but only on certain terms, such as not being irreversibly comatose or suffering prolonged and excruciating pain. Heroes and martyrs are celebrated for giving up their lives for whatever they value more. Drug addiction, smoking, and alcohol in excess significantly shorten life, yet millions are addicts, smokers, and heavy drinkers. If the speed limit were lowered to say forty miles per hour, many lives would be saved, nonetheless the law would be scorned and unenforceable. Obesity, sunbathing, spelunking, boxing, unsecured rock climbing, mining, and construction work lead to the loss of many lives, yet they are permitted, sometimes even encouraged, and are part of the lives of countless people who know the dangers. Those who are involved in these practices show by what they do that they do not believe that human life has absolute value, regardless of what their sanctimonious rhetorical statements might claim. Of course, such people need not go so far as to agree with Eleazar that God's law, rather than human life, has absolute value. But they do value something more than human life, and whatever that may be has a better claim to being what they think of as the absolute value than life itself.

We may admire Eleazar for the fidelity of his actions to his evaluation, but we may also have doubts about it. Although Eleazar had reasons for his evaluation, there were also reasons against it. He and his sons accepted torture and death rather than swallow even a mouthful of pork. Yet the prohibition of it by God's law seems arbitrary. Millions of people eat pork and are none the worse for it. Perhaps in biblical times, in a warm climate and no refrigeration, trichinosis was a serious danger. The law against eating pork would then have been reasonable. But times have changed, and the law should also change. Moreover, Eleazar chose certain and very painful death, rather than the much more remote danger of being poisoned by ingesting a small amount of pork. If this is the reason why we think that his evaluation was mistaken, then we miss why Eleazar acted as he did.

The reason is that Eleazar's evaluation was motivated by his unconditional commitment to following God's law, not by wanting to avoid being poisoned by pork. It was psychologically impossible for him to question God's law because he thought that it was from it that all reasonable evaluations ultimately followed. It defined what was good and bad, permissible and prohibited, reasonable and unreasonable.

He could no more have found acting according to it unreasonable than he could have found that what he saw he did not see. Such ineluctable certainty is involved in making an unconditional commitment to an absolute value. Eleazar no doubt valued other things, including his and his sons' life, but all his other commitments were conditional on his unconditional commitment to what he regarded as the absolute value of following God's law.

This is a powerful line of thought, but there are reasons against it. One is that there is a difference between believing that God's law has absolute value and the truth of that belief. Eleazar was no doubt sincere in his belief, but sincerity is no guarantee of truth. Even a cursory reading, say, of *Leviticus* or *Deuteronomy* includes among God's laws detailed prescriptions of how, when, and which animals to sacrifice to assuage God's anger; how to treat slaves; which of the then familiar birds should and should not be eaten; to whom may loans be given and at what interest rate; which conquered people should be killed; and so on and on. God's law included hundreds of rules meant to guide the everyday life of a nomadic people in the Near East many thousands of years ago. Some of the laws may have been written in stone, but surely many others were not absolute but changeable. It is not easy to believe that part of the absolute value is killing everyone in a conquered city, sacrificing animals, keeping slaves, identifying edible birds, and setting interest rates.

Another reason for doubting that Eleazar's choice was reasonable and that God's law has absolute value is that there are and have been many different beliefs about what God's law is. Think of the lamentable history of religious wars waged by defenders and proselytizers of what they were convinced was the absolute value. The mere belief that a particular law of God is right is not a sufficient reason for preferring it to other ways of understanding God's law. And there are and have been many non-religious values that were supposed to be absolute.

Happiness, human rights, justice, liberty, pleasure, rationality, truth, and virtue, among others, have all been believed by thoughtful people to have absolute value. But only one of them could be the real thing, and then all the other beliefs about what the supposedly absolute value is would be mistaken. Even if there were an absolute value to which it is reasonable to be unconditionally committed, there would still be many beliefs about what the absolute value is and many unconditional commitments to other supposedly absolute moral, personal, political, or religious values. How could we tell which of them is the right one?

Consider finally a fifty-years-younger but also devout Eleazar who was forced to make the same choice as the old Eleazar. Suppose that he has been married only for a few years, had young children, was the sole support of his family, his aged parents relied on him in many ways, and, unlike the old Eleazar, he was not yet a renowned leader who set an example that his people followed, but merely one of the many faithful. He knew that eating pork violated God's law. But he also knew that the choice was forced on him by enemies of God's law, that his family depended on him, and that God would understand and excuse it if he swallowed a mouthful of pork and otherwise continued to live a God-fearing life. So he chose life rather than torture and death.

We can understand and perhaps even sympathize to some extent with the old Eleazar's evaluation. We can accept that he had reasons for it. But surely the young Eleazar also had reasons for the opposite evaluation. How could we decide which of these conflicting evaluations was reasonable? Do differences in age, social standing, and circumstances between the old and the young Eleazar make a difference to whether God's law is the absolute value that reason requires everyone, always, everywhere to follow? If we think that the differences make no difference to it, what reason do we have for it? If we think that they do make a difference, then God's law is conditional on these differences, and since an absolute value must be unconditional, God's law could not have absolute value.

Perhaps the old Eleazar's evaluation was mistaken. His unconditional commitment to it is not enough to make his evaluation reasonable. It is vitally important not to be mistaken if we make such a life-changing unconditional commitment. And I do not mean just the one Eleazar had made, but any unconditional commitment to any supposedly absolute value.

It matters a great deal to be able to evaluate the relative importance of the reasons for and against the choices Eleazar and his younger self might have made. It is not so much that it matters how we evaluate *them*, what matters is how we personally evaluate the relative importance of the values that guide how *we* personally think we should live. We also have to make choices, even if they are usually less difficult than theirs was, about whether we should be guided by an absolute value, whatever it may be, or whether all of our evaluations are conditional on who we are and in what context and circumstances we live. We have to make life-changing evaluations, for instance, about marriage, raising children, our moral, personal, political, religious, and other allegiances, about the importance we attribute to ambition, death, health, leisure, money, sex, work, and about how we should live given what we take to be our possibilities.

Surely, it makes a difference to the resulting evaluations whether we have to make them in time of domestic tranquility or in the midst of an emergency created by some natural disaster, epidemic, or war; in the context of a strict or permissive society; in a largely law-abiding or crime-ridden context; in a harmonious religious society or where sectarian strife rages; when there is a shared conventional morality or when the consensus is breaking down; whether the available resources are ample or scarce; and so on for a multitude of contingent circumstances.

The reasons I have considered for and against belief in the absolute value of human life are inconclusive and lead to further questions. We may believe, for instance, that happiness, justice, good will, human rights, or compassion has absolute value. Or that all values are conditional, and none is absolute. And we may believe it at one time in one context and then change our mind and believe something else. Does it merely depend on our evaluation whether human life has absolute value? Perhaps we recognize that there are reasons both for and against whatever our evaluation happens to be, but we find that the balance of reasons, or our opinion of their balance, shifts as we and our circumstances change. Are our evaluations about absolute value arbitrary? Are they based on reasons? How can we tell which reasons are good or bad, stronger or weaker, personal or impersonal?

We can tell, but only by going deeper and thinking about the assumptions on which these evaluations rest. The expanded form of the hard question this chapter is about is: given the persons we are, the context in which we live, and the reasons we have available, should we make an unconditional commitment to what we take to be the absolute value, be it human life or something else?

THE CASE FOR ABSOLUTE VALUE

Those who think that there is an absolute value and reason requires everyone to be unconditionally committed to live according to it recognize of course that many of us fail to do that. That is just the reason, they think, why so many of us are dissatisfied with our lives. We want our lives to be better, but if we get what we mistakenly think would make it better, we are soon disappointed and want something else. The result of our failure is that we doom ourselves to a life that is a ceaseless pursuit of satisfactions from birth to death. As Hobbes put it:

> there is no such *Finis ultimus* . . . nor *Summum Bonum* . . . as is spoken of in the Books of the old Morall Philosophers. Nor can a man any more live, whose Desires are at an end, than he, whose Senses and Imagination are at a stand. Felicity is the continuall progresse of the desire, from one object to another; the attaining of the former, being still but the way to the later. The cause whereof is, That the object of mans desire, in not to enjoy once onely, and for one instant of time; but to assure for ever, the way of his future desire (69–70).[2]

Others are unconditionally committed to what they take to be an absolute value, but they are mistaken about what it is, as we know from the lives of moral, political, and religious fanatics. They have caused and are causing immense harm to innocent people by pursuing what they mistakenly regard as the absolute value. And there are also others who are perhaps not mistaken, yet fail to live as they know they should because they are weak, inconsistent, thoughtless, fearful, or succumb to self-deception, fantasy, or depression.

Reasonable defenders of the right absolute value acknowledge how widespread these mistakes are but deny that they cast doubt either on the one and only genuine absolute value, or on the importance of unconditional commitment to it. The mistakes show that we may be motivated by false or inconsistent beliefs; excessive, deficient, or misdirected emotions; or destructive or unrealistic desires. But such mistakes are caused by our defects. They no more cast doubt on the absolute value than mistakes in addition cast doubt on arithmetic.

---

2. Thomas Hobbes, *Leviathan*, ed. Richard Tuck (Cambridge, UK: Cambridge University Press, 1651/1991), chapter 11.

The search for the absolute value has dominated Western moral, political, and religious thought from biblical times to the present. There have been deep disagreements about what the absolute value is and how it should be interpreted and followed. But those who searched for it have agreed about the basic assumption that the absolute value is there to be found, reason requires everyone to seek it, and the goodness of all of our lives depends on how closely we approximate it. Eleazar was unconditionally committed to this basic assumption, although we are not told enough about him to know whether he was aware of it.

Why should we accept this basic assumption? Because unless there were an absolute value, we would have no guide to how we should resolve conflicts between moral, personal, political, religious, and other evaluations. We would not know how to answer the hard questions we face, and we would be doomed to lifelong dissatisfaction. We need a clear guide in life to be able to give reasonable answers to hard questions and cope with conflicts between evaluations, and that is what the absolute value provides. A classic expression of it is Plato's:

> It's the reality of goodness . . . which everyone, whatever their temperament is after, and which is the goal of all their activities. They have an inkling of its existence, but they are confused about it and can't adequately grasp its nature.[3]

If we are not confused about it, we know that reason requires following it. As Kant, reiterating Plato's view, writes: his purpose is

> nothing more than the search for the establishment of the *supreme principle of morality* [in which] the highest and unconditional good alone can be found.[4]

---

3. Plato, *Republic*, trans. Robin Waterfield (Oxford: Oxford University Press, 1993), 505d–e.
4. Immanuel Kant, *Groundwork of the Metaphysics of Morals* in *Practical Philosophy*, trans. Mary J. Gregor (Cambridge: Cambridge University Press, 1785/1996), 47 and 56.

Mill agrees with Kant that supreme principle is needed:

> there must be some standard by which to determine the good-
> ness or badness, absolute and comparative, of ends, or objects of
> desire. And whatever that standard is, there can be but one: for
> if there were several ultimate principles of conduct, the same
> conduct might be approved by one of those principles and
> condemned by another; and there would be needed some more
> general principle, as umpire between them.[5]

Plato, Kant, Mill, and their many followers agree that reason requires
everyone to follow the principle that leads to the absolute value, although they disagree about what the absolute value is. Kant thought
that it was the good will:

> It is impossible to think of anything at all in the world ... that could
> be considered good without limitation except a *good will* (49) ... it
> is good in itself and ... is to be valued incomparably higher than all
> that could merely be brought about by it (50) ... [This] is a prac-
> tical law which commands itself absolutely ... the observance of
> this law is duty ... [the] practical unconditional necessity of action
> and it must therefore hold for all rational beings (76)[6]

According to Mill in *On Liberty*, the absolute value is utility, by which
he means general happiness:

> I regard utility as the ultimate appeal on all ethical questions; but
> it must be utility in the largest sense, grounded on the perma-
> nent interests of man as a progressive being (10)

5. John Stuart Mill, *A System of Logic* in *Collected Works of John Stuart Mill*, ed. J.M. Robson
(Indianapolis: Liberty Fund, 1843/2006), vol. 8, 951.
6. Immanuel Kant, *Groundwork of the Metaphysics of Morals* in *Practical Philosophy*, ed. Mary J.
Gregor (Cambridge, UK: Cambridge University Press, 1785/1999).

and in *Utilitarianism* he explains

> as between his own happiness and that of others, utilitarianism requires him to be as strictly impartial as a disinterested and benevolent spectator . . . so that not only he may be unable to conceive the possibility of happiness to himself, consistently with conduct opposed to the general good, but also that the impulse to promote the general good may be in every individual one of the habitual motives of action (218).[7]

There are, then, two questions that defenders of the absolute value need to answer. One is: what exactly is it? Is it good will, as Kant thought? Utility as Mill claimed? God's law, for which Eleazar gave up his life? Or, is it human rights, justice, love, pleasure, rationality, virtue, or something else? Only if it is known what has absolute value could reason require everyone, always, everywhere to be unconditionally committed to it.

The other question concerns the reason for accepting the assumption on which the search for an absolute value is based: Why should we think that there is an absolute value at all? Hobbes denied it, and so did many others who thought and continue to think that there are many values, some in some conditions are more important than others, but there is no absolute value. According to them, the question of whether we should be unconditionally committed to living according to a supposed absolute value does not arise because there is no absolute value. The search for it is like the alchemist's search was for the philosopher's stone that would turn everything into gold.

---

7. John Stuart Mill, *On Liberty* (Indianapolis: Hackett, 1859/1978) and *Utilitarianism* in *Collected Works of John Stuart Mill*, ed. John M. Robson and Jack Stillinger (Indianapolis: Liberty Fund, 1861/2006).

These two questions are connected. If the absolute value were identified, then the question of whether it exists would thereby have been answered. If, however, reasonable disagreements about what the absolute value is persist, as they have for millennia, then there are two possibilities. Either there is an absolute value, but we have not found it, or there is not, and that is why we have not found it. In either case, it is unreasonable to be unconditionally committed to living according to a supposedly absolute value whose identity is disputed and which may not even exist.

It should not be thought that disputes about whether there is an absolute value are philosophical abstractions far removed from how we actually live. We need to contend with such disputes because we often face conflicts between our own moral, personal, political, religious, and other evaluations, as we all know from daily life. If we try to find reasonable ways of resolving such conflicting evaluations, we quickly discover that we have to go deeper. We have to ask why we attribute the importance we do to the various evaluations to which we are or think we should be committed.

These conflicting evaluations lead to the hard questions I discuss in this book. It is difficult to evaluate reasonably the conflicting answers to them because the evaluation we might accept will be contrary to some of our other evaluations. We then have to ask ourselves which of these conflicting evaluations is more important to us and why we think that one of them is more important than any of the others. If we get this far, we have arrived at the question of whether there is an absolute value to which we should be unconditionally committed and on which our most important evaluations are based.

I am not supposing that such questioning is a description of how we actually face hard questions. We often have to make urgent choices about our conflicting values, conformity, civic duty, justice, responding to evil, forgiveness, shame, being true to ourselves, and the importance of intentions and morality. And these are the hard questions this book is about. We often do not have the luxury or the inclination for prolonged reflection and have many other things to do, like earning a living, raising our children, and so forth. I am suggesting that if we want to evaluate the possibilities open to us as reasonably as we can, then we will encounter ever deeper questions, until we reach the hard question of whether or not there is an absolute value that we do or should follow unconditionally. And then we will see that defenders and critics of the search for the absolute value give incompatible answers to it.

DOUBTS ABOUT ABSOLUTE VALUE

Disputes between defenders and critics of the search for the absolute value have been going on for thousands of years and show no sign of abating. At first, it was among religious thinkers who sharply disagreed about whether the absolute value was prescribed by one God rather than several, what exactly did it require or prohibit, if indeed it or they were the kind of entities that could have requirements. Subsequent thinkers were more philosophical and less explicitly religious, but their disputes continued on and on. In their accounts of the absolute value, moral, personal, and political evaluations played increasingly more significant roles than religious ones.

Eudaimonists, like Plato and Aristotle, had one view. Stoics and Epicureans had their own incompatible candidates. Augustine Christianized Plato's views. Natural law theorists, like Aquinas and his disciples, mingled Aristotelian thought with Christian theology. Muslim and Jewish thinkers gave their own accounts. Leibniz and Spinoza developed different metaphysical theories about it. Kant, Hegel, and the Utilitarians proposed their own sharply different versions. And then there were also the conflicting poetic visions of Homer, Virgil, Dante, and those of the great ancient Greek and

Roman tragedians, and there were also numerous Greek, Viking, African, and American Indian myths.

Embedded in each was a view of an absolute value. Only one of these views could be right, although all could be wrong. Yet no way has been found of making reasonable decisions about which of these views, if any, is the right one that reason requires everyone to follow. It is not implausible to suppose in the light of these unending arguments that the absolute value has not been found because there are many conflicting values and none is absolute.

Doubts strengthen when we realize that even if those who agree about what the absolute value is, disagree about its interpretation. Jews are split into orthodox, conservative, and reform sects; Muslims are divided into Sunnis and Shiites; Christians are split into Catholic, Anglican, Lutheran, Calvinist, and various low church Protestant sects; and then there are Quakers, Mormons, Rosicrucians, and so on, all agreeing that God's law is the absolute value. Kantians disagree about which of the five versions of the categorical imperative is the right interpretation of the absolute value. Utilitarians are split between Bentham, Mill, Sidgwick, and their various followers. And other consequentialists are divided about whether the absolute value is to be arrived at by means of an ideal theory, cost benefit analysis, or rational choice theory.

If we consider these passionately held but disputed interpretations to which their defenders claim we should be unconditionally committed, we may be willing to take to heart Isaiah Berlin's denial

> that all men have one true purpose, and one only, that of rational self-direction; second, that the ends of all rational beings must of necessity fit into a single universal, harmonious pattern, which some men may be able to discern more clearly than others; third, that all conflict . . . is due solely to the clash of reason with the irrational . . . and that such clashes are, in principle, avoidable,

and for wholly rational beings impossible; finally, that when men have been made rational, they will obey the rational laws of their own natures, which are one and the same in them all, and so be at once law-abiding and wholly free. . . . Despite the fact that it rules the lives of more men than ever before in its long history, not one of the basic assumptions of this famous view is . . . true (154).[8]

There is yet a further reason for doubting that there is an absolute value. Assume for a moment that all the questions about its identity and interpretation have been satisfactorily answered. Disputes about its application still remain. Say that the absolute value is general happiness, as some consequentialists claim, or good will, as Kantians suppose. We still have to decide what would contribute most to the general happiness, or what should good will prompt us to do in a particular situation.

The difficulty in the way of deciding what the right application of whatever the absolute value is supposed to be is that we are typically guided by a variety of evaluations each of which represents a point of view different from the others. Our evaluation may be, for instance, moral, personal, political, or religious. Each prompts us to act in a particular way. And if we act in one of these ways, we cannot act in the other ways. But we are typically committed to several of these evaluations, and whichever we rely on, we cannot also rely on the conflicting ones. This is what makes the application of the absolute value difficult, to put it mildly, and this difficulty remains even if, unlikely as that is, we were to agree about what the absolute value is. All the hard questions that the appeal to the absolute value was meant to answer reemerge as questions how to resolve conflicts between evaluations.

---

8. Isaiah Berlin, "Two Concepts of Liberty" in *Four Essays on Liberty* (Oxford: Clarendon Press, 1969).

Defenders of the absolute value may say that the way out of this difficulty is to recognize that the right evaluation follows from the absolute value. If consequentialist or Kantian absolutists are right about the absolute value, then the right evaluation is moral, and it should override personal, political, religious, or any other evaluation that conflicts with it. This may seem like a sensible approach to finding the reasonable evaluation, but only until we ask about the force of the "should" in the claim that one kind of evaluation should always override conflicting ones. Why should it?

The reasonable answer cannot be that the force of the "should" is moral, because that would simply assume what is in question, namely whether a moral evaluation should always override nonmoral evaluations if they conflict with it. And, of course, the force of the "should" cannot be personal, political, or religious either, because then one of them would override the others, and the question of why it should override them remains to be answered. So the force of the "should" cannot be reasonably supposed to derive from any of the evaluations. It seems, then, that defenders of an absolute value do not have a reasonable answer to the hard question of which application of the rightly identified and interpreted absolute value should override other possible applications.

There is no reason to suppose that any kind of evaluation meets the supposed requirement of reason that it should always override all the conflicting ones. Why should a moral evaluation always be more important than, say, an economic or medical one, if starvation or many deaths would follow from the moral evaluation? Why should a relatively unimportant moral evaluation, say about keeping a promise or paying a debt, be always more important than averting blindness, murder, sacrilege, or the destruction great works of art?

As we have seen, there are reasons both for and against there being an absolute value. The reasons for it are that it would be the best guide we could have for living as we should. It would enable us to answer hard questions reasonably. The reasons against it are, first, that no absolute value has ever been found acceptable by all, or even most, reasonable people. And, second, that even if agreement about it has been miraculously reached, hard questions about conflicting evaluations that follow from it would remain. It seems to me that the case for the search for an absolute value has not been able to overcome these doubts. If this is right, we should look for a better approach to answering hard questions.

THE CASE FOR CONDITIONAL VALUES

If we think further about differences between how the old and the young Eleazar evaluated the choice between living and dying, we can see that the old Eleazar chose death because he was unconditionally committed to what he thought was God's law that was the absolute value. The young Eleazar valued God's law, but was not unconditionally committed to it, as shown by his choice to swallow the pork and live because the welfare of his family depended on his support.

Both had reasons for and against the evaluations between which they had to choose. The weight of reasons, however, depended on the differences between the circumstances of the old and the young Eleazar. The old Eleazar had behind him a long life. He was a respected leader of his people. His life set an example that inspired others. The young Eleazar had a life ahead of him. He was not a leader, only one among the God-fearing many. He had a young wife and children, and his parents relied on his help. Both Eleazars wanted to live according to God's law. But when they faced the hard question of whether God's law was the absolute value, they answered it differently. The old Eleazar's commitment to God's law was unconditional. The young one's was conditional, dependent on the context and the circumstances, including his youth, the needs of his family, and his faith in God's forgiveness of his violation of the dietary law.

This brings us to the core of the alternative to relying on a supposed absolute value. It comprises the critical claim of denying that there is an absolute value and the constructive claims that there are numerous reasonable evaluations, they often conflict, and all evaluations are conditional on the context and the personal and social conditions in which conflicts between evaluations have to be resolved.

The rejection of absolute value is not the rejection of reason. Of course we are committed to our various evaluations and should weigh the reasons for and against them. But the reasons depend on what the particular evaluations are, what evaluations conflict with them, what other commitments we have made, what past circumstances have formed us, and what the present context and circumstances are in which we need to resolve the conflicts. We, our evaluations, our personal circumstances, and the context of our life all change: sometimes fast, sometimes slowly. Our reasons and their relative weight changes with them. To recognize that reasons change is not to reject the importance of reasons. It is to reject the mistaken view that there always is an overriding reason that follows from the absolute value and that we should rely on it to find the answers to the hard questions that hold for everyone, always, everywhere.

Reasonable defenders of the conditionality of values accept that there are areas of life, such as logic and science, in which some of the requirements of reason are general, unchanging, and hold in all contexts. But the reasons relevant to answering the hard questions involved in how we should live concern conflicting evaluations, not logical inferences or causal connections. Our moral, personal, political, and religious evaluations need to conform to the basic and uncontroversial requirements of logic and science, but it is part of the essence of evaluations that they go far beyond them. The purpose of evaluations is not to add to our understanding of the nature of world but to help us live in it as we think we should.

The hard questions I am concerned with are hard because we have reasons for and against the conflicting evaluations and because they concern important life-changing choices. The reasons that guided the old and the young Eleazar not only happened to be different, it was right that they were different. This is not to say that they made a reasonable choice. Rather, they were right in recognizing that different reasons were relevant to the evaluations they have chosen to act on.

The question nevertheless remains: did they make a reasonable choice? On balance, I think they did, but my reason for thinking that is not that they had made the choice that reason requires everyone in their situation to make. In this situation, or in any other involving a hard question, there is no answer that reason requires everyone to accept. Young and old Eleazar made a reasonable choice given who they were, where and when they lived, and the evaluations to which they were committed. Someone else, in a different context, at different times, in different personal and social circumstances, and having different values and commitments may have weighed the relevant reasons differently. And that person may also have chosen reasonably. Reason does not require everyone to arrive at the same answer to a hard question. There may be reasonable yet different answers, depending on our personal circumstances and context.

Nevertheless, reasonable answers must be within certain limits defined by the minimum requirements of the elementary rules of logic, the acceptance of well-established causal connections, and basic physiological, psychological, and social needs whose satisfaction is required by all human lives regardless of context and personal circumstances. I have in mind such basic requirements as, for instance, the need for nutrition, oxygen, and rest; for human contacts and the use of language; for nurturing babies, physical security, some division of labor, leisure; and so on.

This view of the conditionality of values and the minimum requirements that reasonable evaluations must meet is contrary to the assumption that there comes a point at which we run out of reasons we can give for evaluations. Beyond that point we have nothing else to rely on than the prevailing evaluations themselves in the context in which we live. As Wittgenstein put it:

> If I exhausted the justifications I have reached bedrock, and my spade is turned. Then I am inclined to say: 'This is simply what I do'. [At that point,] what has to be accepted, the given, is—so one could say—forms of life.[9]

It gives no pause to those who accept this view that a form of life may be vicious, dogmatic, or unreasonable because it fails to meet the minimum requirements that all reasonable evaluations must meet. It is unreasonable to do what is simply done if what is done is contrary to the basic rules of logic, to the acceptance of well-established causal connections, and the avoidable failure to satisfy basic needs.

Conditional values are not arbitrary. Reasons can be given for and against them, but beyond the minimum requirements, there is no overriding reason that must be followed by everyone, always, in all contexts, because personal attitudes, evaluative frameworks, and the prevailing conditions differ from context to context. Our task is not the epistemological one of seeking more and more reasons for our evaluations until we reach an absolute value but the practical, personal, context-dependent one to evaluate the reasons we have, make the most reasonable choice we can on the basis of how we think we should live, and act accordingly.

9. Ludwig Wittgenstein, *Philosophical Investigations*, trans. G.E.M. Anscombe (Oxford: Blackwell, 1986), 217 and p. 226.

Defenders and critics of the continued search for an absolute value agree that no matter how reasonably we act, we may be misled by our false beliefs, misguided emotions, or ruinous desires. Our mistake is neither the failure to follow the absolute value, nor to follow the evaluations that happen to be customary in our form of life. If we make mistakes, as we tend to do, it is that we fail to consider all the relevant reasons, or we make mistakes in evaluating their relative importance to living as we think we should, or that the evaluations are themselves mistaken. We can find out whether or not we are in some way mistaken by considering whether when we are living as we think we should, we continue to think that we should live that way. Of course, we may be mistaken about that as well. But we can do no better than our best to try to avoid making such mistakes.

Contrary to as it first may seem, the case against the search for an absolute value is compatible with making an unconditional commitment to some moral, personal, political, religious, or other value. Individuals may have good reason to make such a commitment, and they may regard it as more important than anything else in their lives. They may even have reasons to die for it, as Eleazar did. What is incompatible with the rejection of the absolute value is the claim that whatever it is to which an individual may be unconditionally and reasonably committed is one that reason requires everyone, always, in all contexts to be unconditionally committed. Making an unconditional commitment to some value is a matter of individual decision that may or may not be reasonable, given the person, the context, and the particular value. But it is not a commitment that reason requires everyone in all contexts to make to that particular value.

I mention in passing that the case for the conditionality of values has as long a history as the case for an absolute value.

Some of those in the past who implicitly or explicitly accepted it were Heraclitus, Herodotus, Pyrrhonian skeptics, Lucretius, Montaigne, Vico, Hume in some of his *Essays*, Herder, arguably Nietzsche in most of his works, and, closer to our time William James, Max Weber, Michael Oakeshott in *Rationalism in Politics*, Isaiah Berlin, Stuart Hampshire, and Bernard Williams. They differed, of course, in many ways, but they agreed about denying that there is an absolute value, acknowledging that there are numerous often conflicting evaluations and held that reason does not require us to be unconditionally committed to the evaluation of anything.

A PROPOSAL

One consequence of the rejection of absolute value is the need to find a reasonable approach to answering hard questions. How we live and how we think we should live depend on some combination of moral, personal, political, religious, and other evaluations. These evaluations conflict, the relative importance we attribute to them changes as we and the conditions of our lives change. If we cannot rely on an absolute value to guide how we resolve such conflicts, then we must find reasonable ways of coping with them even though

> we have no coherent conception of a world without loss... goods conflict by their very nature, and there can be no incontestable scheme for harmonizing them (xvi). . . . There is a pressure to . . . remaining conscious of these conflicts and not trying to eliminate them on more than a piecemeal basis: that pressure is the respect for truth (xvii). . . . Consciousness of the plurality of values is itself a good. . . . One who properly recognizes the

plurality of values is one who understands the deep creative role
that these various values play in human life (xviii).[10]

I accept this view. But agreeing about the centrality of conflicts in
our lives is a long way short of finding reasonable responses to them.
Conflicts among evaluations give rise to hard questions, and we need
to find some reasonable way of answering them. What follows is an
outline of a proposal of such a way. It is only an outline. Its details will
be gradually filled in by the chapters that follow.

The proposal is not a theory that reason requires everyone to accept. A reasonable answer to a hard question cannot be generalized
from one person and context to another. What can be done, I think,
is to recognize that reasonable answers must be particular and vary
from person to person and context to context.

The first step is to accept that conflicts between evaluations are
not out there in the world but within us whenever our evaluations
conflict. The reason why we find it difficult to answer hard questions
is that we are committed to each of the conflicting evaluations and
whatever we do, we have to act contrary to something we value.
There is no answer to hard questions that does not involve the loss of
something we value and do not want to lose. That is why we find the
questions hard. Our evaluations conflict because we are conflicted.

If we think that one of our conflicting evaluations was more important than the other, then conflicts between them would have obvious
resolutions. But the conflicting evaluations are often incommensu-
rable. There is no standard independent of the evaluations themselves that we could rely on—given who we are, our experiences and
preferences, and the context in which we live—to tell us whether any
one of our moral, personal, political, religious, or other evaluations is

---

10. Bernard Williams, "Introduction" in *Concepts and Categories*, ed. Henry Hardy (London:
Hogarth, 1978).

more important then and there than a conflicting one. The choices we have to make between them are often urgent, and then we just have to make them as it seems best in that context. Whether urgent or not, the choice we make may turn out to be mistaken because the evaluations we choose not to follow may prove later to be more important than the one we choose to follow. What, then, should we do to answer hard questions reasonably?

We should ask and answer the question of which of the particular and conflicting evaluations is more important from the point of view of living as we think we should. We will unavoidably lose something we value, but by following this proposal we have a way of deciding which of the conflicting evaluations is more important to us for living as we think we should. If I am an artist, aesthetic evaluations will tend to be more important than others that conflict with them. If I am seriously ill, medical evaluations may loom larger than others. If I aim at wealth, economic evaluations will become crucial. If I am a moralist or a politician, I will resolve conflicts in favor of moral or political evaluations. If I am deeply religious, I will regard religious evaluations as overriding. According to my proposal, the answer to hard questions must be particular, personal, and context-dependent.

To avoid misunderstanding, I stress that although this proposal depends on how we personally think we should live, it need not be self-centered. How we think we should live may be deeply committed to moral, political, religious, or other evaluations, not just to self-centered ones. And these evaluations may be so important in some contexts as to override conflicting ones—but only in some contexts, not always and not for everyone.

Following this proposal will point to a way of answering the hard questions, but, I repeat, there is no guarantee that it will lead to the right answer. We may be wrong about how we think we should live. Even if we are right about it, we may still make mistakes in deciding which of the conflicting evaluations is more important for us. We may be benighted by self-deception, wishful thinking, or depression; overpowered by boredom, ambition, or hatred; misled by prejudice, indoctrination, stupidity, or thoughtlessness. Many things can go wrong. The proposal is far from foolproof. It is only a reasonable although fallible one, and that is more than what the search for an absolute value has yielded.

It may be thought that what the proposal amounts to is just another absolute value added to the long list of the unconvincing others. This would be a mistake. In the first place, defenders of an absolute value think that reason requires everyone, always, everywhere to resolve conflicts by aiming at the same absolute value. The proposal assumes that persons and contexts differ, and reasonable answers to hard questions will also differ. Secondly, it is not an absolute value but one conditional on our evaluations and on the possibilities of the contexts in which we must answer the hard questions. Thirdly, we and our evaluations and contexts not only differ but also change. So that even if we arrive at a reasonable answer at one time in one context, it may not remain reasonable at another time in another context.

It may also be thought that the proposal implies that it is merely a matter of personal attitude what is good or bad, valuable or the opposite. It is certainly true that how we think we should live involves a personal attitude. But it also involves reasons for and against the evaluations to which we are committed, and whether our evaluations are reasonable is not a matter of personal attitude. There are reasons for and against our evaluations, and we are often mistaken about the reasons because we rely on false beliefs, misguided emotions, and unwise desires.

In the chapters that follow, I endeavor to show in many different ways how by following this proposal we can answer hard questions reasonably.

A human life . . . is, in the first place, an adventure in which an individual consciousness confronts the world he inhabits, responds to what Henry James called 'the ordeal of conscious-ness', and thus enacts and discloses himself. This engagement is an adventure in a precise sense. It has no pre-ordained course to follow: with every thought and action a human being lets go a mooring and puts out to sea on a self-chosen but largely unforeseen course. It has no pre-ordained destination: there is no substantive perfect man or human life upon which he may model his conduct. It is a predicament, not a journey. A human being is a 'history' and he makes his 'history' for himself out of his responses to the vicissitudes he encounters.[11]

THE ANSWER

Where does this leave us in answering the hard question posed in the title of this chapter: Is there an absolute value? I think that the answer is: no. There are many circumstances in which it may be reasonable to act contrary to any value.

Whether such actions are really reasonable depends on the bal-ance of reasons we have in the particular context in which we have to answer a hard question. And we may be right or wrong about our evaluation of the reasons we have.

Not even human life has absolute value. It is true that other values presuppose human life because unless we are alive we cannot value anything. But valuing human life presupposes other things as well: a functioning body and brain; some understanding of what we do and do not value; some freedom of choice; not being forced at gun-point, by drugs, or by indoctrination; interacting with other people;

---

11. Michael Oakeshott, *The Voice of Liberal Learning*, ed. Timothy Fuller (New Haven: Yale University Press, 1989), 22–23.

learning from the past and planning for the future; possessing and using an evaluative vocabulary; having been raised and taught; and so on for countless facts and capacities we normally take for granted. Our evaluations are conditional on such facts and capacities, so that we can value human life, or anything else, only conditionally, not absolutely.

That human life has only conditional value does not mean that we cannot value it unconditionally. Such a commitment, however, is only allowed but not required by reason. It is the result of our beliefs, emotions, and desires, which need not be shared by others. Commitment to an unconditional evaluation is a personal attitude, and others may evaluate something else unconditionally or have only conditional evaluations. But whether there is an absolute value is independent of our conditional or unconditional evaluations. Although I do not think that there is an absolute value, I readily acknowledge that various people in various contexts may be unconditionally committed to some moral, personal, political, religious, or other evaluations. An absolute value, if it existed, could not be conditional on anything, but human life is dependent on a multitude of conditions. The unconditional evaluation of human life, then, must be a personal attitude, and others may reasonably evaluate it differently.

Chapter 3

Must We Conform?

THE QUESTION

The question needs explanation. Must we conform to what? To the moral, personal, political, religious, and other evaluations of the context in which we live. We are initiated into these evaluations by our formal and informal education. The same is true of our family, friends, colleagues, neighbors, casual acquaintances, and the rest of our fellow citizens whom we encounter frequently, occasionally, or never. The evaluations become part of our personal attitude, and we rely on them to evaluate the possibilities and limits of how we should and should not live and act; to distinguish between what is good and bad, better or worse, what our rights and responsibilities are; and to know what we can count on from others and what we owe them.

These evaluations taken together is the evaluative framework within which social life takes place. It deeply informs our personal attitude, but we also chafe under it. The possibilities it provides make our lives better, but the limits it sets—its laws, rules, principles, requirements, and prohibitions—curtail us and interfere with how we could live. It channels and restricts the flow of life, regulates our desires, the expression of our emotions, and it makes us confident, ambivalent, or uncertain about our beliefs. The evaluative framework provides benefits we need, imposes burdens we have to bear, and we cannot enjoy the one without having the other.

The burdens often get too heavy and the benefits too meager. Then we ask: why must we conform to the evaluative framework that is so burdensome? We must because we cannot reasonably do otherwise. The evaluative framework is not just an essential part of social life in our context, it is also within us, embedded in our personal attitude that guides how we think we should live. It informs our preferences and aversions and how we evaluate our experiences. We derive from it the evaluative vocabulary we use in daily life. It helps us transform our inarticulate velleities, habitual assumptions, and vaguely felt needs into articulate beliefs, emotions, and desires. And it enables us to distinguish between good or bad, better or worse, permissible or forbidden possibilities of life. It has a formative influence on who we are and how we live.

But if we come to doubt that these benefits are enough to compensate for the burdens, why must we then conform to the evaluative framework? We could repudiate it and reject the prevailing moral, political, religious, and other evaluations. But we cannot participate in social life and reject the entire evaluative framework. We cannot maintain even casual, let alone intimate, relationships without it, because living with others presupposes some shared view of how we should and should not treat one another.

We could leave the context in which we have lived, abandon the prevailing evaluations, and move to some other context that seems less burdensome. Millions of immigrants, exiles, refugees, and travelers seem to have done just that. The key word is "seem." We can certainly leave one context and live in another. But that would not free us from conformity. Wherever we go, we carry with our personal attitude large segments of the evaluative framework that has formed our attitudes to ambition, beauty, comfort, death, food, friendship, health, honor, money, privacy, sex, toleration, work, and so on. Such attitudes are parts of who we are. And even if we embark on the virtually impossible task of total self-transformation, the evaluations that have formed us stay with us even if we reject them, because we are still responding to the evaluations, only our responses have changed from acceptance to rejection.

Furthermore, even if we were to succeed in purging from ourselves all the evaluations that have formed us, we will still not escape conformity. For then we would have to conform to the evaluations of the new context into which we move. If we do not want to be troglodytes, we have to live in some social context, and it will have its own evaluative framework to which we have to conform.

If we must conform, then why is: Must we conform? a hard question. Because there is a perennial conflict between the various evaluations that follow from the prevailing evaluative framework and the beliefs, emotions, and desires that form our personal attitude. We all know from our personal experience that the beliefs, emotions, and desires that form our personal attitude often conflict with the moral, political, and religious evaluations in our context. The more we conform to the evaluative framework, the less we can follow our personal attitude, and the more we follow our personal attitude, the less we will conform.

Our personal attitude is the outcome of our achievements, aspirations, experiences, failures, fears, hopes, relationships, successes, talents, and traumas. These experiences make us both the persons we are and different from others. The source of the conflict between our personal attitude and the prevailing evaluations is that throughout our life we have to struggle with the relative importance we attribute to following, on the one hand, our beliefs, emotions, and desires and, on the other hand, the moral, political, and religious evaluations of our context. If in doubt, consider how often we are prevented from doing what we want by limits set by moral, political, religious, and other evaluations.

The conflicts, however, are not only between our personal attitude and the prevailing evaluations. Our beliefs, emotions, and desires also often conflict with one another, and so do the moral, political, religious, and other evaluations. Our personal attitude is formed by how we resolve these conflicts in the course of our efforts to decide how we should live and then in trying to live that way.

The question of whether we must conform is hard because these multiple conflicts are at the core of our being. They compel us again and again to make difficult choices between two often conflicting influences on how we live. Whichever we choose, it will stifle a valued part of ourselves. And if we consistently favor either part, then we become alienated either from our personal attitude or from the evaluative framework of the context in which we live.

It makes coping with the conflicts even harder that both our personal attitude and the prevailing evaluations may be mistaken. The source of our conflicts may be false beliefs, misdirected emotions, or misguided desires, or it may be anachronistic, impoverished, prejudice-ridden, or rigid moral, political, religious, and other evaluations that follow from the prevailing evaluative framework. And the mistakes may lead to unreasonable responses to changing circumstances. It adds to the hardness of hard questions that if our dissatisfactions make us doubtful of the reliability of our personal attitude and evaluate framework, then we can resolve our doubts only by relying on the beliefs, emotions, and desires that are parts of our personal attitude and deeply informed by the evaluative framework of the context in which we live. The only ways we have of resolving our doubts and coping with our dissatisfactions are to rely on our beliefs, emotions, and desires of which we are doubtful. We are trying to lift ourselves out of the mire we suspect we are sinking into by relying on our frayed bootstraps.

These are some of the reasons why "must we conform?" is a hard question and the conflicts between conformity to the prevailing evaluative framework and to our personal attitude are difficult to resolve. These general and introductory remarks need to be made concrete. I will do so by comparing two very different people who answered this hard question and resolved their conflicts differently. The point of the comparison is to understand the reasons they had and those they might have had for their answers. I hope thereby to enable us to give a more reasonable answer to the hard question as we face it in our context.

PASSIVE NON-CONFORMITY: BARTLEBY

Bartleby is the main character in Melville's short story, "Bartleby, the Scrivener."[12] He is a lowly clerk employed by an unambitious lawyer to copy legal documents. The time is the mid-nineteenth century, and the place is New York City. The copying job is poorly paid and tedious, but jobs are scarce. The lawyer becomes curious about Bartleby who is a very odd person. He discovers that Bartleby has no home, family, or friends; no money apart from the pittance copying pays; he subsists on cheap cookies, sleeps in the office after work, and speaks only when spoken to and even then in monosyllables. He has no interest in anything, spends his spare time staring at the brick back wall of an adjacent building, and absolutely refuses to cooperate with other clerks in checking the accuracy of the copied documents. When asked why he refuses, he responds: "I prefer not to."

Bartleby reiterates this phrase again and again in answer to all questions put to him. The lawyer is decent and tolerant but eventually

---

12. Herman Melville, "Bartleby, The Scrivener" in *Herman Melville*, ed. Harrison Hayford (New York: Library of America, 1853/2000), 641–678.

gets fed up with Bartleby's utter passivity and fires him. But Bartleby does not leave even when urged ever more forcefully to do so. His response is always: "I prefer not to." Like an incubus, he continues to occupy the office, and when he is ejected, he sleeps in the vestibule of the building. Finally the police are called who remove him to the Tombs, the central prison in New York. The food he is given there is not enough to sustain him. The lawyer visits him in the prison, offers to pay for better meals, but Bartleby prefers not to accept it. The lawyer is told that Bartleby spends all his time staring at the brick back wall of yet another building, talks to no one, and although he eats the little he is given, he is otherwise totally passive. He eventually curls up and dies.

Lifelong loneliness, futility, poverty, lack of knowledge, interests, and opportunities, a miserable life without hope, enjoyment, and preferences combined to leave Bartleby an empty shell of a man. He was lethargic, barely functioning, indifferent to his past and his future, and his attitude to life was perfectly expressed by the reiterated phrase: "I prefer not to." He preferred not to have the miserable life he had, and he slowly expired through inanition. He had no conflict between conformity to the prevailing evaluations and his personal attitude because his circumstances left him without beliefs, emotions, and desires that might have formed his personal attitude. He did not find it hard to answer the question of whether he must conform because he preferred not to conform to the miserable circumstances in which he lived throughout his life. Nonconformity was not a difficult choice for him because he saw no acceptable alternative to it.

Melville shows us a human being without a personal attitude who has reached the end of the tether that connected him to life. Our reaction to Melville's portrayal of Bartleby may well be disbelief. We may think that it is implausible that there might be a sane human being who has no beliefs, emotions, or desires about his life beyond preferring that it ends. Bartleby's life was certainly wretched, but how could that not have angered him, or made him ashamed, or left him unwilling to try or at least to hope to change his circumstances? How could he have remained indifferent to kindness, hunger, elementary hygiene, sex, insults, hostility, sympathy, and other natural human reactions? How could he not have complained or tried to make the sympathetic lawyer understand his plight? How could he have been without some pleasant memories or fantasies about a better future? How could he be so utterly passive to what is happening to him? He had a body and physiological needs, but he preferred to ignore them insofar as it was possible. He was alive, but his life was a living form of death.

It might be tempting to say that he was crushed by the society in which he lived. But that is not so. Melville describes other copyists working in the lawyer's office who were lively enough, and their responses to their circumstances were very different from Bartleby's. He could have sought their friendship, accepted the lawyer's offer of help, looked for another job, become a criminal or prayerful, joined the army, read books or newspapers, raged, followed a charismatic leader who promised salvation, and so on. His circumstances were crushing, but they did not crush some others. They crushed Bartleby because he was a cipher without a personal attitude.

Melville does not tell us enough about Bartleby to make his plight psychologically plausible. But we know enough to realize that he faced a choice between conformity and death, and, by being utterly passive, he in effect chose death. He thereby answered the question of whether he must conform by denying that he must since he did not want his miserable life. He chose to die instead, and he did, albeit slowly by way of passive non-conformity. But there is a better way of answering the hard question and responding to conflicts between our personal attitude and the prevailing evaluations.

HYPOCRITICAL CONFORMITY: SARPI

Paolo Sarpi lived from 1552 to 1623.[13] He was a historian, scientist, political philosopher, mathematician, and a Servite friar who was appointed in 1606 as the state theologian of Venice. He was also a closet materialist, determinist, and atheist who believed that there is no reason to believe in God, that everything has a natural cause, and that religion is a tool in the hands of priest-politicians who use it as a means of social control. His great work was the *History of the Council of Trent,* published in 1619. It was one of the most celebrated historical works of its time.

The Council of Trent was summoned to consider whether and how the Catholic Church should be reformed to meet the challenges of the Reformation. It sat between 1545 and 1563! Sarpi's approach to its history was to treat it as a failed attempt to reform the Church. The *History* made clear to attentive readers that Sarpi was opposed to clerical interference with secular affairs, to religious persecutions, and to doctrinal intolerance. Sarpi also kept a *Pensieri,* a diary of his reflections. It remained unpublished during his lifetime. He recorded in it his private opinions, which he could not express publicly.

Sarpi could not express them because during his life the Inquisition was in full force. It aimed to eradicate all challenges to the supremacy of the Catholic Church and the Papacy, including those of the Reformation and of the Catholic reformers in Italy and elsewhere. The Inquisition had virtually unlimited power to imprison, torture, and execute people suspected of any form of heterodoxy. Sarpi was thus forced to dissimulate his real opinions, and he did so throughout his life. He was a hypocrite and a liar in order protect his

---

13. My account of Sarpi is deeply indebted to the fine biography by David Wootton, *Paolo Sarpi* (Cambridge, UK: Cambridge University Press, 1983). References are to the pages of this work.

personal attitude, go on with his scholarly and scientific work, and get away with a semblance of conformity to religious orthodoxy. His hypocritical conformity enabled him to live an active productive life. His inner resources were far greater than Bartleby's.

One of the ways in which Sarpi could come closer to expressing his true views was to take Venice's side in the disputes with the Papacy. In this way he could attack the Papacy by defending Venice's challenges to its supremacy. He was careful not to incur the suspicion of the inquisitors, but he came as close as circumstances allowed to express what he really believed. He took advantage of the fraught political conflicts of his time to carve out as safe a niche for his personal attitude as was then possible. In these circumstances, he lived, worked, and flourished. He wrote to a friend:

> this world of ours has been sick for a long time, and indeed the illness was believed incurable. But there was small crisis in the progress of the disease, which led people to think that it could be cured . . . [but] serious diseases require extreme remedies (99)

The sickness was in the prevailing evaluations and the extreme remedy was to deny the supremacy of the Church and the Papacy. But this could not be expressed because the power of the Inquisition sustained the Papacy. The Inquisition unintentionally encouraged hypocrisy. As Sarpi put it:

> In other centuries hypocrisy was not uncommon, but in this one it pervades everything (112). [Sarpi explains]: My character is such that, like a chameleon, I imitate the behaviour of those amongst whom I find myself. . . .I am compelled to wear a mask. Perhaps there is nobody who can survive in Italy without one (119).

Wootton writes about Sarpi's mask:

> Sarpi had insisted that the wise man must act the hypo-
> crite because he cannot openly acknowledge the truths of
> philosophy (123).

he quotes Sarpi's *Pensieri*:

> Your innermost thoughts should be guided by reason, but you
> should act and speak only as others do (128).

and then he sums up:

> Sarpi's greatest achievement was his life itself, a life lived in defi-
> ance of the cherished assumptions and unquestioned doctrines
> of his age, and the most notable thing about his life was the
> *Pensieri* . . . in which he expressed the ideas and arguments which
> gave coherence to his actions (132–133). . . . Sarpi, though a
> great master of deception, longed for a society in which men
> could feed upon the truth (134).

There is much that we can learn from Sarpi about answering the
hard question: Must we conform? His answer was that when
circumstances demand it, we should maintain the appearance of
conformity in order to protect our personal attitude. Conflicts between personal attitudes and conformity to the prevailing evaluative
framework will be frequent in contexts in which a moral, political, or
religious evaluation is thought to be always overriding. But conflicts
are avoidable in contexts in which we are allowed to be guided by our
personal attitude to decide for ourselves the relative importance we
attribute to conflicting evaluations of how we think we should live.
Then there is room to live according to our personal attitude. And

then the hard question has an obvious answer: conformity is reasonable because it allows us to live as we think we should. If necessary, we should pretend to conform, and thereby make it possible to follow our personal attitude and enable us to try to have a worthwhile life.

In Sarpi's context, this answer was difficult give because his personal attitude and the prevailing religious evaluations conflicted. If he had openly favored his personal attitude, he would have soon been put to death by the Inquisition, which he reasonably wanted to avoid. And if he had conformed to what he thought were mistaken religious evaluations, he could not have lived and worked as his personal attitude led him to think he should. Because Sarpi's intellectual resources were great, he found an adroit way of avoiding both of these unacceptable alternatives. He paid the price of having to live a life of hypocrisy, which is not easy, but he thereby gained a protected private sphere in which he could cultivate his personal attitude, and work as a historian, scientist, and a canny counselor of Venice.

GOING DEEPER

Bartleby and Sarpi faced the hard question and answered it differently. Sarpi chose conformity because his considerable intellectual resources enabled him to follow his personal attitude surreptitiously. Bartleby could not make the same choice because he had no personal attitude and virtually no intellect. And he would not choose conformity to the prevailing evaluations because they doomed him to a miserable life. He chose passive non-conformity and death as a way out. There were reasons for the answer each had arrived at. Sarpi was aware of some of the reasons; Bartleby was not. But their reasons were independent of the extent of their awareness of them. How reasonable their answers were depends on the balance of the reasons for and against them. We need to go deeper to understand how not just they but also we can arrive at a reasonable evaluation of the balance of reasons when we face a conflict between our personal attitude and conformity to the evaluations in context in which we live.

The beginning of such deeper understanding is to recognize that there can be no reasonable answer to the hard question that holds in all contexts and for everyone. A reasonable answer must take into account how reasonable are the particular beliefs, emotions, and desires that form our personal attitude; the significance of the gains and losses our conformity would involve; the relative importance of the particular conflicting evaluations that follow from our personal attitude and the prevailing evaluations of how we think we should live; and what the particular circumstances are in our context. In all these respects, Bartleby and Sarpi differed greatly, and so did the reasons for and against the different answers they gave. But it was not only their answers that were different; so also was the hard question they answered. There are two kinds of hard questions, although they are expressed in the same grammatical form. Bartleby faced one kind, Sarpi another.

Hard questions may be internal or external to the evaluative framework as it is in a particular context. Sarpi asked and answered a hard question internal to the prevailing evaluative framework. The moral, personal, and political evaluations he accepted in sixteenth- to seventeenth-century Italy conflicted with the religious evaluations he rejected. He rejected them because, in his view, they were doubly mistaken. First, because they were mistaken in assuming the existence of God and the authority of the Papacy. And second, because they arbitrarily overrode all non-religious evaluations that conflicted with them. But all of them, including Sarpi's rejection of religious evaluations, were parts of the evaluative framework of his context. He could not reject them explicitly, so he hypocritically conformed to them in order to protect his life, personal attitude, and continued work. He did as well as he could in the context of his life.

Hard questions may also be external to an evaluative framework. They may force us then to face the conflict between accepting or rejecting all the prevailing evaluations and thus the entire evaluative framework of our context. This was the kind of hard question Bartleby faced, and his answer was to reject it. He could not finesse his answer, as Sarpi did his, because he had no personal attitude he could protect and knew no alternative to the evaluative framework he rejected. His rejection took the form of passive non-conformity and death, rather than continuing to live a miserable life in miserable circumstances.

The evaluative framework of nineteenth-century New York City was not kind to poor, lonely, uneducated, miserable people. In Bartleby's case, however, the lack of kindness was exacerbated by his inability to recognize the meager opportunities of which a more enterprising person might have taken advantage. Sarpi did well despite what he took to be the mistaken religious evaluations that dominated in his context. Bartleby was crushed by the combination of prevailing evaluations and his personal shortcomings.

The internal hard question Sarpi answered was not as hard as the external one that Bartleby faced. Sarpi knew about and could rely on moral, personal, and political alternatives to religious evaluations. Bartleby faced an external question about whether he must conform to his entire evaluative framework, not just parts of it. He could not rely on alternatives to the prevailing evaluative framework because he did not know of any. Sarpi was able to answer the internal hard question he faced by relying on the considerable resources of his intellect, practical savvy, and personal attitude. Bartleby had no such resources and was disabled by lacking them. Bartleby's situation was tragic, and his only way out of it was death. Sarpi's situation was manageable, and he managed it adroitly.

As far as I can tell, neither Bartleby nor Sarpi thought about the larger significance of the conflict they faced between personal attitudes and the prevailing evaluations. Understandably enough, they were concerned with the immediate conflict they had to cope with. But we, as spectators, have some distance from them. We can think more deeply about how they answered the hard question. We can understand how difficult it is to live in a context whose overriding evaluations we regard as mistaken. And we can also understand that this difficulty is not an exceptional episode in the history of the many different evaluative frameworks in the context of which human beings had to make what they could of their lives. All hitherto known evaluative frameworks are mistaken in some ways. Part of the hardness of the question is to evaluate reasonably just how serious are the mistakes of our evaluative framework and what, if anything, we can specifically do about it beyond handwringing and loud complaints.

We find it mistaken because some of the prevailing evaluations prevent us from living as we think we should. We are dissatisfied with one or more of the prevailing moral, personal, political, and religious evaluations. And then we ask whether we should conform to them. We may interpret the question as asking for reasons internal or external to our evaluative framework. If we are asking for internal reasons, we will be inclined to conform in the hope that the mistakes of the evaluating framework can be corrected or somehow avoided. This is what Sarpi did. Or we may be asking for external reasons because we suspect that our evaluative framework and all its evaluations are incorrigibly mistaken, which is what Bartleby in effect did. A deeper understanding will enable us to consider these internal and external reasons for and against the hard question. And then, perhaps, we will try to find a reasonable way of balancing these conflicting reasons.

INTERNAL QUESTIONS AND REASONS

One influential approach to internal questions is virtually the official doctrine of anthropologists, sociologists, and social historians. A particularly clear philosophical formulation of it is by Peter Strawson[14]:

> Inside the general structure or web of human attitudes and feelings . . . there is endless room for modification, redirection, criticism, and justification. But questions of justification are internal to the structure or relate to modifications internal to it. The existence of the general framework of attitudes itself is something we are given with the fact of human society. As a whole, it neither calls for, nor permits, an external "rational" justification.

If Strawson is right, then all hard questions are internal to the evaluative framework as it is in a particular context. The very idea of asking external questions and seeking external reasons for an evaluative framework is mistaken. All our reasons for or against how we answer the hard question must be internal. This is not to accept the archconservative view that the evaluative status quo must be accepted as is. There can certainly be reasons for and against existing evaluations. But, according to Strawson, the reasons must be based on some evaluation, and whatever the evaluation is it must be part of our evaluative framework.

It is a reason against some evaluations, for instance, that they encourage moral rigidity, personal irresponsibility, political corruption, or religious strife. But these reasons must be internal to and follow from some moral, personal, political, or religious evaluation we

14. P. F. Strawson, "Freedom and Resentment" in *Freedom and Resentment* (London: Methuen, 1962/1974), 23.

accept and whose violation we deplore. If the reasons were derived from the evaluative framework of a context other than our own, we would think that they have force only if the evaluations on which the reasons rest agree with our own evaluations.

We know, for instance, that reincarnation, revenge, flogging offenders, the iconic status of some animals, witchcraft, the evil eye, arranged marriages, ritual purification, the interference of the dead inhabiting a nether world with human lives are valued or feared in some contexts. That, however, we would not regard as an external reason against our evaluations that we neither value nor fear them. We may acknowledge that they are valued or feared by others in other contexts, but that has no effect on how we evaluate them in our context.

Internal reasons within an evaluative framework are often against some evaluation that has become overriding and stifles valuable possibilities of life. Bartleby's case may be taken to suggest that economic evaluations in nineteenth-century New York mistakenly overrode moral, personal, political, and religious ones. Sarpi thought that religious evaluations in sixteenth- and seventeenth-century Italy mistakenly overrode personal and political ones. Those who thought that economic or religious evaluations ought to be overriding concluded that the internal reasons for them were decisive because all evaluations presuppose and rest on economic resources or on God's law. And the market or the Inquisition was there to protect the economy or God's law against those who are opposed to it.

A reasonable answer to the hard question of whether we must conform to the evaluative framework in our context depends on the balance of reasons for and against it. The hardness of the question is not specific to any particular evaluative framework. There are and have been contexts in which moral, political, or religious evaluations were assumed to be overriding. And in all these contexts there usually emerged an institution, like the Inquisition, whose task it was to

compel conformity to whatever the overriding evaluation was sup-
posed to be. The results were the repressive regimes of Franco in
Spain, Salazar in Portugal, the colonels in Greece, the Ayatollahs in
Iran, Castro in Cuba, and the like elsewhere.

Those who think that reasons for and against evaluative
frameworks must be internal will, of course, acknowledge that repressive regimes are bad. But they would claim that their fault is not
that they follow internal reasons but that they fail to find a reasonable
balance between contrary internal reasons. They are motivated by the
fear that if the evaluation they favor does not override the others in
case of conflicts, then the very survival of the evaluative framework
will be endangered. And they will say that it is in everyone's interest
in that context, whether they understand it or not, to conform to the
overriding evaluation because the evaluative framework that makes
it possible for them to live as they think they should depends on it.
What seems repressive to those who fail to understand this, they
would claim, is in fact a defense of the very possibility of living a
civilized life.

If God's law, the categorical imperative, the greatest happiness
principle, virtue, natural law, democracy, or cost-benefit analysis is
elevated to the status of the overriding evaluation that takes precedence over anything that conflicts with it, then it would be the key to
how everyone, always, everywhere should live. And the failure to live
that way would be to reject the overriding evaluation whose acceptance enables us to live as we should. Thus the defense of the overriding evaluation turns into the defense of a repressive regime under
which no reasonable person would wish to live.

What has gone wrong with this lamentably familiar line of thought
is the assumption that if some particular evaluation is not accepted
as overriding all other evaluations that conflict with it, then the very
possibility of the evaluative framework and all its evaluations would
be endangered. There would perhaps be strong internal reasons for

making this assumption if no better way were available of making reasonable choices between conflicting evaluations. But in fact there is a much better way. It is to recognize that reasons for and against conflicting evaluations depend on always-changing possibilities of life; on our beliefs, emotions, and desires as we are trying to resolve the conflict we face; and on the time, place, and the circumstances in which we face the conflicts. Sometimes one of the conflicting evaluations is more important than the others, at other times, their relative importance shifts.

It makes a great difference to the relative importance of conflicting evaluations whether the conflict occurs in time of war or peace, prosperity or poverty, religious harmony or strife, rigid or permissive morality, general law-abidingness or widespread criminality, politics as usual or revolutionary unrest, adequate health care or a threatening epidemic, and so on. The balance of internal reasons for and against a particular evaluation depends on the prevailing circumstances. Whatever the circumstances are, there will be some reasons for and against the various alternatives, so the resulting evaluation will not be arbitrary. But it will be difficult because we often have to choose between conflicting evaluations when we are committed to both. We will choose to act according to one of them, but that does not change the fact that we will have to act contrary to one of our evaluations.

Nor does it change the fact that even our most reasonable choice may turn out to be mistaken because we may make it on the basis of false beliefs, misguided emotions, unwise desires, that are part of our personal attitude, or on the basis of mistaken evaluations. And if they are in some way mistaken, we may be unaware of their mistakes, otherwise we would not be motivated by them.

This way of making reasonable choices between conflicting evaluations recognizes their context-dependence. The contrary way does not. It insists on the importance of accepting that some particular evaluation should always, in all contexts, be overriding. One reason in favor of accepting the context-dependence of evaluations and denying that there is an evaluation that is overriding in all contexts is that it does not lead to a regime that tends to become repressive in the name of some evaluation that supposedly should guide how everyone, always, everywhere lives.

Another reason is that in our daily life we in fact treat evaluations as context-dependent without adverse consequences. We constantly and competently choose whether we should be guided by moral, personal, political, religious, or some other evaluation in a particular context. Most of the time we can resolve conflicts between the evaluations we accept by asking which of them is more important in that context than the others to living as we think we should.

The answer we give, of course, may be mistaken. That is one reason why it remains a hard question whether we must follow our personal attitude or conform to the prevailing evaluations when they conflict. Another reason is that the deeper is our understanding of the reasons for and against protecting our personal attitude and conforming to the prevailing evaluations, the stronger the reasons seem to become. For we realize then that how we think we should live depends both on living as we believe, feel, and desire that we should—and in accordance with the evaluations that have partly formed our personal attitude and on which we rely to evaluate the moral, personal, political, and religious possibilities and limits of life in our context. If we also realize that both our personal attitude and the prevailing evaluations may all be mistaken, and yet we have to choose between them, then the resulting uncertainty makes answering the hard question even harder.

This uncertainty, I think, is a strong reason for concentrating on the conflict between some belief, emotion, or desire of ours and whatever evaluation conflicts with it. We can do this without assuming that the right reason must hold for everyone, always, in all contexts. This makes it easier to answer the hard question by recognizing that the reasonable answer to it is going to be particular and context-dependent.

The fact remains, however, that our personal attitude is constituted of whatever our beliefs, emotions, and desires happen to be. To be human is to be motivated by them, regardless of whether they are mistaken. We can question them, but we must do so in terms of our other beliefs, emotions, or desires, which may also be mistaken.

Our connection to the prevailing evaluative framework is much looser. We can abandon it because we think that it is hopelessly mistaken, as Bartleby did, or because, unlike Bartleby, we do not think that death is the only other alternative to rejecting it. We can become committed to another evaluative framework we regard as better. This possibility is not allowed by the view that all evaluations and all reasons for and against them must be internal to the prevailing evaluative framework. But the possibility obviously exists. Some evaluative frameworks are unacceptable for excellent moral, personal, political, or religious reasons external to them. I now turn to this possibility and to external questions about and reasons against any evaluative framework, including our own.

EXTERNAL QUESTIONS AND REASONS

Obvious sources of external reasons for or against our evaluative framework are comparisons between our own and another. We may find that ours is better or worse than the ones with which we compare it. If we do find ours better, it is because we compare the evaluations that follow from our own evaluative framework with those of others in particular respects, such as education, health care, lawfulness, liberty, life expectancy, prosperity, the protection of rights, political stability, religious toleration, security, and so on. We may then find that in these particular respects ours is better or worse than the other with which we compare it. Of course there may be yet further respects in which the evaluations that follow from another evaluative framework are better, for instance in respect to the security and loyalty of tightly knit extended families, fewer conflicts, uncomplicated sexual relations, better behaved children, less corruption, more compassion, and so forth.

The result of such comparisons may or may not favor us. However, the very possibility of comparisons shows that external reason for and against our evaluative framework and its evaluations can be found. And that means that the balance of external reasons may tilt heavily against some of our own evaluations and in favor of others with which we compare them. In the light of the possibility of such comparisons, I find it odd that first-rate thinkers, like Strawson and many others who agree with him, could say of any of our evaluations that it neither calls for, nor permits, an external "rational" justification.[15]

Suppose for a moment that defenders of evaluations that lead to the murder, torture, and enslavement of countless innocent victims would say if asked for reasons for their evaluations that they neither call for, nor permit external justification, or that this is simply what they do, or that what they are doing is fine, given their criteria of logic.

How could it be unreasonable to look at such evaluations from the outside and condemn them? But this is precisely what would be unreasonable if there were no external reasons for or against the evaluations that follow from an evaluative framework, including our own. Indeed, we may find that the external reasons against our own are overwhelming, and then we may not conform to it any longer. Or we may choose to die if we find our own evaluative framework unacceptable and know of nothing that would be better, as it happened to Bartleby. Or we could conform to the mistaken evaluative framework

---

15. Strawson, "Freedom and Resentment," 23.

hypocritically, as Sarpi did, in the hope that we can escape the vigilance of its enforcers and live the only life we have as well as possible in bad circumstances.

Those who deny both the possibility and necessity of external reasons for or against evaluative frameworks and their evaluations will say that however we answer the hard question of "Must we conform?" we will do so by following internal reasons we derive from our own evaluative framework and its evaluations. That is why we condemn atrocities like the murder, torture, and enslavement of innocent victims. We may not be aware of doing this. We may think that the reasons we have against the atrocities are external to our evaluative framework, but they think that we would be mistaken.

There is a trivial sense in which this denial of the possibility of external reasons is right. But there is also a far more important sense in which it is wrong. The trivial sense is that when we give reasons for or against anything, it is we, the persons we are, who give the reasons, and we give them on the basis of the beliefs, emotions, desires we have and which have been formed in part by our of evaluations. The important sense the denial of external reasons misses is that there are some external reasons whose force must be recognized by all evaluative frameworks.

These external reasons express the minimum requirements (briefly discussed already in the preceding chapter) of the continuation of human lives. Some examples of such requirements are conformity to elementary rules of logic, such as the acceptance of the conclusion that follows from true premises; of undeniable facts, like having a head; and of causal connections, for instance between hunger and eating. The minimum requirements also include the satisfaction of basic needs for nutrition, rest, the use of language, nurturing infants, and so on. And they include as well such basic evaluations as that adequate nutrition is better than starvation, health better than sickness, happiness better than misery.

All evaluations are human evaluations. External reasons for and against them partly depend on whether they meet these minimum requirements. The atrocities I mention above are deplorable because they fail to meet them. The reasons against them are not internal ones we derive from our evaluations. They are reasons whose force all reasonable evaluative frameworks must accept. There could no more be a reasonable evaluative framework that fails to meet these minimum requirements than there could be a system of logic that does not meet the minimum requirement of consistency, or a scientific system that does not accept what is supported by overwhelming evidence. Conforming to the minimum requirement is not just something we in our context happen to accept. Accepting them is part of being human, regardless of how much we differ in our other beliefs, emotions, desires, and evaluations.

There are further external reasons that can be derived from comparisons between the evaluations of different evaluative frameworks. The ones based on the minimum requirements are obvious. Evaluative frameworks that prohibit the murder, torture, and enslavement of innocent people are better than ones that do not. Comparisons become more complex, however, if they go beyond simple evaluations and concern the cumulative effect of several detailed comparisons: such as, for instance, how good or bad are the protections of justice, liberty, peace, prosperity, public health, security, stability, toleration and so forth. We can compare evaluative frameworks on the basis of the extent to which they recognize the importance of these external reasons.

The comparisons will not allow us to conclude simply that a particular evaluative framework is better than another. But they make it possible to say that in a particular respect one evaluation of an evaluative framework is better than another. It may well happen that in another respect the other is better. Still, external reasons can be cumulative, and we can reasonably conclude in some cases that overall, taking into consideration all the relevant respects in which comparisons can be reasonably made, one evaluative framework is better than another. And we can reasonably conclude this even though both conform to the minimum requirements of human lives.

We can also compare evaluations on the basis of what follows from them for those who for some reasons fail to be able to live according to the prevailing evaluations. This is a mixed group that includes those who are uneducated, insane, handicapped, or incapacitated by misfortune, failure, grief, loneliness, and so on. Their treatment is likely to be more or less appropriate to the causes of their plight. But, allowing for differences in what is regarded as appropriate responses to them, the comparisons allow us to say that they are treated with more or less kindness or cruelty, pity or blame, with more or less understanding, generosity or meanness, strictness or neglect. Evaluations can be better or worse depending on such external reasons for or against the way they treat unfortunate people in the context.

If we face the hard question of whether we must conform to our mistaken evaluative framework, then we can give a reasonable answer on the basis of the balance of internal and external reasons for and against them. I now turn to how we may do this.

THE ANSWER

A reasonable answer depends, first, on finding a fit between our personal attitude that guides how we think we should live and the evaluations that follow from the evaluative framework of our context. If our personal attitude were formed entirely by the prevailing evaluations, then the fit would be built into our personal attitude, and there would be no need try to find it. But, of course, our personal attitude has been formed also by our genetic predispositions, experiences, history and preferences, successes and failures, talents and weaknesses, and our relationship with our family, friends, lovers, teachers, and colleagues. The overlap between our personal attitude and the prevailing evaluations is only partial, and the parts that do not overlap often conflict with those that do because they often motivate us to act in different ways, and leave us uncertain about what we should do. The answer to the hard question depends on finding reasonable ways of resolving these conflicts and uncertainties.

A reasonable answer also depends on recognizing that although the evaluations in our context are given and not optional, it is optional whether we act according to them. It is not optional whether we are committed to some among the moral, personal, political, religious, or other evaluations of the evaluative framework of our context. They are, as I have stressed, essential parts of living a human life. Without them we could not distinguish between what is good and bad, better or worse, prohibited or permissible. But it is optional what the particular evaluations are to which we commit ourselves. And it is optional also how strongly we are committed to them.

If we live in any social context, evaluations of some kind must be part of our life. In that respect, there are no differences between the personal attitudes of human beings. Our personal attitude, the respects in which we differ from one another, consists in what our particular beliefs, emotions, desires, and evaluations are and in how strongly we are committed to them. Resolving the conflict between our personal attitude and conformity to the prevailing evaluations depends on whether the evaluations aid or hinder us in living as we think we should, but there is no doubt that if we live with others, we must make compromises. Montaigne, I think, was right about this:

> We must live in the world and make the most of it as we find it (774). He who walks in the crowd must step aside, keeps his elbows in, step back and advance, even leave the straight

way . . . according to the time, according to the men, according to the business (758). [But] we must reserve a back shop all our own, entirely free, in which we establish our real liberty and our principal retreat. . . . Here our ordinary conversation must be between us and ourselves. . . . We have a soul that can be turned upon itself (177).

It is in that back shop that our personal attitude resides and sets limits to how far we should go in conforming to the prevailing evaluations. Bartleby had no such back shop. He found his life miserable without it, and he preferred death to such a life. Sarpi was adroit enough to protect his back shop and personal attitude by hypocritical conformity, and he not only survived but lived an admirable and productive life. We can learn much, as I have tried to show, from thinking about the success and failure of these two experiments in living.

A reasonable answer also depends on abandoning the futile search for a general answer to the hard question and accepting that it depends on the particular beliefs, emotions, and desires that form our personal attitude and on the prevailing moral, personal, political, religious and other evaluations. All of them are by their very nature particular, context-dependent, vary in strength, often conflict, and are subject to the countless non-evaluative circumstances of our context.

It is because of such particularities that there can be no general answer to the hard question: "Must we conform?" But from this it does not follow that it is arbitrary how we answer it. We can and should consider the reasons for and against our answer, but the reasons must be particular. They cannot be generalized from one person to another, or from one context to another. We, the different persons we are, have to find our own answer. It should be based on reasons, but it will vary with persons and contexts. And, unfortunately, unavoidably, and importantly, our particular answers may be mistaken because they may be based on mistaken evaluations, beliefs, emotions, and desires. Both our personal attitude and the prevailing moral, personal, political, and religious evaluations not just may be but are likely to be mistaken in some ways because we are all, individually and collectively, fallible and far from being as reasonable as we should be. This is part of the reason why the question is hard and why so many of us are dissatisfied with our lives.

Chapter 4

Do We Owe What Our Country Asks of Us?

THE QUESTION

Let us begin with two apparently simple but contrary answers. One is that we owe whatever our country asks of us. The other is that we owe no more than we think is reasonable. Neither is as simple as it may first seem. A country is not the sort of entity that can ask anything. The asking is done by the people who run the government on behalf of the country. Their powers are great, and they have the means to exact compliance with what they ask. But asking is one thing, owing it is another. Why should we owe anything? Because if our country is well ordered, its government provides many of the services we need for living as we think we should, such as education, public health, defense, security, a system of justice, the upkeep of the infrastructure, and the regulation of employment, finance, trade, foreign relations, commerce, and torts. If the government fails to provide many of these services, the country is badly ordered. What we think we owe, then, depends on how well or badly ordered our country is. If it is well ordered, it provides these services, and then we owe what it asks of us. Thereby we do our part to live in a well-ordered country.

What we might owe then are not just taxes but also some measure of our allegiance, loyalty, and support of at least some of its institutions, laws, and traditions. We identify to some extent its general interests with our own, and we follow some of the prevailing moral, political, religious, or other evaluations. What we owe, if we owe anything, creates obligations to do what it asks of us. But it is not just a matter of obligation. It is also in our interest to have the services and to recognize that bearing some burdens is a condition of having them.

What we owe goes beyond the expediency of keeping an unwritten contract. It involves our emotional engagement with our country's landscapes, ceremonies, comforts derived from the language, colloquialisms, and jokes we share with others, familiarity with its art, music, and popular sports, the diet that has shaped our culinary tastes, and a sense of belongingness derived from the generally fulfilled expectation that we can count on others and they on us in the dozens of casual encounters of daily life. We usually take for granted these ties and become aware of them only when they are broken or when we visit or live in another country. Once there, unfamiliar conventions and practices permeate the usual interactions and make us wish for what we have left behind: the unspoken reciprocal recognition of one another as fellow citizens.

There is yet more that underlies the obligation, interests, emotional ties, and the personal attitude we have toward our country. It is the sense of "us-against-them" when our country or fellow citizens are attacked, challenged, or mistreated. We feel that we are entitled to be critical of our country from the inside and resent it when others do it from the outside. We feel that reasonable criticisms can come only from those who are familiar with our country's evaluative framework, priorities, and with the possibilities and limits that have emerged in the course of its history.

Anthropologists, sociologists, and visitors can certainly describe our evaluative framework, but we are and they are not affected by the motivating force of these descriptions. They are passive observers, while we are active participants. And when our country is criticized by outsiders, we take it personally. Our *amour-propre* is involved. Such obligations, interests, and emotional ties are reasons for owing what our country asks of us, provided it is good. Then the government has the authority to decide, within appropriate lawful limits, what we owe.

Of course the government often governs badly. Its authority to ask anything of us then becomes questionable. Positive emotional ties to it become looser and are gradually replaced by anger, resentment, disaffection, or cynicism. Our identification with our country is then weakened and perhaps even broken. Countless refugees, emigrants, and frustrated reformers came to think and feel reasonably enough that they no longer owe anything to their country.

We are thus brought back to the other simple-minded answer that it is up to us to evaluate what we owe our country. We have a life to live, our only life, and we make of it what we can. If the government prevents us from it, then it is not a friend but a foe. We are then entitled to protect ourselves by reform, revolution, or emigration. If the government misrules, then we have good reasons against accepting its authority and owing what it asks of us. Its misrule threatens our efforts to live as we think we should. A bad government often claims that we owe what is contrary to our personal attitude and to the moral, political, religious, and other evaluations of the prevailing evaluative framework.

However, we may deny that we owe what the government reasonably asks of us because we are selfish, greedy, self-indulgent, opportunistic free-riders; envious or jealous of others; enraged by the successes of others; ashamed of our failures; flaunt what we have and withhold what we owe; and so forth. Both the government and we may be unreasonable.

The upshot is that we often have good reasons for and against both answers to the hard question this chapter is about. These conflicting reasons explain why it is a hard question to answer what we owe our country. Reasonable answers depend on how well or badly our country is governed and how important are the particular respects in which it is good or bad. These are complex matters of evaluation. Both simple answers ignore the complexities.

It makes the question of what we owe even harder that most governments do well in some respects and badly in others. We all have to evaluate again and again whether what we owe is commensurate with the services we receive. How we answer this question depends on our evaluation of how well the government provides the services we need, how strong are the obligations we feel, how important are our interests that may or may not be met, how deep are our emotional ties to our country, and how reasonable we think are the criticisms of our country by us, our fellow citizens, and those outside of it. And then, having weighed the reasons for and against them, we have to decide whether we owe all that the government asks, only some of it, or nothing at all.

I now consider the Kamikaze and the Draftee, who answered the hard question and evaluated what they owed their country very differently. The reason for doing so is not to praise or blame them, but to probe their answers, evaluations, and reasons in order to come to a deeper understanding of why the question is hard. And we can also understand better how we, in our context, might answer the hard question more reasonably.

THE KAMIKAZE AND THE DRAFTEE

Ohnuki-Tierney, the author of *Kamikaze Diaries*, is a Japanese-American anthropologist who has written a remarkable book about the Kamikaze pilots.[16] It is based on the extensive diaries, notes, and letters six of them left behind, and their families preserved. All of them kept a diary in which they recorded their closely similar attitudes to life, to the war Japan waged against Allied forces in World War II, and to their coming death. They were twenty-one- to twenty-three-year-old university students, among the elite of the Japanese educational system. They read extensively and rapidly English, French, and German works. According to Ohnuki-Tierney,

> [their] readings ranged from the works of classical writers such as Aristotle, Plato, Socrates . . . Rousseau, Martin du Gard, Gide, and Rolland; Kant, Hegel, Nietzsche, Goethe, Schiller, and Thomas Mann (15). . . . They began seeking psychological comfort in an aesthetics of nihilism; the aesthetic of death and its symbols . . . The stance of nihilism offered them powerfully poetic ways to understand, or, in fact, to avoid understanding the death in which they lived (17).

But they read superficially, even if allowances are made for their youth. They were not taught to think critically about what they read. They read in order find an inspiring answer that would give meaning to their life and death, rather than to consider whether what they read was reasonable. They yearned for an emotionally satisfying answer given to them by an authority.

> They examined the meaning of being a member of a society . . . the individual's responsibility to society . . . they debated

---

16. My sources are Ivan Morris, *The Nobility of Failure* (New York: Farrar, Straus and Giroux, 1975); Yukio Mishima, *The Way of the Samurai*, trans. Kathryn Sparling (New York: Basic Books, 1967/1977), and, most importantly, Emiko Ohnuki-Tierney, *Kamikaze Diaries* (Chicago: University of Chicago Press, 2006).

whether patriotism can be understood as the sacrifice of the self for a greater cause (17).

They found the answer in a version of romanticism mixed with two formative influences deeply embedded in Japanese sensibility as it then was: the samurai ethic and the aesthetic symbol of cherry blossom. The Kamikaze chose and embraced this heady mixture from among the many they knew about because they found them more inspiring than the others.

The samurai were legendary warriors in Japanese history: swordsmen serving a master whose authority they unquestioningly accepted. The identity of the master or the cause they were fighting for mattered little to them. Their overriding concern was with the fight itself. They were committed to victory or death in their fight with their opponents, usually other samurai. Their motto was: the way of the samurai is death. And few of them reached old age. If they were conclusively defeated, they committed *hara-kiri* or *seppuku*, meaning "belly-cutting." It was an excruciatingly painful form of ceremonial self-mutilation and death. By this manner of death they proved their courage, redeemed their honor, and showed contempt for life that was disgraced by defeat.

Another formative influence on the Kamikaze was the symbol of cherry blossom. Ohnuki-Tierney describes it as:

the exact time of blooming in unpredictable, and the blossoms last only a short time. . . .[It] offers a medium for soliloquy. Individuals reflect on life and death; love and loss . . . while composing poems in which the cherry blossom serves as the medium for their deliberations. . . .The flower represents processes of life, death, and rebirth. The most salient characteristic of the cherry blossom is their gorgeous but very brief life . . . closely linked to the sublimity of pathos and ephemerality (26–27).

The Kamikaze were imbued with this redolent mixture of the life and death of the samurai, the ephemeral beauty of cherry blossoms, and the superficially understood romanticism they found in Western works.

At the same time—surprisingly enough, at least to me—they were opposed to the war which the militarist Japanese government initiated with the unprovoked attack on Pearl Harbor and waged against Allied forces. The Kamikaze knew by the time they were conscripted in 1944 that the war was lost, and they did not want to die. Nevertheless, throughout their young lives they willingly accepted their government's authority and that they owed what it asked of them.

Their willingness was powerfully reinforced by the samurai ethics, cherry blossom aesthetic, and romanticism, and led them to see their lives and coming deaths in the lost war as honorable and beautiful. They were bewitched by death, and it silenced their doubts about the war and death. Wearing the image of cherry blossom on his flying suit, each flew alone in a makeshift plane loaded with explosives, intending to crash it on an Allied warship and destroy it. They were not given enough fuel for a return flight, and they all died.

The answer they ended up giving to the hard question was that they owed what the government asked of them. It asked for their death in the war, and they gave up their young lives. They did that, even though they were opposed to the war, knew that it was lost, and realized that their death served no military purpose. As it mattered little to the samurai who their master was, so it mattered little to the Kamikaze that they disagreed with their government's policies. They thought they owed what it asked of them because they accepted its authority. As they saw it, theirs was not to question why but simply to do or die, and, as it happened, to do and to die. Their extant writings testify to their evaluation of the reasons for and against owing their lives, and they found the reasons for it much stronger than the reasons against it.

This reconstruction of how the Kamikaze thought about the hard question is of their evaluations as they were in the 1940s during the war. I do not mean to suggest that their evaluations were shared then by all Japanese. And I have no doubt that all the many and various evaluations have changed in various ways since the many things that happened in Japan and the world since then.

Then and there, however, the Kamikaze were overwhelmed by their ideal of an honorable and beautiful death. It prevented them from recognizing that there were strong reasons against accepting the authority of their government, the morbid samurai ethic, and the use of the ephemeral beauty of cherry blossom as a metaphor for their lives. Given their youth, their acceptance of the authority of the government and its demands, the long years of war that dominated Japanese society, and the coming military defeat, perhaps it is too severe to fault the Kamikaze for not examining the reasons they had. But the pressure of wartime circumstances combined with the samurai ethic and cherry blossom aesthetic led them to give up their lives willingly, even though it accomplished nothing apart from their death.

They had reasons for their actions, but there were also reasons against them. If they had questioned their reasons, they might have realized that they did not owe what a bad government asked of them, that a meaningful life need not include seeking death, and that honor and beauty may have other sources other than the ones that beguiled them. These other sources included valuing life itself; moral, personal, political, and religious evaluations quite different from those of the samurai one; and life-affirming rather than life-denying aesthetic appreciation. We are, then, left with the question of how reasons for or against answers to the hard question could be reasonably evaluated. I will come back to it after considering the Draftee.

He was a young American in the 1970s during the war in Vietnam. He was over six feet tall, much too thin, weighing about 140 pounds.

He received a draft notice and had to appear before the draft board in three weeks. He then stopped eating and during the ensuing three weeks, apart from drinking water, lived without any nutrition. By the time he was required to appear before the draft board, he weighed less than a hundred pounds. Since he was thin to start with, after having lost a lot of weight, he became as skeletal as inmates of Nazi concentration camps. The draft board deemed him medically unfit for military service.

There were many young men of draft age who wanted to avoid the draft, but neither I nor anyone else I asked or read about had heard of someone else who did what this Draftee did. I know him personally, and many years later, I asked him why he did what he did. His answer was that he wanted to protect his autonomy and avoid having to kill someone else. His reason was not opposition to the war and to the government's policy, nor fear of being killed or injured, nor having to interrupt his education: his reason was commitment to his autonomy and to the overriding value of human life. It guided his answer to the hard question.

The Kamikaze accepted and the Draftee did not that they owed what their government asked of them. The Kamikaze derived his evaluations from the authority of his government, the samurai ethic, and the cherry blossom aesthetic. The Draftee derived his from the importance of human life and autonomy. Both relied on the evaluative framework of his society. But in the Japanese framework, human life and autonomy were much less important than the samurai ethic, cherry blossom aesthetic, and an honorable and beautiful death. In the Draftee's evaluative framework, autonomy and human life had great importance, while the government's authority did not.

These were the reasons why the Kamikaze and the Draftee based their very different answers to the hard question of whether they owe what their country asks of them. The Draftee thought that we have the final authority to make an autonomous decision about whether we owe what the government asks of us. The government asked that he should be willing to kill in the war in Vietnam, but the Draftee thought that this was unreasonable. He valued more his autonomy and human life than doing what the government asked. The Kamikaze subordinated their autonomy to the government's authority because they valued life much less than an honorable and beautiful death.

I have far more sympathy for the Draftee's answer than for the Kamikaze's. My interest, however, is not in taking sides but in evaluating the reasons they had for their answers. My view is that their reasons were inadequate. They failed to consider reasons that might have led them to give a different answer to the hard question they faced. They had reasons for and against their answers, and they evaluated the reasons they gave. But they could and should have considered additional reasons, and yet they did not. Their evaluations of their reasons were not reasonable enough.

THE EVALUATION OF REASONS

The evaluation of reasons involves considering all the relevant reasons generally available in the context, avoiding mistakes in their evaluation, basing reasons at first on the widely accepted moral, personal, political, and religious evaluations that follow from the evaluative framework in the context, and then revising the evaluations as it seems best on the basis of further reasons for or against them.

Part of the problem with the evaluation of the reasons the Kamikaze and the Draftee had was that there were relevant reasons unavailable to them. The Kamikaze did not know that there was disagreement on the highest level of the Japanese government about whether Japan should surrender, put an end to the lost war, and avoid further loss of life. And the Draftee did not know that secret peace negotiations with the Viet Cong were under way. If these reasons had been available to the Kamikaze and the Draftee, they would have been able to evaluate more reasonably what they should do. They might have still done the same thing, but they would have had better reasons for it.

In fact, their evaluations of the reasons for and against what they owed to their country were mistaken, although not because any fault of their own. It was the secrecy of their government that kept them from considering relevant reasons, and they cannot be blamed for that. If there is blame, it lies with the secrecy of the government. But it is difficult to say whether the secrecy was warranted. The fact remains that the evaluations of the reasons by the Kamikaze and the Draftee were mistaken because they based their actions on incomplete reasons.

Another reason why their evaluations of the reasons they had were mistaken was that they relied on moral, personal, political, religious, and other evaluations—some of which were mistaken. They led them to over- or underestimate the importance of some of the relevant reasons. The Kamikaze's government deliberately underestimated the risks involved in waging the war. It set in motion a propaganda machinery that glorified the samurai ethic and the cherry blossom aesthetic and used them to indoctrinate the young men they conscripted to believe that they owed it to their country to sacrifice their lives in the senseless war. But the Kamikaze were not their blameless dupes. Their personal attitude was informed by romantic obsession with beautiful death as the ideal they thought would give meaning to their lives and that readily lent itself to abuse by the propaganda machinery. The Kamikaze colluded in misjudging the importance of the reasons they had against owing what the government asked of them.

The Draftee's evaluation of the reasons he had was significantly different from those of the Kamikaze. The Kamikaze readily identified their evaluations with those of the government's. The

Draftee did not. His moral, political, and other evaluations left room for the possibility that his personal evaluations could conflict with them. And it was that possibility that allowed the Draftee to decide that he did not owe what the government asked of him. He thought that his personal evaluations overrode moral, political, and other evaluations. Whether his evaluation was reasonable depends on the reasons for and against the personal and the conflicting moral, political, and other evaluations involved. For the moment, I will say only that his personal evaluation was questionable. More needs to be said before I can return to it.

Another consideration is whether the evaluative framework from which the moral, political, religious, and other evaluations are derived is itself reasonable. If it is reasonable, it enables those in this context to live as they think they should. It may, of course, be unreasonable for a variety of reasons of which I mention only a few: the evaluations that follow from it conflict, and they provide no reasonable way of resolving their conflicts; or it arbitrarily regards one kind of evaluation as always in all contexts overriding; or it is insufficiently flexible and unable to respond reasonably to changing circumstances; and so on.

Let us assume, however, that the evaluative framework is not mistaken, nor are the evaluations that follow from it. This would not by itself guarantee that the answers to the hard questions that follow from them would be reasonable, because personal attitudes may prevent acting on reasonable answers and come between the evaluations of reasons for and against the possible answers. Personal attitudes may also be mistaken. Those whose attitudes they are may be too fearful, too prone to self-deception or wishful thinking, too susceptible to unrealistic illusions or to other psychological ruses that prevent them from acting on reasons that are available and rightly evaluated by their evaluative framework. It did not occur to the Kamikaze that they allowed their overwrought emotions to silence their reasons. And the

Draftee did not realize that there were many circumstances in which killing human beings is the only way of saving many innocent lives.

The best case is when the evaluations of reasons for and against owing what the government asks meet these conditions, and the personal attitudes of those concerned are based on true beliefs, rightly directed emotions, and life-enhancing desires. It is, I think, not unduly pessimistic to say that the best case is never realized. Governments and the people they govern should aim to be as reasonable as possible, but both parties always and unavoidably fall short. The moral, political, and religious evaluations of an evaluative framework are always less than fully reasonable. And even if they were fully reasonable, they may often conflict, and there would be reasons both for and against resolving their conflicts in favor of one or another of them. Moreover, we are all fallible, prone to having faulty beliefs, emotions, and desires, and even the most reasonable beliefs, emotions, and desires will conflict, leave us ambivalent and uncertain: this is because whatever we do, we will lose something we value and do not want to lose.

Fallibility, conflicts, and unavoidable loss make the evaluation of reasons difficult and often mistaken. And even if the reasons we arrive at are free of these mistakes, they cannot be generalized from one context to another. The evaluative framework, reasonable evaluations, and personal attitudes vary and change with contexts, persons, times, and circumstances, and that makes reasons context-dependent. Nevertheless, we can and should evaluate the reasons for and against possible answers to the hard question of what we owe our country. The Kamikaze and the Draftee did not do a good job of it.

Reasonable answers to the hard question also depend on the evaluation of constructive reasons for and critical reasons against possible answers. Constructive reasons tell us why we should accept a particular answer but not why we should not accept other answers. Critical reasons tell us why we should not accept some answers, but not which one we should accept. We need both constructive and critical reasons because each is incomplete without the other. This, however, was not obvious to the Kamikaze and the Draftee. They failed to give sufficient weight to critical reasons, and their answers were vitiated by the same mistake.

The Kamikaze did not consider critical reasons against the samurai ethic, cherry blossom aesthetic, and the romanticism that motivated them. And the Draftee did not consider critical reasons against autonomy and the overriding value of human life that motivated him. Both thought that their constructive reasons were strong, but the very strength they attributed to them prevented them from considering the critical reasons against their evaluations. Why did the Kamikaze and the Draftee make this mistake and what can we learn from them to avoid repeating it?

REASONS AND THE KAMIKAZE

The Japanese evaluative framework included many aesthetic, moral, and religious ideals in addition to those of the samurai and the cherry blossom. A small sample of them includes Zen Buddhism; haikus; Kabuki; family loyalty; the arts of flower arrangements, the presentation of food, and rock gardens; the ever-growing literary tradition beginning with *The Tale of the Genji*, and so on.[17] As to the version of Western romanticism that appealed to the Kamikaze, why choose it rather than the bourgeois morality they found in Mann's *Buddenbrooks*, or the pacifism of Romain Rolland, or the individualism of Nietzsche, or the love of life in Goethe, or the critical questioning of Socrates, or the celebration of practical reason

17. For a wonderful study of these and other Japanese ideals, see Donald Keene, *Appreciations of Japanese Culture* (Tokyo: Kodansha International, 1971/1981).

by Aristotle and Kant? The Kamikaze knew of these Japanese and Western ideals, but when it came to facing the hard question of whether they owed what their country asked of them, they ignored them and followed the samurai, cherry blossom, and romantic ideals in the willing acceptance of the constructive reasons for honorable and beautiful death that the government asked of them. Their tacit assumption was that the other ideals they knew of were appropriate in peace—but not in war and not in the face of death.

These constructive reasons followed largely from the Japanese evaluative framework. If we think of evaluative frameworks as ranging between authority at one end to autonomy at other end, then we can situate the Japanese evaluative framework close to the authority end of the continuum. And authority then gained added importance because they were at war when the authority of the government became overriding. It asked them to die, and die they did. They believed that the survival of their country was at stake, and that made the examination of critical reasons against the authority of the government unacceptable to them. They suppressed whatever doubt they had.

Of course the Kamikaze also had autonomous personal attitudes and reasons that followed from them. They had doubts about the war, and they wanted to live and continue their education. But those were peacetime concerns. They were at war and were overwhelmed by the potent mixture of the government's propaganda machinery, of respect for authority that was a defining characteristic of the Japanese evaluative framework, and of the inspiration they derived from the ideals of romanticism, samurai ethic, and cherry blossom aesthetic. That mixture was the source of their constructive reasons, and their strength overwhelmed whatever critical reasons they may have had. This, however, was not all.

Another defining characteristic of the Japanese evaluative framework was its aestheticism. The authority that pervaded their evaluations was concerned not so much with the content of evaluations, but with their form. It defined how whatever is done should be done, and that form was aesthetic. This is what led Keene to write of the

elevation of aestheticism to something close to a religion. Aestheticism spread from the court to the provinces, and from the upper classes to commoners (50).

The closer their evaluations came to the end of the continuum where authority was dominant, the farther behind were left evaluations of the opposite end where autonomy was dominant. Given the importance of authority and form, rather than autonomy and content, the reasons for honorable and beautiful death their government asked of them was overriding. That was what motivated the Kamikaze and that was why they did not consider critical reasons against how they answered the hard question. Given their evaluative framework, they had strong constructive reasons that silenced their weak critical reasons. And that made it easy for them to answer the hard question.

In this they were mistaken. Even if in their evaluative framework authority was dominant, they could and should have considered critical reasons against the government. Surely, no matter how dominant the government's authority was, it could be reasonable to accept its authority only if it was not bad. But the wartime militarist Japanese government was bad.

The survival of Japan was at stake only because the militarist government embarked on a senseless war they could not win. After early victories, they suffered defeat after defeat, and they were responsible for the death of millions of soldiers and civilians both Japanese and foreign. The government got into power by suborning the opposition of many high-ranking officers, diplomats, and economists who understood Allied capabilities, of many respected cultural leaders, and the Emperor himself, on whose heavenly sanctioned authority the military claimed, falsely, to be acting. The military planners knew that oil was essential to the war effort, that they had only a two-year supply of it, and that they had to gain control of the Dutch oil fields thousands of miles away. When they failed, their supply of oil was gradually depleted; at this point they knew that the war was lost, and yet they persevered fighting. Like the samurai, they sought an honorable death. But they took with them millions of people who just wanted to live in peace.[18]

We situate our evaluations much closer to the end of the continuum where autonomy is dominant. Most of us find moral, personal, political, or religious evaluations more important than aesthetic ones, and we regard the content of evaluations far more important than their form. Our evaluative framework makes it hard for us to understand why well-educated young men would answer the hard question of what they owe their country and choose between life and death as the Kamikaze did. We should understand that what they did followed from their evaluative framework in which the wartime authority of their government was dominant. But even in terms of that evaluative framework, their answer was insufficiently reasonable. The militarist government was bad in terms of Japanese evaluative framework, and no reasonable evaluative framework could require accepting an authority that is known to be bad.

The Kamikaze, however, did not see that. They were blind to critical reasons against owing what their bad government asked of them because their evaluative framework was mistaken. Their unquestioned obedience to authority and the aestheticism of form prevented them from going beyond constructive reasons in favor of the authority of the government and considering also critical reasons against it.

---

18. On the Japanese decision to start the war, and the internal opposition to it, see Ian Kershaw, *Fateful Choices* (New York: Penguin, 2007), chapter 8.

REASONS AND THE DRAFTEE

The Draftee's evaluations were close to the autonomy end of the continuum, and he thought that their content was far more important than their form. He wanted to avoid killing human beings. Unlike the Kamikaze, the Draftee was quite willing to consider critical reasons against how he answered the hard question. But he was certain that his constructive reasons for valuing human life were overwhelmingly stronger than any critical reason that may be given against it. In his personal attitude autonomy took precedence over any consideration by any authority that conflicted with it. It is doubtful, however, that he realized the force of the critical reasons against the answer he gave.

Why did he choose fasting as the way of avoiding the draft, rather than other ways? He might have become a forthright conscientious objector, or renounced his citizenship and emigrated, or volunteered for the non-combatant medical corps, or refused service and served jail time. Thousands opted for one of these ways, but he did not. The reason is, I think, that his way allowed him to get on with his life with much less disruption than any of the other ways would have involved. He did not just want to avoid killing, he also wanted to have as little inconvenience as was possible when he acted as his autonomous personal attitude dictated. If he had been more critical of the promptings of his autonomy, he might have considered these other possibilities and examined the critical reasons against his personal attitude.

Furthermore, he was not opposed to killing, so long as it was done by others. He raised no objection to the police lawfully killing violent criminals in order to protect their intended victims; nor to suicide and euthanasia; nor to addictions that killed large numbers of people; nor to killing in self-defense. He did nothing to prevent killing, if it was done by others. That did not interfere with his life, while being drafted would have. He ignored the critical reasons that might have led him to question his personal attitude.

He did not consider what his opposition to killing included and excluded, nor what critical reasons there were against the exclusions and inclusions. He could not have known whether his refusal to owe what the government asked was reasonable unless he had considered critical reasons against it. But he did not consider them. He acted on a strong constructive reason he believed he had, and he no more considered critical reasons he should have considered than the Kamikaze did.

It might be thought that he was opposed to killing only in the Vietnam war but not to other forms of killing. That, however, is not what he said. He said that he was opposed to killing any human being. But then he was inconsistent in failing to act on what he believed. He should have been opposed to all forms of killing, not just those in the war in Vietnam.

Nor did he consider whether there were acceptable moral, personal, political, religious, and other evaluations that allowed him to carry on with his life, while others disrupted their own. They took the risks he did not and did the killing he believed he should not do. To what extent was it really his autonomous evaluations rather than *sauve qui peut* that motivated his non-compliance with the government's demands? Was he perhaps guided by false beliefs, misdirected emotions, or selfish desires? These questions are not meant to imply that the Draftee was insincere. They are intended to point to the need to consider both constructive and critical reasons for and against deciding whether the Draftee was motivated by autonomy, or by self-interest, or by some not easily ascertainable mixture of the two.

The consideration of these reasons was even more pressing because the Draftee was motivated by two conflicting considerations. One was that he valued his citizenship from which moral and political obligations followed, the many services the government provided, and he had strong emotional ties to the language, landscapes, customs, mentality, cuisine, and institutions of his country and of his region. The other was that he was also motivated by the unquestioned certainty that he should avoid killing. Gauging the relative strength of these conflicting reasons leads to the hard question of what the Draftee owed to his country.

The Draftee, like the Kamikaze, did not see that the question was hard. He considered only some of the constructive reasons for avoiding killing, but not the constructive reasons for doing what the government asked of him. Nor did he consider the critical reasons against the answer he gave. He did not ask to what extent might his answer be motivated by self-interest. The point is not that it is unreasonable to be motivated by self-interest. We are all often and reasonably motivated by it. What is unreasonable is to fail to consider the reasons that motivate us when we make crucial decisions about how we should live. Only by taking into account the surely relevant constructive and critical reasons could we reasonably evaluate the Draftee's answer.

I repeat: I am not concerned with agreeing or disagreeing with the Draftee's answer, nor with the reasons for and against waging the war in Vietnam. I am concerned with understanding what needs to be done in order to find a reasonable answer to the hard question of whether we owe what our country asks of us. Understanding this is difficult because it involves the evaluation of the relevant constructive and critical reasons for and against both our evaluative framework and our personal attitude. A reasonable answer depends on that evaluation.

When the question is about how we should live, there is a constant temptation of self-deception, wishful thinking, and the simplification of complex problems. They may lead to a misleading emphasis on some reasons or to a self-imposed blindness to some of them. It is not just observers of the Draftee who may be misled in these ways but also the Draftee himself. The evaluations of both constructive and critical reasons for and against the personal attitude that may have motivated the Draftee make it very unlikely that either we or the Draftee could be confident of just what the right balance of reasons is. The Draftee, however, was confident. He was certain that the answer he gave was more reasonable than the alternatives to it. But he was mistaken. Even if his answer had been reasonable, he could not have known without taking into account the relevant constructive and critical reasons. And that he did not do.

I conclude that the answers the Kamikaze and the Draftee gave to the hard question of what they owe their country were not reasonable enough. They assigned far too much weight to one of the constructive reasons they had and far too little to other constructive reasons they also had and to the critical reasons they could and should have taken into account.

If this is right, then a reasonable answer to the hard question remains to be found. Such an answer involves comparing the Kamikaze's and the Draftee's evaluative frameworks. The Japanese evaluative framework during World War II and the American evaluative framework during the war in Vietnam were, of course, very different. But they were alike in being complex, including moral, personal, political, and religious evaluations. They were also different in the substantive content of their evaluations, as well as in the relative priority they attributed to them. In the Japanese evaluative framework, most of the time conflicts were resolved in favor of aesthetic evaluations of how what was done should be done. In the American evaluative framework, moral, personal, and political evaluations usually took precedence over other conflicting evaluation. One difference, then, between the two evaluative frameworks was that they attributed different priorities to kinds of evaluation they both had.

Another significant difference was that on the evaluative continuum that ranges between authority at one end and autonomy on the other, the Japanese evaluative framework in wartime favored the government's authority, while the American evaluative framework gave priority, even in wartime, to autonomy. The consequence was that the Kamikaze felt they owed what the government asked of them, while the Draftee did not. When it mattered, as in the midst of war, the Kamikaze's attitude was, "my government right or wrong"; while the Draftee's attitude was, "my autonomy right or wrong."

It seems to me, however, that the Draftee's mistake had the right aim, although it was wrongly pursued, while the Kamikaze's mistake had the wrong aim wrongly pursued. So I think that the Kamikaze were, as it were, more deeply mistaken than the Draftee, because the Kamikaze failed to understand that individuals are concrete, while governments are abstractions. The government is a collection of individuals who are supposed to regulate the affairs of their country. But if the government does it badly, then the obligations of citizens are null and void, their interests become contrary to the government's, and their emotional ties to their country are weakened or broken. The Kamikaze were mistaken in feeling that they owed their lives when their bad government asked for it. And they were prevented from recognizing it by their evaluative framework in which authority dominated autonomy, and form dominated content.

In the Draftee's evaluative framework, autonomy took precedence over authority. Obedience to the government was conditional on the evaluation of whether it was doing its task well, badly, or somewhere in between. The Draftee's mistake was that he failed to consider constructive reasons for owing what the government asked and the critical reasons against his personal attitude in which autonomy was dominant. It may be that if he had corrected these mistakes, his answer to the hard question would have remained the same. But he could not have known that without actually evaluating all the relevant constructive and critical reasons. He failed to do that because he unquestioningly acted on the ingenious expedient that allowed him to escape the draft and to do what he thought he ought to do, which ignored his obligations to his country and fellow citizens and coincided with his interest.

The salient point I am making is that the domination of authority and autonomy may both be mistaken and avoiding the mistake depends on considering the critical reasons against and the constructive reasons for the domination of either authority or autonomy. Neither the Kamikaze nor the Draftee did that. Although they had some reasons for the different answers they gave to the hard question they faced, their answers were not reasonable enough.

THE TWO CONFLICTS AND HARD QUESTIONS

I have been discussing the Kamikaze and the Draftee in order to learn from understanding their mistakes how we might avoid making the same mistakes. The deepest source of their mistakes were two conflicts which they tried but failed to resolve reasonably. One was between their personal attitude and the evaluative framework in their context. The other was between the constructive and the critical reasons they had or should have for and against how they should answer the hard question they faced. But these conflicts were not just theirs. They are ours also. Our personal attitude and the evaluative framework also often conflict, as do the constructive and the critical reasons we have or should have for and against how we should answer the hard questions we face. It is these conflicts that make the hard questions hard. And I mean all the hard questions I discuss in this book.

These conflicts are not symptoms of some underlying mistake. They are not signs of irrationality, nor the results of false beliefs, overwrought emotions, or destructive desires. They are not indications of some political malaise in our context or in our psychological functioning. The conflicts between our evaluative framework and personal attitude, and between our constructive and critical reasons are normal parts of life in a civilized society. They can be resolved, but they cannot be avoided. They are in us, and make us conflicted.

They are unavoidable because we are the kind of beings who can live a worthwhile human life only in some social context or another, and because we do not just live but evaluate how we should live. In the normal course of events we evaluate it from moral, personal, political, religious, and other points of view. Our evaluations guide how we should live, but they conflict, make us conflicted, and we must decide which we should or should not follow. And we do decide, but rarely arbitrarily.

We decide on the basis of the various evaluations embedded in our upbringing, education, traditions, customs, experiences, and innate or acquired preferences in which the evaluative framework of the context in which we live and our personal attitude are inseparably mixed. These evaluations give us the constructive and critical reasons for and against the decisions we make about how we should live. Our evaluations and reasons are many, and their conflicts lead to the hard questions we face, including the one about what we owe to our country. These questions are hard because the conflicts are between our own evolutions and our own reasons for and against them. Whatever we decide, we must say no to some of our own evaluations and reasons in order to say yes to others.

This, I believe, is an accurate description of our situation if we are not handicapped in some way and live in a civilized context. The terms used in my description of our situation are unimportant. Those who would prefer to use terms other than evaluative framework, personal attitude, constructive and critical reasons, conflicts, and evaluations should feel free to substitute the terms they favor. And to those who doubt the accuracy of the description on the grounds that most of us are not aware of these conflicts, I say that awareness of what we do is not a condition of doing it. We are engaged in countless physical, physiological, and psychological activities without being aware of them. Making decisions based on reasons and evaluations we have gained in the course of a lifetime is one of these activities. We become aware of them only when we realize that we face a hard question whose answer has an important effect on how we should live.

The Kamikaze and the Draftee became aware of it, and yet their answers were not reasonable enough. Their constructive reasons overwhelmed their critical reasons. The Kamikaze's personal attitude was overwhelmed by their corrupted evaluative framework. And the Draftee's evaluative framework was overwhelmed by his ill-considered personal attitude. Their mistake was that they failed to find the right balance between their conflicting constructive and critical reasons and between the evaluations that followed from their evaluative framework and personal attitudes. In closing, I turn to Montaigne whose life is a wonderful example of how the right balance can be maintained.[19]

THE ANSWER

Montaigne's answer to the hard question was based on his experience as a magistrate for many years, as a mayor of Bordeaux who served two terms, and as a mediator who was respected by both sides in the religious civil war that ravaged France. He excelled in practical reason. And it enabled him to give a balanced answer to what he owed his country. He thought that autonomy is to have

> a pattern established within us by which we test our actions, and, according to this pattern, now pat ourselves on the back,

---

19. All references are to the pages of Michel Montaigne, *Essays* in *The Complete Works of Montaigne*, trans. Donald M. Frame (Stanford, CA: Stanford University Press, 1588/1943).

now punish ourselves. I have my own laws and court to judge me, and I address myself to them more than anywhere else (613). My actions are in order and conformity with what I am and with my condition (617). To compose our character is our duty. . . and to win, not battles and provinces, but order and tranquillity in our conduct. Our great and glorious masterpiece is to live appropriately (850–851). It is an absolute perfection and virtually divine to know how to enjoy our being rightfully (857).

But he recognized that autonomy unavoidably depends on a social context. He bore the unwanted burden of being for many years a public official. He wrote,

> I do not want a man to refuse, to the charges he takes on, attention, steps, words, and sweat and blood if need be. . . .But this is by way of loan and accidentally, the mind holding itself ever in repose and in health, not without action, but without vexation, without passion. . . . But it must be . . . with discretion (770).

He had no illusions. He saw clearly that he was living in a corrupt society:

> Our morals are extremely corrupt, and lean with a remarkable inclination toward the worse; of our laws and customs, many are barbarous and monstrous (497). Consider the form of this justice that governs us: it is a true testimony of human imbecility, so full it is of contradiction and error (819).

Yet he remained true to his autonomous personal attitude and could say that

> I have been able to take part in public office without departing one nail's head from myself, and give myself to others without taking myself from myself (770). I do not involve myself so deeply and entirely (774).

How could he do this? By offering

> only limited and conditional services. . . . I frankly tell them my limits (603). . . . The mayor and Montaigne have always been two, with a very clear separation. . . . An honest man is not accountable for the vice and stupidity of his trade, and should not therefore refuse to practice it: it is the custom of his country. . . . We must live in the world and make the most it such as we find it (774)

I think that Montaigne was right about all this. We are obligated to do what our country asks of us but only up to the point at which it becomes incompatible with our autonomy. But autonomy is reasonable only if it is based on our evaluation of the constructive and critical reasons for and against it. The remarkable thing about Montaigne is that he not only did it, but he left a record of doing of it. The *Essays* are that record. It is Montaigne's lifelong evaluation of the constructive and critical reasons for and against how lived, and of the changes, second thoughts, and revisions of his personal attitude.[20] As he wrote of it:

---

20. For a record of these revisions, see the remarkable scholarly edition of Frame's translation in which revisions Montaigne made in various versions of the *Essays* are clearly indicated.

I have no more made my book than my book has made me—
a book consubstantial with its author, concerned with my own
self, an integral part of my life (504). . . . I believe in and conceive
a thousand ways of life . . . insinuate myself by imagination into
their place (179). I put myself into [their] place, I try to fit my
mind to [their] bias (183). [Thereby] we may strengthen and
enlighten our judgment by reflecting upon this continual variation in human beings (216).

This is the comparative case study approach that I have been following
in this chapter and will continue to do so in subsequent chapters. It
enables us to find and evaluate the constructive and critical reasons
for and against possible answers to the hard questions we face.

Chapter 5

Must Justice Be Done at All Costs?

THE QUESTION

Justice is customarily thought to require treating like cases alike and different cases differently. This is a purely formal and not very helpful way of understanding justice. It does not specify what cases are and are not matters of justice, nor what likenesses and differences are relevant to it. Surely, justice has to do with what human beings do or what is done to them, and with the particular likenesses or differences that are relevant to what they deserve. This chapter, then, is about justice as it concerns human beings, intentions and actions; as well as the larger social institutions and practices we create, maintain, or participate in, as well as entire societies. Justice requires treating them alike or differently depending on what they deserve on the basis of how good or bad they are. It also requires that their treatment should be proportional to their goodness or badness. The question is whether justice, understood in this way, is necessary for life in a civilized society: one that protects the requirements that enable us to live as we think we should.

Why should we think that justice is necessary? Consider the sequence: intention-action-consequence. We have an intention, perform an action that follows from it in order to bring about a certain consequence. Each component of this sequence may be good or bad.

If our intention and the action are both good, we expect that their consequences will also be good. But the consequences are often not good for a variety of reasons. One of them is that bad people, actions, institutions, or practices disrupt the sequence and disappoint our reasonable expectation that the intended good consequence will follow. The aim of justice is to make it more likely that good intentions and actions will have good consequences and bad intentions and actions will have bad ones.

If we could not count on justice, it would be pointless for us to form any intention and act on it. We would have no reason to suppose that the consequence we intend to bring about would follow. Human activities have a point only because intentions and actions much of the time lead to their intended consequences. Justice is thought to be necessary and valuable because it makes this more likely. And injustice is regarded as bad because it disrupts the intention-action-consequence sequence.

If we live in a civilized society, we typically have a sense of justice, even if we are sometimes unjust. We generally recognize its importance, want people to have what they deserve, and are indignant or worse if undeserved good things are enjoyed by bad people and undeserved bad things are suffered by good people. Nevertheless, we do not want justice to be strict and relentless. We want it to leave room for exceptions: for instance, when justice would cause more harm than good; or when two or more requirements of justice conflict and only one of them can be met; or when unjust acts should be excused on the grounds of ignorance, illness, low intelligence, or other incapacities; or when justice conflicts with other things we value even more, like love, pity, or peace; or when we face extreme situations in which our own or our beloveds' survival is threatened. But we do think that in the absence of reasonable exceptions, justice should obtain: we should get what we deserve, not what we do not deserve, and it should be proportional to our goodness or badness.

However, if there are reasonable exceptions to justice, then justice is not necessary but conditional on whether exceptions to it are reasonable. The fact is that it is often controversial whether an exception is reasonable. Is justice necessary? is a hard question partly because we are uncertain about what consequences, conflicts, or incapacities would constitute reasonable exceptions.

In struggling with the question, we should distinguish between cosmic and human justice. Cosmic justice is thought to be inherent in the scheme of things. It is like the laws of nature in being universal and unavoidable, but it is also unlike them in being evaluative rather than descriptive. Those who think that there is cosmic justice also think that how good or bad our life is depends on how closely we conform to cosmic justice. Christians, Jews, and Moslems, among others, think that cosmic justice is the order created by God. But cosmic justice need not be thought of in religious terms. Plato, the Stoics, Spinoza, and their many followers all thought that cosmic justice permeates all there is, but it is not made by God or the gods, and certainly not by us. We and all else are subject to it. And we can no more free ourselves from it than we can free ourselves from the laws of nature. Conformity to it is good, deviation from it is bad, because cosmic justice is simply the order that governs all there is and determines what is good. All the bad things in our lives are thought by defenders of cosmic justice to be caused by our failure to conform to it.

Is it reasonable to believe in cosmic justice? Note the crucial ambiguity of this question. Is the *belief* in cosmic justice reasonable? Or is it reasonable to believe that cosmic justice *exists*? The belief may be reasonable, even if cosmic justice does not exist. Consider an analogy. It may be reasonable to believe in the perfectibility of human life, even if its perfection is unattainable. Mere belief in it may motivate us to do what we can to make human life less imperfect. Similarly, belief in cosmic justice may be reasonable even if cosmic justice does not exist, because it may prompt us try to bring human justice come closer to what cosmic justice would be if it existed. And that may be reasonable regardless of whether cosmic justice exists.

How does this bear on the hard question of whether cosmic justice is necessary? A reasonable answer cannot be that it is necessary because we do not even know that it exists, let alone whether its existence is necessary. A multitude of incompatible theories about its existence, about the possibility of human knowledge of it, and about what it prescribes and prohibits have been proposed throughout the millennia, and they leave us uncertain about the right answer.

What about human justice? Human justice is imperfect. We often do not get what we deserve and get what we do not deserve. Is human justice, given its imperfections, necessary? No, because, as we have seen, there are reasonable exceptions to it. Is imperfect human justice then necessary when there are no reasonable exceptions to it?

The answer to the hard question is inconclusive: human justice is sometimes necessary, sometimes not. When it is and when it is not necessary depends on the evaluation of the reasons for and against the supposed exceptions; on how good or bad are the consequences that follow from doing what justice requires; on the severity of the disabling incapacities that may excuse unjust actions; and on the relative importance of justice and other evaluations that conflict with it. This balancing, judging, and weighing must be done by the persons we are, in the context in which we live, and we must do it from the point of view of how we think we should live. It makes the answer to the question even harder that these contrary evaluations depend on our beliefs, emotions, and desires, each of which may be misguided.

I will now discuss how Creon and Antigone in Sophocles's *Antigone* and the Sherpas in Nepal answered the hard question in their very different contexts. Creon thought that human justice is necessary because life in a civilized society is impossible without it. Antigone thought that it is conditional on its conformity to cosmic justice, which was necessary. The Sherpas thought that human justice is not only unnecessary for a civilized society, but actually detrimental to it, although they also thought that cosmic justice was necessary.

I discuss them in order to evaluate the reasons that might be given for and against their answers, regardless of whether they were actually aware of these reasons. The point is not to justify or criticize how they lived and acted but to understand their reasons and to compare them with the reasons we might give for how we think about the necessity of justice. We can learn from these comparisons and from the mistakes of Creon, Antigone, and the Sherpas to give a more reasonable answer to this hard question.

CREON VS. ANTIGONE

The majority view of *Antigone* is that it is about the tragic life and death of Antigone who dies rather than obey what Creon proclaimed is required by justice. Antigone is the heroine, and Creon the villain. The majority view is not so much mistaken as simple-minded. At the center of *Antigone* is not Antigone but the conflict between Antigone and Creon. Both are tragic figures. Hegel thought so.[21] So did Kitto:[22]

the centre of gravity does not lie in one person, but between two.... there is not one central character but two, and that of the two, the significant one to Sophocles was always Creon (126). The chief agent is Creon; his is the character, his the faults and merits. (129)

And Knox, who writes that Creon seems at first sight to be the hero of the play.[23]

21. See G. F. W. Hegel, *The Phenomenology of Mind*, trans. J. B. Baillie (New York: Harper, 1807/1967), 464–499.
22. H. D. F. Kitto, *Greek Tragedy* (London: Methuen, 1939).
23. Bernard M. Knox, *The Heroic Temper* (Berkeley: University of California Press, 1964).

He is the one who, like the Aristotelian

tragic hero, is a man of eminence, high in power and prosperity, who comes crashing down from the pinnacle of greatness, and it is he who speaking in terms of the length and importance of his role ... is the protagonist. .... Creon is now in the position of the hero whose will is thwarted. (67–68)

Antigone and Creon have reasons for acting as they do, both are flawed, both do what they think is right, and both are destroyed by it. This is a minority view of *Antigone*, but I think it is the right one.

Creon thought that human justice is necessary because it sustains the social context in which we can live as we think we should. All other evaluations presuppose human justice because it establishes and protects the conditions in which everything else can be evaluated. Creon says[24]:

I now possess the throne and all its powers.
... whoever assumes the task,
the awesome task of setting the city's course,
... Remember this;
our country is our safety (194–211)
[he adds later] that man
the city places in authority, his orders
must be obeyed, large and small,
right and wrong.
                         Anarchy –
show me a greater crime in all the earth!

24. Sophocles, *Antigone* in *The Three Theban Plays*, trans. Robert Fagles (New York: Viking, c.441 BC/1982). References are to the lines of this translation.

> She, she destroys cities, rips up houses,
> ... we must defend the men who live by law. (748–756)

Creon is not alone in Thebes in having this view. The Chorus, speaking for the citizens, says

> Man the master, ingenious past all measure
> past all dreams, the skills within his grasp—
> he forges on, now to destruction
> now again to greatness. When he weaves in
> the laws of the land, and the justice of the goods
> that binds his oaths together
> he and his city rise high. (406–412)

As Creon saw it, Antigone challenged his legitimate rule, endangered the possibility of life in a civilized society, and raised the specter of anarchy, all because of her personal relationship with her now dead brother, Polyneices, who was a traitor to the city. Antigone wanted to honor him by proper burial, which Creon forbade. Dead patriots ought to be honored, unlike dead traitors who ought to be condemned, regardless of who they are. Human justice must be impersonal. It must apply to everyone equally, regardless of personal relationships. Antigone put her personal relationship above human justice, and for that she must take the blame, as she knew she would have to do.

Antigone thought that human justice can protect a civilized society only if it recognizes that personal relationships are part of it. And Creon's rule was unjust because he thought that some personal relationships were challenges to it. Human justice can be right or wrong, and Creon's conception of it was wrong because it was contrary to cosmic justice. She disobeyed Creon's proclamation forbidding Polyneices's burial because

It wasn't Zeus, not in the least,
who made this proclamation—not to me.
Nor did that justice, dwelling with the gods
beneath the earth, ordain such laws for men.
Nor did I think your edict had such force
that you a mere mortal, could override the gods,
the great unwritten, unshakable traditions.
They are alive, not just today or yesterday:
they live forever. (499–507)

Antigone would not have challenged human justice if it had
conformed to cosmic justice. She challenged Creon's flawed version
of it because it violated cosmic justice by failing to recognize that personal relationships were essential parts of it.

The conflict between Creon and Antigone was between two intransigent, willful people. Each was utterly convinced of being right
and the other wrong. One appealed to the necessity of human justice,
the other to the necessity of cosmic justice. They had no doubt, however, that justice rightly understood was necessary, that following its
requirements took precedence over anything that may conflict with
it, and that it allowed no exceptions. They both scornfully rejected
friendly suggestions that their certainties were misplaced. Ismene,
her sister, tells Antigone

You're wrong from the start,
you're off on a hopeless quest. (106–107)

And Tiresias, the blind seer, tells Creon

Take these things to heart, my son, I warn you.
All men make mistakes, it is only human.
But once the wrong is done, a man

can turn his back on folly, misfortune too,
. . . Stubbornness brands you for stupidity—
pride is a crime. (1132–1137)

But Creon and Antigone remain undaunted. Sophocles shows the ruinous consequences of their dogmatism. Creon and Antigone are tragic figures who brought their ruin on themselves by their uncompromising certainty about the necessity of what they took to be justice. Sophocles conveys through them a warning to all dogmatists—from Plato to Rawls—who think that justice has priority over anything that may conflict with it, and that there can be no reasonable exception to it.

THE COMPLEXITIES OF JUSTICE

I think that Sophocles is right both about the dangerous consequences of dogmatism and about Creon and Antigone being wrong. Of course human justice is an important part of a civilized life, but it is not the only necessary part. Adequate resources, cooperation, the division of labor, the education of children, fellow feeling, liberty, loyalty, peace, pity, public health, trust, and other civic virtues are also important parts of civilized life. And as we all know from daily experience, they often conflict. There is no reason to suppose that when human justice conflicts with something that is also a necessary part of a civilized life, then it should always override whatever conflicts with it. Justice is overriding in many cases, but not in all cases because there are exceptions to it. It is true that justice should be protected. But it is also true that education, liberty, peace, and so forth should be protected. The adequate protection of some things we value is often possible only by compromising other things we value. And which of the things we value should override which keeps changing because the conditions of our life keep changing. In some conditions, one of the things we value should have priority to the others, in different conditions, priorities will be different.

As soon as we get beyond abstract generalizations about justice, or about any of our other evaluations, we must take into account exceptions in particular cases—consequences, excuses, incapacities—and we must consider whether we should give priority to justice or to something else we value in some particular context in some particular circumstances. To make this more concrete, consider what must surely be part of human justice: the prohibition of murder and treating people as they deserve to be treated. It is easy to feel righteous and proclaim that murder is wrong and that murderers should get what they deserve. A little thought and some experience of life will soon make us realize the obvious difficulties of making reasonable generalizations about murder and desert.

Start with murder. Central cases of it involve the premeditated, maliciously intended killing of a human being. Is the prohibition and punishment of murder not a necessary part of justice? No, it is not. For the murder may be committed in self-defense; or as the only way of saving many innocent lives; or involving soldiers on one side murdering soldiers on the other side; or done by the police in the course of apprehending dangerous armed criminals; or to prevent the abduction of children; or to stop a lynching mob.

Nor is it a straightforward matter how long a time is required to count as premeditation; how to distinguish between malicious intent and intent motivated by anger, indignation, resentment, or jealousy; or how much malice and how long a premeditation must there be for a killing to become a murder? Law courts and lawyers spend much time in evaluating the complexities of such difficult cases and deciding what the requirements of justice are. It will not avoid these and other complexities to say that if the law courts have decided that a killing is a murder, then it is a necessity of justice to punish it. For the murder may still be excused or even justified in the sort of cases I have just mentioned.

Think also about the difficulties involved in treating people as they deserve, not as they do not deserve, and doing so proportionally to how good or bad they or their actions are. Might not avoiding war be more important than punishing an enemy soldier? And what would be the proportional punishment of mass murderers, or the reward of a benefactor of humanity who discovered the cure for a deadly disease, or of compensation of someone who was blinded in an accident, or of children whose beloved parents died, or of ideologues who create a climate of hatred and intolerance? And is it a necessity of justice not to be led by gratitude, compassion, or love to treat people better than they deserve?

These questions are not intended to cast doubt on the importance of justice. Of course justice is important. Of course it is important to prohibit murder and to treat people as they deserve. But stressing their importance is not to stress their necessity. The kind of dogmatism that motivated Creon and Antigone and continues to motivate theorists of justice does more harm than good by glossing over the context-dependence of justice and the complexities involved in the reasonable evaluation of exceptions that justice unavoidably involves.

Consider some among many theorists who exemplify this dogmatism. Here is Kant's extraordinary claim that

> Even if a civil society were to dissolve itself by common agreement of all its members . . .the last murderer remaining in prison must be first executed, so that everyone will duly receive what his actions are worth and so that the bloodguilt thereof will not be fixed on the people because they failed to insist on carrying out the punishment (102).[25]

---

25. Immanuel Kant, *The Metaphysical Elements of Justice*, trans John Ladd (Indianapolis: Bobbs-Merrill, 1797/1965).

What could this champion of the Enlightenment mean by blood-guilt? If civil society were dissolved, why would bloodguilt, whatever this ominous phrase means, be fixed on members of the dissolved civil society? Why must murderers be executed, rather than imprisoned? And then there is Mill's pronouncement:

> Justice is a name for certain moral requirements, which, regarded collectively, stand higher in the scale of social utility, and are therefore of more paramount obligation, than any others (259).[26]

Why is the social utility of justice higher than of cooperation, education, adequate nutrition, or the protection of public health? Mill does not say. He is carried away by his dogmatic convictions, which prevent him from recognizing the importance of what he cannot fail to know.

And there is also the assumption Rawls begins with

> Justice is the first virtue of social institutions ... laws an institutions no matter how efficient and well-arranged must be reformed or abolished if they are unjust. (3)[27]

Why is justice the first virtue? Why not keeping the peace, maintaining order, protecting national security, or raising and educating children? And why must social institutions have a first virtue? Why should they not have several important virtues, none of them being the first? These questions remain without a reasonable answer in the seven-hundred-plus pages of this celebrated book.

---

26. John Stuart Mill, *Utilitarianism*, chapter 5, (1861/2006) in *The Collected Works of John Stuart Mill*, Vol. 10 (Toronto: University of Toronto Press).

27. John Rawls, *A Theory of Justice* (Cambridge, MA: Harvard University Press, 1971), and repeated in the revised edition of 1999.

How we should deal with the complexities of justice depends on the prevailing circumstances, on conflicting considerations, and on unforeseeable but reasonable exceptions to it. If we recognize these complexities, we can see that impassioned proclamations about the necessity of justice substitute rhetoric for the reasonable consideration of the particular cases in which justice is necessary and those in which it is not. And we can see also that in all cases, human justice is conditional on the consideration of possible exceptions, conflicts, and excuses.

THE SHERPAS

The Sherpas live in the highlands of northeastern Nepal.[28] They do not think that human justice is necessary. They care far more about social harmony and the unruffled temper of personal relationships. The anthropologist, Furer-Haimendorf (Furer for short), writes that the Sherpas place great value on

> courtesy, gentleness and a spirit of compromise and peacefulness. The Sherpa does not admire the strong and ruthless man. . . .The whole system of village government with its insistence on the allotment of office in rotation is designed to curb such tendencies, and the annual selection of village officials by informal consultation assures that reasonable and considerate

---

28. My sources are C.W. Cassinelli & Robert B. Ekvall, *A Tibetan Principality* (Ithaca: Cornell University Press, 1969); Christoph von Furer-Haimendorf, *The Sherpas of Nepal*, (Berkeley: University of California Press, 1964); Robert A. Paul, "The Place of the Truth in Sherpa Law and Religion," *Journal of Anthropological Research* 33, no. 2 (1977): 167–184; and Robert A. Paul, "Act and Intention in Sherpa Culture and Society" in Lawrence Rosen, ed. *Other Intentions: Cultural Context and the Attribution of Inner States* (Santa Fe, NM: School of American Research Press, 1995), 15–45. References in the text are to the pages of these works.

people rather than aggressive personalities are placed in positions of authority (283). The sentiments of tolerance and consideration for the interests and feelings of others are central to Sherpa morality, find their outward expression in courtesy and good manners (285).

The other sources I rely on confirm this view of the Sherpas. It is against this background that the remarkable case I am about to discuss should be understood.[29] As far as I know, the case has been first described by Casinelli and Ekvall (171–176).

Two Sherpas quarreled, and bad feelings between them persisted. On one occasion, both had a lot of beer at a celebration and began to fight seriously; however, they were separated, went home drunk, and slept. The wife of one reports that she woke up in the middle of the night and her husband was gone. She looked and found him lying in front of the house bruised and dead. The woman raised an alarm and she and the neighbors demanded that the dead man's enemy appear before them, but he was not at home. He said later that he was visiting a relative. The brother of the dead man accused him of murder.

The case was treated by the Sherpas as

a dispute between two private parties to be resolved by an agreement between the parties based on an equitable payment, in the form of life indemnity, for the damage done by the killing (172).

The suspect protested his innocence. He was then flogged as part of the standard treatment of suspects who claimed to be innocent when accused, rather than pay indemnity. It was thought that he should

29. I first heard about this case from a talk David Velleman gave. Since then it has been published as part of J. David Velleman, *Foundations of Moral Relativism* (OpenBook Publishers, 2015), 23–36. Unlike Velleman, I do not think that this case and others like it have relativist implications.

have stopped disrupting social harmony. But he continued to maintain his innocence. The authorities were stumped. They had no way of proving or disproving that the suspect committed the murder. He was flogged again to see whether he would change his story, but he did not. The floggings were severe, and they left the suspect limping for the rest of his life. But he still did not change his story. Then the accuser was flogged, but he did not retract the accusation. This left the local authorities powerless.

> The dispute over the claimed life indemnity could not be resolved without an agreement between the parties (175).

They then appealed to the highest authority in the land. It ordered that the decision should be based on the suspect and accuser rolling two dice three times. Whoever had the highest score won. This was done. The suspect's overall score was higher, and he was declared innocent.

> A document . . . directed the accuser to apologize to the accused and to give him a token gift . . . and ordered them to keep the peace and engage in no reprisals. No further incident between the two occurred. . . . The case was closed (176–177).

And that was the end of the matter.

What are we to make of this case? Why where the authorities powerless? Why was there not a proper trial with a judge, witnesses, and so forth? Why were they both flogged before their guilt or innocence was decided? How could guilt or innocence be determined by rolling dice? What kind of closure is it that treats both the suspect and the accuser without regard to what they deserve? We find the whole case outrageous. But that is because we do not understand how the Sherpas think about human justice. They do not think that it is necessary. They value social harmony far more. They are tolerant of each other and want to resolve conflicts before they disrupt personal relationships.

> The object of their conflict-resolving efforts is to . . . allow social life to go on with minimal disruption . . . setting off a permanent category of guilty criminals is a social impossibility. . . .The conflicts are resolved not by office-holding professional judges, but by friendly third parties who try to find some grounds upon which the disputants might come to terms (Paul 1977, 174). . . . The aim of conflict resolution . . . is not the establishment of objective truth and the . . . assignment of blame for a crime but rather the establishment of a workable basis for future social relations, the means of conflict resolution are conciliation, compensation. (Paul, 1995, 24)

Conflict-resolution, conciliation, and indemnity are arranged by peace-makers

> It is considered meritorious to act as peace-makers. Many quarrels are settled by persons without official status, who far from deriving any profit from their activities in the interest of social harmony, incur considerable expense in providing the drink necessary to bring the parties together. What they gain is . . . social approval. It is significant that Sherpas admire a skillful mediator and a man of peace more than a 'strong' man. Their ideal is not the heroic personality, but the wise, restrained and mild man (Furer, 275).

The Sherpas would not think well of Creon or Antigone. And if they had heard of the views of Kant, Mill, and Rawls, they would have rejected them out of hand as signs of grievous ignorance of what matters in life. And that is

> warmth and cordiality which pervades the relations between friend and fellow villagers . . . intensified among close kinsmen, and the atmosphere in the average Sherpa home is one of relaxed and affectionate cheerfulness. . . .There is an emphasis on broad-mindedness and tolerance. . . .Tolerance and an innate respect for the individual determines also the attitude of parents to their children. . . . harmonious relations with members of his family, kinsmen and fellow villagers are in Sherpa eyes one of the main facets of the good life (Furer, 287–288).

The conflict between the accuser and the suspect disrupted social harmony, and everyone agreed that it was a bad thing. The intransigence of both parties to the conflict made matters worse. They were not flogged to determine guilt or innocence but to make them resolve their conflict. Higher authorities eventually stepped in but only when amicable alternatives were not found by peace-makers, and they resolved the conflict, not to do justice, but to reestablish social harmony. The Sherpas certainly did not think that human justice was necessary.

But they did think that cosmic justice is necessary. And it is their belief in a relentless and unavoidable cosmic justice that made possible the social harmony they so highly valued. The Sherpas believe in reincarnation:

> fate in the life to come [depends] solely on the balance of merit and guilt which he accumulated in the course of his life on this earth. It is his moral conduct which ultimately determines his reincarnation. . . . Throughout a man's or woman's life, good and bad deeds make their mark on the person's record sheet. . . .At

a man's death the account is made and the balance of . . . marks determines his fate in the next world (Furer, 272). . . .The locus of all sanctions . . . lies outside of the human sphere, and a man's kinsmen and co-villagers do not arrogate to themselves the right to forestall this transcendental judgement. (280)

The Sherpas call cosmic justice karma.

There is no way, then, once a crime has been committed, for karmic retribution to be averted. It can never be cancelled out. All one can hope to do is perform meritorious actions to attain positive rewards in future lives. But these do not average out: one must still suffer for all one's sins, and then enjoy rewards for one's good deeds. . . . Punishment is certain, and the fact of the crime requires no lawyers or jury to establish it. . . . On a cosmic level, then, justice is taken out of hands of men; and Sherpas are remarkably unwilling to take action to sanction wrongdoing among themselves. (Paul 1977, 171–172)

There are implications that follow from thinking about the Sherpa view of justice, and they have important consequences for trying to find a reasonable answer to the hard question: Is justice necessary? First, human justice is not necessary for civilized life. Sherpa society was civilized and human justice had negligible importance in it. This, I think, is a sufficient reason for rejecting dogmatic claims about the necessity of human justice. It is simply not true that

if legal justice perishes, then it is no longer worth while for men to remain alive on this earth (Kant 1797/1965, 100), [or] justice is . . . of more paramount obligation than any others (Mill 1861/ 2006, 259), [or] justice is the first virtue of social institutions. (Rawls 1971, 3)

Second, the Sherpas thought that cosmic justice is necessary. Yet there is no reason to believe in its existence, in reincarnation, in a transcendental book-keeping system, or in a tit-for-tat strategy being built into the scheme of things. It would have made no difference to the life the Sherpas actually lived if cosmic justice did not exist. What would have made a great difference to them is if their *belief* in cosmic justice had been abandoned or seriously questioned. That would have basically affected their lives because the belief was crucially important in the context of Sherpa society. Unquestioned commitment to it was essential to living as the Sherpas thought they should live, which was

> courtesy, gentleness and a spirit of compromise and peaceful-
> ness . . . [and] the sentiments of tolerance and consideration for
> the interests and feelings of others are central to Sherpa morality,
> find their outward expression in courtesy and good manners
> (Furer, 282, 285).

Third, as far as we are concerned, in our own contemporary context, not even the *belief* in cosmic justice is necessary. Many of us do not hold it, and yet try to live in a way that by and large conforms to the prevailing evaluations, including the requirements of justice. Of course, we often fail, but then we know or can be told that we have and should not have failed and be held responsible for it. No mention needs to be made of cosmic justice. Many of those with religious commitments do believe in cosmic justice. But very few of them believe that it is necessary. Most of them think that God is loving, good, and merciful and, if we repent, will forgive our trespasses.

The reasonable answer to the hard question "Is justice necessary?" is that human justice is not necessary. It is conditional on the context in which the question is asked, on what, if anything, it conflicts with; on whether there are reasonable exceptions to it; and on what good or bad consequences follow from acting justly. Of course human justice remains important, even if it is conditional. As to the necessity of cosmic justice, its existence is questionable, questioned, and so is its necessity. Belief in the necessity of cosmic justice may be important for some of us, especially those who are religious, but not for many others, and our civilized life can go on without belief in cosmic justice.

If these answers to the hard question are reasonable, then we must consider how to resolve conflicts between reasons for and against following the requirements of justice. These conflicts are important because getting what we deserve and not what we do not deserve depends on making them reasonably.

DECENTERING JUSTICE

I have been considering the evaluations of justice by Creon, Antigone, and the Sherpas in order to compare our evaluations of it with theirs. The comparison gives us a point of view at some distance from our immediate concerns. By relying on it we can evaluate more critically our reasons by considering alternatives to them. I have claimed that the reasons of Creon, Antigone, and the Sherpas were faulty because, in different ways, they were all unreasonably dogmatic.

Creon thought that human justice is necessary and the security of the city, which justice protected, had priority to whatever conflicted with it, including personal relationships. He was ruined by thinking this way. All the personal relationships that mattered to him were destroyed by his uncompromising certainty. He failed to see that personal relationships and the protections of the security of the city are both important parts of justice. When Antigone's disobedience forced him to face the conflict between them, he insisted that the security of the city was and personal relationships were not part of justice. He thought that justice must be impersonal.

Antigone was also dogmatic and no less intransigent than Creon. She thought that human justice is conditional on conformity to cosmic justice, which is necessary, eternal, and prescribes the obligations of personal relationships. Cosmic justice, on her view, overrides whatever conflicts with it, including human justice if it fails to conform to it, and even if it protects the security of the city. She thought that the true interests of a city cannot be contrary to cosmic justice, no matter what Creon thought. She also came to a bad end when she failed to recognize that Creon was the legitimate ruler of Thebes, his obligation was to protect the security of the city on which everyone depended. He had a good reason for condemning Antigone's brother: he betrayed the city and endangered everyone's security. Antigone failed to see that the obligations of personal relationships can be fulfilled only if the city protects the conditions in which personal relationships are sustainable.

Creon and Antigone were both motivated by a particularly intransigent view of justice. In their conflict, one opted for security over personal relationships, the other for the reverse. They rightly questioned each other's view, but they did not question their own. They did not ask themselves how they could be so certain that justice required what they thought it did and that what the other thought was contrary to it. That is why they became tragic figures. But they brought their tragedy on themselves. And that, I think, is what Sophocles shows.

What could Creon and Antigone have done to avoid the tragedy? They could have given up their dogmatic view of justice. They could have realized that justice is concerned with many of the requirements of civilized life, not just with security or personal relationships, and that these requirements may conflict, and that the conflicts rarely force us to make either-or choices. Much of the time prudent more-or-less choices are available. Creon could have excoriated Antigone and pardoned her. Antigone need not have provoked Creon by publicly calling him a fool. They should have realized that the reasonable approach to coping with such conflicts is not to make dogmatic judgments and then stick to them through thick and thin, but to evaluate calmly the reasons for and against the alternatives, and listen to the advice of others. In the words of Aristotle, they were without the knowledge and the skill of how to treat

> the right person, to the right extent, at the right time, with the right aim, and in the right way (91109a23–29)[30]

Such prudent decisions depend on asking and answering such questions as how serious are the present threats to the city? How dangerous are its enemies? What specifically is the obligation of the personal relationships involved? How serious is the harm that might follow if the obligation is not honored?

They should have realized that the reasons for and against the alternatives are context-dependent and that excludes their dogmatic view of justice that cuts across contexts and assumes that there is one and only one reasonable answer that holds for everyone, always, everywhere. Nor should they have assumed that when justice conflicts with social harmony, pity, public health, happiness, toleration, and resistance to vicious enemies, then justice should always prevail. And they should have realized also that although justice is important, there are also other values that are important and that sometimes one or another of the important values is more important than the others. They should have decentered justice, stopped insisting that it must always be more important than anything else, that their view of justice was universally and impersonally applicable, and that it enabled them to know when it is or is not more important than conflicting considerations.

---

30. Aristotle, *Nicomachean Ethics*, trans. W. D. Ross, rev. J. O. Urmson, in *The Complete Works of Aristotle*, ed. Jonathan Barnes (Princeton, NJ: Princeton University Press, 1984).

The Sherpas were certainly not intransigent. They did not think much about or of human justice. What they cared about was social harmony, which they thought was necessary for maintaining the amiable civilized society in which they valued living. They were cheerful and considerate, in marked difference from the cheerless zealotry of Creon and Antigone. But for living as they did, the Sherpas had to pay the price of the frequent disruption of the intention-action-consequence sequence in their context. They and others often did not get what they deserved and got what they did not deserve, as in the case I have described.

In that case, the murderer did not get what he deserved, and the innocent got what he did not deserve. Both were flogged, although not for the murder but because they have disrupted social harmony. Social harmony soothed the indignation that, being human, even the victims of injustice must have felt. Amiable social harmony compensated them for a quotidian social life in which the consequences of their actions were uncertain and unpredictable. But they could be soothed only because they believed in the existence of cosmic justice that guaranteed that ultimately, not in this life, but in the course of an endless succession of past and future reincarnated lives, everyone is really getting what he or she deserves. They were not dogmatic about human justice, but they were dogmatic about cosmic justice and reincarnation. They were not as intransigent as Creon and Antigone were, but they did not have to be because they believed that cosmic justice was certain and unavoidable, regardless of what they did.

HUMAN JUSTICE

Neither Creon, nor Antigone, nor the Sherpas had reason to believe that cosmic justice existed, that justice will eventually be done, and that sooner or later all human beings get what they deserve and not what they do not deserve. Human justice may be all that we have, and it is a fragile, conditional, imperfect human construct that can, at best, only approximate what perfect justice would be, if only we could have it.

Our thinking about justice is split between those who think that human justice is necessary and others who accept that it is conditional on how reasonably we evaluate the requirements of justice in the light of possible exceptions, conflicts, incapacities, excuses, and good and bad consequences. We certainly care about getting the good things we deserve and not the bad things we do not deserve. However, we do not seem to mind getting good things we do not deserve and not getting bad things we do deserve. But many of us recognize, even as we lament it, that human justice is imperfect. As to cosmic justice, our moral, personal, political, and other evaluations are at most marginally concerned with the existence of cosmic justice or with the belief in it. Religious evaluations are centrally concerned with it, but there is no agreement among religious believers what exactly cosmic justice permits or prohibits. We all agree that justice is important, but we disagree about whether it is necessary or conditional.

I think that the reasons for the conditionality of justice are much stronger than the reasons against it. If justice were necessary, we could not live without it. In fact, we do, even as we lament its imperfections. We certainly recognize its importance, but we recognize as well that other things are also important and they may conflict with justice, and, our intentions, actions, institutions, and practices often go against it. A strong reason against the supposed necessity of justice is that its defenders have disagreed for thousands of years about what justice is, what makes it necessary, how to distinguish between reasonable and unreasonable exceptions to it; how to resolve conflicts between different interpretations of justice and between our evaluations of justice and other things we value; how to evaluate the good and bad consequences to which justice leads; and how to overcome the imperfections of justice that prevent us from getting what we deserve and not what we do not deserve. How could it be reasonable to believe both that justice is necessary and that in many cases there are reasonable exceptions to it?

We certainly want justice, but we also want to recognize that there may be conflicts that make it reasonable in some contexts to give priority to something other than justice. We want justice to allow for the possibility that peace, love, or pity may in some cases be more important than it. We want justice to allow that averting environmental disasters, epidemics, anarchy, and foreign or civil war; resisting aggression; protecting great works of art; making political compromises; or defaulting on debts, contracts, and promises in order to meet more pressing concerns may reasonably take precedence to it. If such reasonable exceptions are allowed, then they would show that justice is not necessary but conditional. And if such exceptions were disallowed, then the consequence would be the kind of uncompromising dogmatic intransigence that doomed Creon and Antigone.

If, however, the answer to the hard question is, as I think, that justice is not necessary, then we must face conflicts, exceptions, and consequences that require giving priority to considerations other than justice. We can reasonably resolve such conflicts by decentering justice, that is by recognizing that our evaluation of justice is only one evaluation among others.

The point is not to decenter justice because something else should replace it in the center. If all evaluations are conditional, then no value or evaluation should permanently occupy the center. In some contexts and in some circumstances one important evaluation should have priority, in other contexts and circumstances the priorities may be different. Justice is important, but neither it nor any other value or evaluation should always, in all conditions, at all times be more important than any other that may conflict with it. How, then, can we evaluate the reasons for and against alternative ways of resolving conflicts between justice and something else?

THE ANSWER

We can evaluate them by reference to the evaluative framework of the context in which we live. It includes all the various moral, personal, political, religious, and other evaluations, as well as the customs, practices, and traditions associated with them. The reasons for and against answers to hard questions—including the one about the necessity of justice—ultimately depend on whether they conform to or deviate from the prevailing evaluative framework.

There are and likely to continue to be, conflicts within an evaluative framework about that as well. I have endeavored to show in this and the previous chapters that these conflicts and the reasonable ways of coping with them are particular and context-dependent. The conflicts will often persist because there will be reasonable disputes about how the context-dependent and particular reasons for and against the available alternatives should be evaluated. The hardness of answering hard questions is the result of reasonable disagreements about how the relative strength of these contrary reasons should be evaluated.

My proposal is that only when this point has been reached can we appeal to our evaluative framework. And the appeal consists in evaluating the relative strength of the contrary reasons from the point of view of whether they strengthen or weaken the entire evaluative framework on which all of us who live together in a context depend. That evaluative framework has partly formed our personal attitudes, it protects the conditions in which we can live as we think we should, and it is one we share with others and thereby belong to the same community.

Of course, the evaluative framework is always changing because the particular moral, personal, political, religious, and other evaluations that jointly form it are changing, often in response to changing environmental, cultural, demographic, international, scientific, technological, and other conditions. But throughout these changes we continue to depend on it. Its continuity is more important than any of its constituent elements because we rely on it to cope with the changes. If there were no continuity, we would have no resources left on which we could rely to evaluate the possibilities of life. The evaluative framework in our context, the only we have, would then disintegrate. That would be a devastating cultural calamity. We would be left with basic needs we would want to satisfy, but we would not know how to make moral, personal, political, religious, and other choices on which living as we used to think we should have always depended. It would be like losing the only language we ever had.

If the evaluative framework in our context does indeed provide these benefits, then we can reasonably appeal to it to resolve conflicts between the relative strength we attribute to conflicting reasons for or against particular answers to hard questions. We could then opt for reasons, answers, and choices that strengthen the evaluative framework, and against ones that weaken it. All of us in our context have a vested interest in resolving conflicts in these ways because the failure to do so weakens the evaluative framework and endangers the benefits we all want to continue to enjoy. The continuity and allegiance to the evaluative framework is more important than any of the conflicting answers we may give to any of the hard question

This appeal to the evaluative framework is more reasonable than alternatives to it, assuming that the evaluative framework does provide the benefits we want to have. But, of course, there have been and are evaluative frameworks that fail to do this. They may be vicious, inconsistent, prejudice ridden, inflexible, serve only the limited interests of a select group, incapable of providing even the basic necessities of life, based on false beliefs, provoke base emotions, and encourage ruinous desires that express atavistic inhuman tendencies. How could we tell whether the evaluative framework is free of these defects?

We can tell by applying to it what may be called the "test on consent." An evaluative framework passes this test if it meets the following conditions. First, it has endured in a society for a long time, measured in generations, not in years. Second, throughout this period there has been sufficient continuity in its evaluations to accommodate the necessary changes that have to be made to adjust to the changing conditions of life. Third, those inhabiting the society by and large adhere to the evaluative framework voluntarily. They have the option to leave the society, or to try to reform it in ways they think are needed, or to protest and organize against particular features of it. They can say then, or it can be truthfully said of them, that if these conditions are met by the evaluative framework, and yet they fail to live as they think they should, then the fault is theirs, not of the evaluative framework.

Assuming that an evaluative framework passes the test of consent, which is a big assumption, what answer follows from it to the hard question: Is justice necessary? The answer is that it is not necessary, but one among a small number of our most important evaluations. It is not necessary because there may be reasonable exceptions to it in particular cases; because it may conflict with other important evaluations that in some contexts are reasonably regarded as more important than justice; and because the consequences that follow from justice in a particular case might be much worse than the consequences of injustice. If the relative strength of the reasons for and against these exceptions, conflict-resolutions, and consequences is controversial, then the controversy can be reasonably resolved by asking which set of conflicting reasons is more likely strengthen rather than weaken the entire evaluative framework in that context. And if we arrive in this way to the answer to the hard question, then we will also have arrived at how we could reasonably resolve conflicts between the reasons we have for and against adhering to or going against justice.

Chapter 6

How Should We Respond to Evil?

THE QUESTION

The "we" in "How should we respond to evil?" is intended to be understood in a personal, not general, sense. The question is how each one of us—the particular individuals we are, given our experiences, context, and personal attitude—should respond to the evil that has been done to us, or what we have directly or vicariously experienced as having being done to others?

One response to evil is called by James "healthy-minded." It dwells on evil as little as possible. This is very hard to do for those who have endured or witnessed evil. It is psychologically impossible to trivialize, ignore, or explain it away because it threatens the very possibility of civilized life in which we can form an idea of how we should live and then do our best to live that way. The experience of evil brings home to us how thin is the layer of security that moral, personal, political, religious, and other evaluations have gradually erected over the centuries to protect us from the barbaric urges that seem to be as much part of us as the civilized ones. If we have experienced evil, we cannot help dwelling

on a sense of disgrace, of outrage, of horror, of baseness, of brutality, and most important, a sense that a barrier, assumed to be firm . . . has been knocked over, and a feeling that, if this horrible, or outrageous, or squalid, or brutal, action is possible, then anything is possible . . . the fear that one may feel is fear of human nature.[31]

The experience threatens everything we value. The hard question I am asking and trying to answer in this chapter is how we should respond to this experience of evil.

Part of the reason why the question is hard is that there are three conflicting answers to it: the pessimist, the optimist, and the realist. The pessimist one is that evil is prevalent because barbaric tendencies are dominant in human nature. But since there is ample evidence that we also have civilized tendencies, a reasonable answer must at the very least assume that our tendencies are mixed. I will, therefore, say nothing further about the pessimist answer.

The optimist answer is that evil is avoidable. The key to it is to respond to evil by finding its cause and then changing it for the better. This must be possible, optimists think, because it has been done both individually by many people who examined and changed their motives for the better, and by societies whose evaluative framework civilized the barbaric tendencies of its inhabitants. What needs to be done is to do more of it and to do it better. Human nature is perfectible. And optimists think that we should respond to evil by doing all we can to make it less imperfect than it is.

The realist answer is that evil has been present in all ages, societies, and conditions, and even if the lives of some people have been free of it, many others have suffered it. Evil is unavoidable because its source is human nature. The enemy is us, as Pogo, that insufficiently appreciated deep thinker, told us. The realist answer should not be confused with

---

31. Stuart Hampshire, "Morality and Pessimism" in *Morality and Conflict* (Cambridge, MA: Harvard University Press, 1983), 89.

the pessimist one. Realists can accept that the scope of evil can be curtailed, perhaps even a great deal, but it cannot be eliminated because its cause is within us. In fearing evil, we fear human nature.

Evil is one of our most severe condemnations. Its force is not just that we personally think badly of whatever we condemn as evil. We also think that others are seriously mistaken if they fail to condemn it. This makes it important to be clear about what we are condemning and why. How does evil differ from what is merely bad, or even very bad? Is the point of view from which we condemn it moral, personal, political, religious, or something else? Are we condemning a person, action, motive, society, custom, or policy? And why are we condemning it? If the force of the condemnation is stronger than a mere personal preference, what is the reason for it? Reasonable optimists and realists can agree about the answers to these questions about what we are condemning when we condemn evil, and yet go on to disagree about what the most reasonable answer is to the hard question: "How should we respond to evil?" I begin, then, with an account of evil that may be shared by optimists and realists.

WHAT IS EVIL?

The primary sources of evil are evil actions. They are worse than bad. They are contrary to the possibility of civilized life in which we can live as we think we should. The force of the condemnation is that victims of evil actions are grievously harmed and, as a result, become unable to live a normal human life. Recovery for them may sometimes be possible, but it takes a long time and favorable circumstances. And even if they can heal physically, the psychological consequences of what they have endured continue to haunt them for a long time, if not forever.

The account focuses on the actions of evildoers, not of groups, on actions that are not isolated episodes in the life of evildoers, but habitual patterns in which the same kind of evil action is repeated again and again. Patterns of evil actions are voluntary. There are alternatives to them and evildoers are aware of at least some of the alternatives. They are not forced to perform the actions, and the immediate consequences of the actions are readily foreseeable. Any even moderately intelligent adult could foresee what is likely to happen if a gun is pointed and the trigger is pulled, an eye is gouged, or a bomb is exploded in a crowd. Lastly, the patterns of evil actions grievously harm people who do not deserve what is done to them. Evil actions then form *patterns*, are *voluntary*, done by *individuals, cause grievous undeserved harm,* and to *innocent* victims.

This account is a description of central indisputable cases of evil actions, not a definition that specifies the necessary and sufficient conditions that make an action evil. It allows that there may be borderline cases, grey areas, evil actions that do not form a pattern, and exceptions when what is normally an evil action may be mitigated, excused, or even justified, although it is not easy to find such exceptions for *patterns* of evil actions. Disputable cases, however, do not cast doubt on central cases that are obviously evil.

I will be concerned with evil actions understood in this way. I will not discuss whether evil actions are accepted or even approved in a context; what degree of responsibility evildoers have; nor whether passively allowing evil actions to be done is as bad as actively doing them. These considerations are important for the evaluation of the evildoers, but I am concerned with patterns of evil actions, not with those whose actions they are.

Here are some examples of evil actions from about 1900 on.[32] Between 1914 and 1918, the Turks massacred about 1,500,000

32. For detailed documentation, see Stephanie Courtois, et al., *The Black Book of Communism* (Cambridge, MA: Harvard University Press, 1999); Martin Gilbert, *The Holocaust* (New York: Henry Holt, 1985); Jonathan Glover, *Humanity: A Moral History of the Twentieth Century* (New Haven, CT: Yale University Press, 1999); Paul Hollander, ed.

Armenians. In 1931, Stalin ordered the murder of prosperous peasants, called kulaks, and about two million of them were executed or deported to concentration camps where they died slowly as a result of forced labor in extreme cold and on starvation diet. During the great terror of 1937–1938, two million more were murdered on Stalin's orders. In 1937–1938, the Japanese murdered about half a million Chinese in Nanking. During World War II, about six million Jews, two million prisoners of war, and half a million gypsies, mental defectives, and homosexuals were murdered in Nazi Germany. After India's independence in 1947, over a million Muslims and Hindus massacred each other. In the 1950–1951 campaign against so-called counter-revolutionaries in Mao's China about a million people were murdered, and the so-called Great Leap Forward of 1959–1963 caused the death of an estimated sixteen to thirty million people from starvation. Pol Pot in Cambodia presided over the murder of about two million people. In 1992–1995, about two hundred thousand Muslims were murdered in Bosnia by Serb nationalists. In 1994, almost a million people were murdered in Rwanda. To this list of mass murders many more could be added from Afghanistan, Argentina, Chile, the Congo, Iran, Iraq, Sudan, Uganda, and numerous other places. And, of course, the examples I have given are only for the last couple of centuries. Countless more could be culled from the history of religions, conquests, tyrannies, colonies, slavery, and persecutions throughout the millennia. I do not see how it could be reasonably doubted that evil has been prevalent throughout human history.

Its prevalence calls into question the very possibility of civilized life in which it is possible to live as we think we should. If we face these atrocities, it will change our personal attitude to the possibilities of life. We come to see that the possibilities are not just life-enhancing

From the Gulag to the Killing Fields (Wilmington, DE: ISI, 2006), and John Kekes, *The Roots of Evil* (Ithaca, NY: Cornell University Press, 2005).

opportunities but also destructive, corrupting, and horrifying threats. And we see also that the customary civilized limits have been violated by repeated transgressions of them. What we took for granted in the past has become questionable. We can no longer count on anything secure in the future because the prevalence of evil has driven home to us the thinness of the layer of civilized life below which lie the horrors of barbaric inhumanity. This is the background against which survivors of massacres, concentration camps, torture chambers, and so on cannot help but ask the hard question and try to answer it.

If we have merely witnessed the evil actions done to others, without having been a victim of them, then the hard question is less intensely personal. We have not endured the evil. But if we are suffi-ciently compassionate and imaginative, we are vicariously assailed by it. We try to understand what it must have been like and form some personal response to it. Nevertheless, even the most perfect em-pathy will keep us at one remove from the direct experience of evil. Vicarious experience is unavoidably second hand.

Still, our personal response to the evil done to others may also be devastating. We too have to try to understand why evildoers have done it. This is the form of the hard question that arises for the family members and friends of the survivors, the police, and soldiers who come face to face with what happened to the victims, and for the clergy or psychological counselors who try to help those who have endured the horrors. The experience forces those who have had it to ask whether civilized life can go on when its very possibility has been called into question by the limits that have been deliberately violated, not once, but again and again, by the patterns of evil actions that have grievously harmed innocent victims.

The following discussion of the hard question involves comparing and evaluating the reasons for and against the responses of two people: Anna and the Priest. Anna's experience was direct, the

Priest's vicarious. They both faced the hard question and struggled with trying to find a reasonable answer to it.

ANNA AND THE PRIEST

The events in question began just before the German occupation of a Central European country in the middle of WWII.[33] Anna is sixteen, the beloved daughter of a happy secular Jewish family. Her father is a high school teacher, her mother a conventional housewife, and she has two younger sisters. She is a charming, vivacious adolescent, as innocent as girls used to be then and there. She is the one with lovely green eyes that gives the title to the novel. The Priest is her father's close friend. They have grown up together in the same neighborhood, went to the same school and university, and the Priest had been a frequent and always welcome visitor who shared many of the family meals. All this came to an end with the German occupation. In a short time, the entire family was deported to one of the death camps. As they arrived in the company of thousands of others who, like them, were packed for days like sardines into cattle wagons. After the train arrived, there was a quick selection process supervised by a Nazi physician. Most, including Anna's entire family, were selected for extermination and gassed in the same day. But Anna was not.

Her lovely green eyes caught the attention of the physician. He kept her to himself for sexual pleasure, used her for a few weeks, and was beginning to tire of her. She knew that her own death was approaching, wanted to live, and because of her youth and

---

33. The discussion that follows is based on a heartrending novel that should be far better known than it is. Its author is Arnost Lustig, *Lovely Green Eyes*, trans. Ewald Osers, (New York: Arcade, 2000). I have altered the original in various ways. I do not think the alterations affect the essential elements of the narrative.

beauty she was taken to a brothel kept for German officers. She was allowed to live there as long as she pleased the officers. Other girls who did not were returned to be gassed. Anna once again survived because she became the favorite of one of the officers who instructed the SS woman in charge of the brothel to feed her well, and make sure she was healthy. In this way she survived for over a year in the brothel until the war came to end. She then had nowhere to go, no one to help her in the postwar chaos. She eventually made her way back to what used to be her hometown. The ravages of the war destroyed her family, her home, and everything in it. She had nothing left except her memories of how sweet life was before the war and what it had become during the hell she had lived through. She happened to encounter the Priest. He, of course, remembered her, took her to his home, and did what he could to look after her.

Words cannot adequately express how traumatized she was by what had happened to her. Slowly, as the months passed, she began to talk to the Priest and tell him what she had endured and what some of the sordid details were of what she had to do to survive. One among the many others was that Anna had to pretend to enjoy what was done to her several times every day for more than year. The Priest was kind, helpful, patient, and understanding, and he did what he could to nurture her back to life. But, of course, he was deeply shaken by what Anna told him. Eventually, little by little, many more months later, she slowly revived from emotional death. Catharsis after catharsis she came to be able to express to the Priest her feelings of rage, humiliation, degradation, shame, pain, and the devastating loss of her childhood and innocence. In this way she came to face the evil that was done to her. But that still left her with the question of how to respond to it and go on with her life.

The Priest was left with the concrete details of the evil he experienced vicariously as he was listening to the terrible things Anna told him. Nothing in his own experience and training for the priesthood had prepared him for the soul-destroying details of what had been done to Anna and of what she had endured. He struggled to reconcile with his faith what happened to Anna. He knew, of course, the Christian view of the problem of evil. But when it came to the awful details that displaced the abstract theological response to evil, then he had to face the demeaning concrete horrors of the evil that was inflicted on and endured by the no more charming, vivacious, and innocent girl he knew before.

He did not know how to console Anna, nor how to respond to his own feelings of despair, indignation, pity of Anna, and rage against those who did to her the evil she had endured. He could not understand how human beings could do what they did to Anna, how the God he believed in could have allowed this to happen. All the theological abstractions and arguments he had learned during his seminary days seemed to him to have been cast in doubt by the concrete details of the evil Anna had endured and he vicariously lived through by compassionately and imaginatively trying to share Anna's experience. He, too, faced the hard question, but he did not know how he should answer it.

Nevertheless he took action. He found out that Anna had some distant relatives living in America. He wrote to them, explaining only that Anna had returned from a death camp, her family was murdered, and she was left alone in the world. He asked the relatives to help Anna. They did, and arranged for Anna to join them. She emigrated and gradually got used to her new life in new circumstances. She told no one what she had to do to survive. She tried to live a normal life as a young new American. She had recurrent nightmares, daytime panic attacks, and rages, but they slowly became less and less frequent and harrowing. She could get on with her new life because she was young, resilient, and found in herself the strength that she did not dream she had. For Anna, the hard question was the personal and practical one of how to get on with her life. She had no interest in the theological complexities of the problem of evil, nor in making theories about what happened to her and to her family. And there, for a moment, I leave her.

RESPONSES TO EVIL

The Priest, however, was obliged to form a religious response to evil. The concrete details of the evil he vicariously experienced could not but challenge his faith. His conscience dictated that he should try to reconcile the evil that was done to Anna with his religious view of the world, but he could not do it. He knew of course God's answer to Job when he complained of what happened to him:

> the Lord said to Job: Shall a faultfinder contend with the Almighty? He who argues with God, let him answer it. Then Job answered the Lord: Behold, I am of small account; what shall I answer thee? I lay my hand on my mouth. I have spoken once, and I will not answer; twice, but I will proceed no further. (Job 40:1–5)

But he found that this answer was no answer at all. It was just a way of silencing the question he himself could not silence. Nevertheless this is the no-answer answer that some thoughtful religious people give. Thomas Reid, a philosopher and a clergyman, wrote:

> Since it is supposed that the Supreme Being had no other end in making and governing the universe, but to produce the greatest happiness to his creatures in general, how comes it to pass, that there is so much misery in a system made and governed by infinite wisdom and power? . . . I confess I cannot answer this

question, but must lay my hand upon my mouth. He giveth no account of his conduct to the children of men.[34]

John Cottingham, a fine philosopher, agreed:

At this point, I think, philosophical argument must come to an end. . . .the opponents of theism may devise ever more dramatic presentations of the problem of evil, and its defenders construct ever more ingenious rebuttals, but one has the sense that neither side in the arguments has any real expectation of changing the opponent's mind.[35]

And Alvin Plantinga and Michael Tooley, hardnosed analytic philosophers who are also among the faithful, say when they write about Job that

the point is not really to convince him that God has his reasons, but to quiet him, to still the storm in his soul . . . the doubts and turmoil abate and once more Job loves and trusts the Lord.[36]

I speculate that these philosophers could evade the hard question because they were not compelled to face the concrete details. They had no direct experience of evil, such as Anna had, nor vicarious experience of it, as the Priest had. But whether or not my speculation is correct, they evaded the hard question.

Anna and the Priest, however, could not evade them. Anna could not because of what had happened to her, and the Priest could not because he tried to come to terms with Anna's experience. What

---

34. Thomas Reid, *Essays on the Active Powers of the Human Mind* (Cambridge, MA: MIT Press, 1814/1969), 349 and 353.
35. John Cottingham, *Why Believe?* (New York: Continuum, 2009), 150.
36. Alvin Plantinga and Michael Tooley, *Knowledge of God* (Oxford: Blackwell, 2008), 183.

compelled them, however, were their personal experiences. Other people, more fortunate than Anna and who have no priestly obligation to try to make sense of evil, need not be compelled to struggle with the hard question. These lucky healthy-minded ones, as James called them, could avoid dwelling on it.

Thoughtful people, however, should not count themselves among these lucky ones, regardless of whether they are religious or secular. They are supposed to think deeply about the human condition, recognize that evil is part of it, and they should not evade the hard question, nor keep it at arm's length by abstractions, and find a reasonable response to it. Williams is right to remind them of it:

> There are areas of philosophy which might be supposed to have a special commitment to not forgetting or lying about the [world's] horrors, among them moral philosophy. No one with sense asks it to think about them all the time, but, in addressing what it claims to be our most serious concerns, it would do better if it did not make them disappear. Yet this is what in almost all its modern forms moral philosophy effectively does.[37]

In the influential works that have shaped contemporary moral and political thought, there is no discussion of evil.[38] Their authors are concerned with constructing theories of what autonomy, equality, happiness, justice, liberty, rights, virtue, and so on, would be if only we had them. They take no notice of evil that is an obstacle to living according to even the most carefully constructed theory.[39] They

37. Bernard Williams, "The Women of Trachis" in *The Sense of the Past* (Princeton, NJ: Princeton University Press, 2006), 54.
38. Isaiah Berlin, Ronald Dworkin, Harry Frankfurt, Alan Gewirth, Christine Korsgaard, Alasdair MacIntyre, Thomas Nagel, Derek Parfit, John Rawls, Joseph Raz, Michael Sandel, and Thomas Scanlon, among many others, mention it barely, if at all.
39. I discuss and criticize this tendency at length in *How Should We Live?* (Chicago: University of Chicago Press, 2014).

ignore the concrete experience of evil to which Anna and the Priest were compelled to respond.

I said earlier that what makes it difficult to choose between conflicting optimist and realist responses to the hard question is that there are reasons both for and against their responses. Those who have to answer the question may not be aware of all, or even many, of these contrary reasons, but there nevertheless are reasons. I will now consider what reasons could be given both for and against Anna's and the Priest's responses.

THE BALANCE OF REASONS

After many months of emotional turmoil and the help of the Priest, Anna accepted the opportunity to remake her life in a new setting. She was able to do this because she was young, resilient, and found in herself unexpected strength and resources that no one, herself included, could have predicted she had. She was not ruined by her experience of evil. The answer she found to the hard question was admirable and reasonable, but it was not based on reasons. She was, after all, a young girl who had understandably passionate reactions to what she had lived through. It was psychologically appropriate for her to have such reactions. Nevertheless, she was not reflective, analytical, or given to examining and evaluating the personal attitude that motivated her response. Although she was not aware of the reasons that made her answer reasonable, there were such reasons.

Foremost among them was her will to live. It enabled her to survive in the death camp, the brothel, the sexual degradation, the murder of her family, to go to her unknown relatives, and begin again. Various psychologically astute thinkers (among them Spinoza, Schopenhauer, Nietzsche, Freud, and more recently Sartre and Frankfurt) regarded the will as the main, or perhaps one of the main, motivating forces in human life. It may indeed be that, but it is not by itself sufficient. The life it enables us to live may not be worth living, especially not when we have to live with the memory and consequences of the evil we endured. The unwillingness to do this has been for more than a few of the victims, unlike for Anna, among the reasons against continuing to live.

In Anna's case, if all her courageous efforts had led to a new life in America that was haunted during the day by her memories of having to pretend to enjoy the daily degradation in the brothel, and by nightmares as she was trying to escape to sleep, then she might have found that the burdens of her life outweighed its benefits. As it happened, they did not. Her reactions began to fade, and new experiences began to preoccupy her consciousness. But when she was in the Priest's house, she could not have counted on this fortunate outcome. If she had been what she was not, a thoughtful and analytical reasoner, she may well have found the reasons for and against living with what happened to her equipoised.

In actual fact, she could not have been concerned with the relative strength of these reasons because she was unaware of most of them. She was concerned with the practical task of putting behind her the past and getting on with life. I stress the point that *she* had this concern. Others, who were older, more reflective, less resilient, weaker, and less courageous than Anna, may well have examined the reasons and found the balance of them tilt in favor of not finding it worthwhile to continue to live with the memory of the evil to which they had been subjected.

The importance of this for us, who are far more fortunate, is that the balance of reasons we have for and against facing evil varies with who we are, at what point in our life and in what circumstances we have to face it, and what we have to live for. This makes the reasons for and against the answer we give vary with persons and contexts. We have reasons for and against the alternatives between which we have to choose, but the reasons are not generalizable to others who have different psychological characteristics, live in different circumstances, and have different aims in life. A reasonable answer to the hard question of how we should respond to the direct or vicarious experience of evil cannot be universally applicable to everyone, always, everywhere.

This brings us to the Priest who searched for but could not find an answer that he could reconcile with his faith in the goodness of God's order. He could not generalize it so as to apply to all or most other victims of evil, and, at the same time, allow him to face the horrifying concrete details of the evil that was done. Unlike Anna, he remained devastated by his experience of evil. It was not his fault that he could not find a reasonable answer to this hard question. Perhaps no one could, but I set aside the theological complications involved in that possibility.

The relevant point is that the Priest could not resolve the conflict, and that left him devastated by the terrible details he could not stop thinking about. He remained in a state of uncertainty, and a persistent crisis of faith gnawed at him. His faith was genuine and strong, but so was the problem of evil. He was unable and unwilling to maintain the sort of distance between himself and his vicarious experience of evil that Reid, Cottingham, Plantinga, and Tooley arrived at. His compassion and imaginative understanding of what it was like for Anna to live through it prevented him from distancing himself. Yet his priestly obligation compelled him to ask what it is in human beings that accounts for the prevalence of evil throughout history.

Optimists and realists give conflicting responses to it and thus to the hard question of whether evil is avoidable. According to optimists, human beings are basically disposed toward the good, but they do evil because they are corrupted by circumstances beyond their control. Realists think that human beings are basically ambivalent, disposed toward both good and evil. Which of their dispositions is dominant depends on their character, experiences, preferences, and the evaluative framework of the context in which they live.

The optimist response is accepted by the majority of those who try to understand why there is evil and whether it is avoidable. This is the response the Priest might have given as a way out of his crisis of faith. It would have allowed him to continue to have faith in the goodness of God's order and blame evil on human beings. The realist response is accepted only by a minority. I will discuss the reasons for and against both responses. My own view is that the reasons for the realist response are much stronger than for the optimist one.

THE OPTIMIST RESPONSE

Numerous first-rate thinkers agree that human beings are basically disposed toward the good. According to Plato[40]

> it's the reality of goodness . . . which everyone, whatever their temperament, is after, and which is the goal of all their activities. They have an inkling of their existence, but they are confused about it and can't adequately grasp its nature.

Rousseau agrees:[41]

> Man is naturally good; I believe I have demonstrated it.

---

40. Plato, *Republic*, trans. Robin Waterfield (Oxford: Oxford University Press, 1993), 505d–e.
41. Jean-Jacques Rousseau, *Discourses on the Origin and Foundation of Inequality Among Man*, trans. Donald A. Cress (Indianapolis: Hackett, 1988/1754), 89.

And again,

> The fundamental principle of all morality, about which I have reasoned in all my works ... is that man is a naturally good creature, who loves justice and order; that there is no original perversity in the human heart.[42]

Kant says that man is

> not basically corrupt (even as regards his original predisposition to good), but rather ... still capable of improvement [and] ... man (even the most wicked) does not, under any maxim whatsoever, repudiate the moral law. ... The law, rather, forces itself upon him irresistibly by virtue of his moral predisposition.[43]

Mill holds the same view,

> The leading department of our nature ... this powerful natural sentiment ... the social feeling of mankind—the desire to be in unity with our fellow creatures, which is already a powerful principle in human nature, and happily one of those which tend to become stronger, even without inculcation.[44]

Rawls writes more recently

> Men's propensity to injustice is not a permanent aspect of community life; it is greater or less depending in large part on social

42. Jean-Jacques Rousseau, *Letter to Beaumont* in *Oeuvres completes*, 5 vols. (Paris: Gallimard, 1959–1995), 935; translated by Timothy O'Hagan in *Rousseau* (London: Routledge, 1999), 15.

43. Immanuel Kant, *Religion within the Bounds of Reason Alone*, trans. Theodore M. Greene and Hoyt H. Hudson (New York: Harper & Row, 1960/1794), 39, 31.

44. John Stuart Mill, *Utilitarianism* in *The Collected Works of John Stuart Mill*, vol. 19, ed. J.M. Robson (Indianapolis: Liberty Fund, 1861/2006), 231.

institutions, and in particular on whether they are just or unjust. a moral person is a subject with ends he has chosen, and his fundamental preference is for conditions that enable him to frame a mode of life that expresses his nature as a free and equal rational being.[45]

Most of our contemporary moral, personal, political, religious, and other evaluations assume, following these influential thinkers, that the primary human disposition is toward the good. They explain the prevalence of evil as caused by bad social arrangements, such as the abuse of political power, discrimination, humiliation, injustice, intolerance, persecution, poverty, prejudice, superstition, and so on. Those who are mistreated in these ways by bad social arrangements become embittered, and, it is supposed, their evil actions express their understandable reactions to the undeserved grievous harm they themselves have suffered.

There can be no reasonable doubt that there are and have been such bad social arrangements that corrupt some people. But this does not come anywhere close to an adequate explanation of the prevalence of evil. First, there are numerous responses other than evil actions to being harmed by bad social arrangements. Some are crushed by them, become lethargic, and lose hope. Others turn to religion for consolation. Yet others join some political movement that aims at reform or revolution. There are also those who side with the evildoers, adopt their ways, and hope thereby to escape being victimized. Some emigrate to another society whose social arrangements, they suppose, are less bad. Those who become evildoers chose to respond in one possible way but not in any of the other available ones.

45. John Rawls, *A Theory of Justice* (Cambridge, MA: Harvard University Press, 1971), 245 and 561.

The question then is: why do some but not others respond by becoming evildoers? The explanation cannot be merely in terms of bad social arrangements. Many who are subject to the same bad social arrangements have not responded the way evildoers have. The explanation, therefore, must include some account of what it is in the motivation of evildoers that disposes them to do evil. And whatever that explanation is, it cannot be that they are basically disposed toward the good because if they were, they would not become evildoers.

Second, many of those who became evildoers have not been victims of bad social arrangements. In fact, many of them have been among those who maintain and benefit from bad social arrangements. It is not at all unusual for terrorists; revolutionaries; perpetrators of nationalist, tribal, ethnic, religious, or political massacres, tortures; and other patterns of evil actions to come from a privileged background. Their evil actions, therefore, cannot be understood as caused by bad social arrangements since they have been favored by the bad social arrangements.

Third, let us assume, counter-factually and only for a moment, that evildoers have become what they are because bad social arrangements have corrupted them. The obvious question remains: why are these social arrangements bad? They are made and maintained by people. Those who made and maintained them, could not be basically good, because if they were, they would not have made and maintained bad social arrangements that abuse power, discriminate, humiliate, persecute, or doom people to a life of poverty, ill-health, fear, and insecurity. It cannot be reasonably claimed that those who made and maintained bad social arrangements have themselves been corrupted by bad social arrangements. People are bound to precede the social arrangements they make and maintain, and they could not have been corrupted by the social arrangements before they made and maintained them.

It seems to me that these considerations count decisively against the widely accepted view that we are basically disposed toward the good and that evil actions are caused solely by bad social arrangements. Many evil actions are not caused by bad social arrangements but by aggression, callousness, cruelty, envy, fanaticism, greed, hatred, ill will, prejudice, rage, stupidity, thoughtlessness, and so on. Why, then, do the optimists I have cited and their many followers continue to hold the implausible view that human beings are basically disposed toward good?

They hold it because they are misled by a false hope that ignores the history of economic, ethnic, ideological, nationalist, religious, territorial, and tribal conflicts throughout the millennia in which millions of people were and continue to be massacred, tortured, enslaved, and persecuted in the name of some ideal. Their false hope is that the construction of yet another theory that defends yet another reformulation of a yet even more abstract ideal, say, of autonomy, duty, equality, God's law, happiness, justice, liberty, reason, rights, and so on, will be sufficient to persuade all who oppose it to transform society to come ever closer to whatever the ideal is.

Their false hope leads them to ignore the past in favor of a glorious imagined future in which all manner of things will be well. They do not seem to realize that the perpetrators of large-scale evil throughout history have been motivated by the same false hope. And their hope, regardless of its content, has been falsified again and again by evildoers who believed that they are doing God's work, or are reforming humanity, or are agents of historical necessity, or are scourges of evil. They do not realize that:[46]

---

46. G. F. W. Hegel, *Reason in History*, trans. R.S. Hartman (New York: Liberal Arts, 1840/ 1953), 26–27.

passions, private aims, and the satisfaction of selfish desires are . . . tremendous springs of action. Their power lies in the fact that they respect none of the limitations which law and morality would impose on them; and that these natural impulses are closer to the core of human nature than the artificial and troublesome discipline that tends toward order, self-restraint, law, and morality. When we contemplate this display of passions and the consequences of their violence, the unreason which is associated not only with them, but even—rather we might say *especially*—with good designs and righteous aims; when we see arising therefrom the evil, the vice, the ruin that has befallen the most flourishing kingdoms which the mind of man ever created, we can hardly avoid being filled with sorrow at this universal taint of corruption.

THE REALIST RESPONSE

Realists think that we should accept the sad fact that evil is prevalent because we are basically ambivalent about the good and the bad. The familiar virtues of compassion, conscientiousness, courage, honesty, loyalty, moderation, wisdom, and so forth dispose us toward what we regard as the good, and the no less familiar vices of cowardice, cruelty, dishonesty, envy, greed, hypocrisy, prejudice, self-indulgence, and so on dispose us toward the bad. The bad often turns into evil if it leads to patterns of voluntary actions that cause grievous harm to innocent victims.

The optimist response focuses on causes external to us that corrupt our disposition to aim at the good. The realist one focuses on the combination of both external and internal causes that jointly lead to evil actions. Corrupting external causes are not by themselves sufficient explanations of evil actions because, as we have seen, different people respond differently to the same potentially corrupting external causes. According to realists, then, the optimist response is only half true: potentially corrupting external causes may or may not be actually corrupting. The response is half true, half false.

The realist response is that our actions are evil when our dispositions to aim at the bad are combined with external causes that encourage us to act on our bad dispositions and discourage us from acting on the good ones. We are neither basically good nor basically bad, but the complex joint products of internal and external causes. The internal ones are our personal attitudes formed of our beliefs, emotions, and desires that reflect our genetic disposition, upbringing, education, preferences, and experiences. The external causes are, among others, demographic, economic, medical, physical, technological; the prevailing moral, personal, political, and religious evaluations; the family into which we are born and in which we are raised; and how fortunately or unfortunately we are affected by the contingencies of life that vary with time, place, and context. The result is that we are rarely basically good saints or thoroughly bad monsters. Most of us are basically complicated and ambivalent. The proportion of our good and bad dispositions and actions, and the extent to which the bad ones turn into evil, vary with external and internal causes and the context in which we live.

The realist response stands in as long a tradition as the optimist one, but its defenders have usually sharply disagreed with one another.[47] Some who have contributed to it are Euripides, Thucydides, the Manicheans, Augustine, Machiavelli, Calvin, Montaigne,

---

47. In *Facing Evil* (Princeton, NJ: Princeton University Press, 1990) and *The Roots of Evil* (Ithaca, NY: Cornell University Press, 2005) I continue in this tradition and say much more about it.

Shakespeare, Hobbes, Nietzsche, and more recently Freud, Stuart Hampshire, and Bernard Williams.

There are several important implications of the differences between the optimist and realist responses. One is that if we were basically good, we would see good actions as natural and requiring no explanation. Evil would then be seen as interference with our basic goodness and contrary to our nature. Evil would be seen then as unnatural. What would need to be explained is the nature of the interference. And it is typically, but as we have seen poorly, explained in terms of bad social arrangements. However, if we are basically ambivalent, as I think we are, then we see both good and evil dispositions as natural, that is, as part of our nature. What then needs to be explained is why one of these dispositions becomes dominant in particular cases. And it is typically explained in terms of the conjunction of internal psychological and external social conditions.

I say that both explanations hold only typically, not universally, because in exceptional cases, some human beings are through and through good or evil. Saints will not be corrupted by bad social arrangements, and monsters are rarely motivated by good dispositions because they do not have them. In the overwhelming majority of cases, however, both explanations are needed. The first is largely social. The second is largely a mixture of psychological and social conditions.

Another significant difference between the implications of the two responses is that if human beings were basically good, optimism about the betterment of the human condition would be reasonable. It would depend on improving the prevailing social arrangements by reforming the corrupting ones. This, in fact, is the aim of social programs favored by the majority of people in the contemporary Western world.

If, however, we, human beings, are basically ambivalent, then the reasonable attitude toward the human condition would be realism, by which I do not mean pessimism. Realists think that some social arrangements will be likely to remain bad because those who make and maintain them are ambivalent. The realist response is not that ambivalence leads us to favor bad social arrangements. Rather, we are often misled by our ambivalence to make and maintain bad social arrangements we mistakenly take to be good. Realists think that the beliefs, emotions, and desires that motivate us are permeated by our ambivalence regardless of whether or not we are aware of it. They do not think that ambivalence makes us monstrous. They think that it makes the social arrangements we favor as prone to mistakes as the dispositions that motivate them. Optimism about the human conditions fails to recognize our ambivalence and fallibility.

Bad social arrangements cannot explain the prevalence of evil throughout human history. Social arrangements change, but these evils remain. They take different forms in different circumstances, and the reasons evildoers give for their actions also vary but not by much. The usual reasons are ideological or religious, regardless of what the ideology or the religion are. Ideologues and defenders of their faith see themselves as defending the human good against its enemies. They think that the harm they do to others is justified by unfortunate necessity.

Not all evil is motivated by ideology or religion that has gone wrong. There is also much smaller-scale evil that people acting on their own behalf do to the innocent victims they grievously harm. They are caused by the familiar criminal acts of murder, mayhem, gang warfare, and so on. But they are less dangerous than ideological or religious evil because their victims are much fewer.

Optimists fail to see that bad social arrangements are the effects of evil, not its causes. They cultivate blindness to the prevalence of evil throughout human history in radically different social conditions. Perhaps their blindness is the result of unwillingness to accept that history falsifies their hopes, or of self-deception, wishful thinking, ignorance of the past and the present, dogmatism in the face of contrary facts, sentimentalism, or to something else. But whatever is the explanation of their failure, their optimism prevents them from facing the fact that human ambivalence remains constant throughout changing social conditions. Realism is a necessary condition of trying to understand evil. As Hume put it:[48]

> Man is the greatest enemy of man. Oppression, injustice, contempt, contumely, violence, sedition, war, calumny, treachery, fraud; by these they mutually torment each other, and they would soon dissolve that society which they formed were it not for the dread of still greater ills which must attend their separation.

That is the significant fact that realism leads us to face and optimism falsifies.

THE ANSWER

We began with the hard question: How should we respond to evil? The answer I have proposed is that evil in general is here to stay because we, human beings, are ambivalent toward the good and the bad, and in some social conditions the bad leads to evil actions. The answer depends on deciding between the optimist and realist responses to evil. The question is hard because there are reasons for and against both responses.

The main reason for the optimist response is that it gives us hope for the future and, although it accepts that there is much evil, it attributes evil to bad social arrangements, not to human ambivalence,

---

48. David Hume, *Dialogues Concerning Natural Religion* (Indianapolis: Hackett, 1779/ 1980), 60.

and thus allows us to think well rather than badly about ourselves. It is an encouraging, humane response that is explicitly or implicitly accepted by the majority in the contemporary Western world. The main reason against it is that its encouragement and humaneness rest on the denial of the truth. Some truths are difficult to accept. As Eliot put it:[49]

> human kind cannot bear very much reality.

And that reality is that,

> The world turns and the world changes,
> But one thing does not change.
> However you disguise it, this thing does not change:
> The perpetual struggle of Good and Evil.

It is undoubtedly difficult to accept this, but it is still better than the alternative.

The main reason for the realist response is that we cannot cope with evil unless we understand its cause. The main reason against it is that it is difficult to live with that understanding. If we are fortunate enough to live in a civilized context, most of us can avoid evil. We know, of course, that there is much that is bad, but it is not, for us fortunate ones, evil, and it does not now threaten the very possibility of civilized life here and now. But it does threaten it elsewhere, and that is what happened to Anna and the Priest. They did not have the luxury of keeping evil at arm's length. They had to respond to it and cope with it because their once civilized society was overtaken by evil. And they did face it courageously and tried to cope with it

---

49. T. S. Eliot, "Burnt Norton" in *Four Quartets* and "Choruses from the Rock" both in *T.S. Eliot, The Complete Poems and Plays* (New York: Harcourt, 1971).

admirably. But their experiences of evil were different: one direct, the other vicarious; and so were their efforts: Anna's were successful, and the Priest's were not. I will conclude this chapter by what I think we can learn from how they responded to evil.

Anna saw the evil that she had endured as a personal, not a theoretical, problem. It happened to *her*, *she* had to bear it, and *she* had to try and recover from it. Despite all that had passed, she remained a young girl without a historical perspective. She knew of no theories about human nature, and she was not committed to any considered moral, personal, political, or religious evaluations. She had only her few good and many awful memories, emotions, and traumas. And she also had, amazingly, great inner resources of strength and courage. Her concern was not with understanding evil but first with surviving it and later with recovering from it. And she did survive and recover.

Her case shows us that a theoretical understanding of evil is not necessary for responding to the experience of it. Direct or vicarious experience of evil comes first, and theories about it can only follow. And whether the theories are adequate depends, in part, on whether their response to evil rings true to those who have endured it. Theories about how we should live must be firmly anchored in concrete experiences. If they are not, they are pretentious intellectualized fantasies, formulated as the supreme principle, the absolute good, or the universal requirement of reason. This is what has happened to the various philosophical theories I have cited earlier about the basic goodness of human nature. They founder on the concrete experience of evil.

What happened to Anna is one of many concrete experiences that do not fit into the view of human nature as basically good. All the other reasons for that view—that it gives us hope, motivates reforms, makes us feel better about ourselves, and so on—are rendered irrelevant by the brutality of the contrary concrete experiences. Anna was right to focus on her experiences and be indifferent to the theories into which she might have tried to make her experiences fit. Like so much else she did, it was not deliberate or thoughtful. Yet her actions enabled her to endure evil and live with its consequences.

The Priest was a compassionate, thoughtful, and good man. It is doubtful that Anna could have recovered if it had not been for the Priest's help. But his indirect, vicariously lived through experience of the evil Anna had suffered left the Priest deeply conflicted. He could not and did not want to falsify the concrete reality of the evil Anna told him about. At the same time, he could not and did not want to deny his faith in God and the goodness inherent in the scheme of things God has created. He felt acutely the conflict between the experience of evil and faith in God's goodness, and he could not resolve the conflict to his satisfaction. He could not make up his mind between accepting and denying that evil dispositions are part of human nature. He was a good but deeply troubled man.

Finally, I hope it will be seen that the comparison between how Anna and the Priest struggled with the experience of evil is not the beginning of yet another theory about evil. I hope that it is vivid enough to convey something of what the experience of evil is like, but it is intended to be more than that. It is there as an essential step in the approach I am following throughout this book, one that is intended as an alternative to relying on theories to evaluate the reasons for and against the answers we give to hard questions. These reasons are evaluated in terms of the comparative cases I discuss in chapters 2 to 11. Which of the contrary reasons are stronger or weaker, or better or worse, does not depend on impersonal, universalizable, context-dependent theories but on whether they help or hinder a particular person in a particular context to answer a particular hard question as reasonably as possible. We do not need theories for that. We need imaginative sympathy that allows us to struggle from a distance with the hard question faced by that person in that context.

This approach is not anti-theoretical. Theories are indispensable in science, economics, medicine, metaphysics, epistemology, logic, and in other areas of life. But they seriously hinder the evaluation of the reasons for or against how we, the particular persons we are, in the particular context in which we live, answer hard questions about how we should live. There can be no reasonable impersonal, universalizable, and context-independent theories about that. Nevertheless, there are reasonable and unreasonable answers. And the approach I follow is intended to show how reasonable ones may be found in particular cases.

Chapter 7

Should We Forgive Wrong Actions?

THE QUESTION

On the one hand, there is the cosmic tit-for-tat strategy of forgiveness that Matthew 6:14 attributes to Jesus:

> if you forgive men their trespasses, your heavenly Father also will forgive you; but if you do not forgive men their trespasses neither will your Father forgive your trespasses.

On the other hand, Matthew in 25:41, 46 has Jesus's unforgiving condemnation of unrighteous trespassers to hellfire:

> Depart from me, you cursed, into the eternal fire . . . And they will go away into eternal punishment.

On the one hand, we have the compassionate view of Jean Hampton, echoing the sentiment held by many Christians and non-Christians that forgiveness involves:

> seeing the wrongdoer as, despite all, a person who still possesses decency and one whom we ought to be for rather than against . . . we come to know and understand the wrongdoer as

an individual, we may retain our hatred of her deeds and of her character traits that led her to hurt another, but still come to feel compassion, and even come to like, the individual herself.[50]

On the other hand, we have the realism expressed by Bishop Butler:

It is necessary for the subsistence of the world, that harm, injustice and cruelty should be punished; since compassion, which is so natural to mankind, would render the execution of justice exceedingly difficult and uneasy; indignation against vice and wickedness is, and may be allowed to be, a balance to that weakness of pity, and also to anything else which would prevent the necessary methods of severity.[51]

On the one hand, Kant, that sage of reason, confidently proclaims that

[Man] is *not basically* corrupt (even as regards his original predisposition to good), but rather . . . still capable of improvement" and "man (even the most wicked) does not, under any maxim whatsoever, repudiate the moral law. . . .The law, rather, forces itself upon him irresistibly by virtue of his moral predisposition.[52]

And three years later the very same Kant, no less sagely and confidently, depopulates the ranks of humanity by denying that those who tell a lie—and who has not?—are human beings.

50. Jean Hampton and Jeffrie G. Murphy, *Forgiveness and Mercy* (New York: Cambridge University Press, 1988), 151.
51. Joseph Butler, *Fifteen Sermons* (London: Bell & Sons, 1726/1953), 130.
52. Immanuel Kant, *Religion within the Bounds of Reason Alone*, trans. Theodore M. Greene and Hoyt H. Hudson (New York: Harper & Row, 1794/1960), 39, 31.

By a lie a human being throws away and, as it were, annihilates his dignity as a human being. A human being who does not himself believe what he tells another . . . has even less worth than if he were a mere thing. . . .Communication of one's thought to someone through words that yet (intentionally) contain contrary of what the speaker thinks on the subject is an end that is directly opposed to the natural purposiveness of the speaker's capacity to communicate his thoughts, and is thus a renunciation by the speaker of his personality, and such a speaker is a mere deceptive appearance of a human being, not a human being himself.[53]

Inconsistent as they are, all these views rest on conflicting reasons for and against forgiveness. Forgiveness involves not blaming people for their wrong actions; justice involves blaming them. A strong sense compassion favors forgiveness, and a no less strong sense of justice opposes it. This is partly what makes the question hard. I begin to struggle with it by trying to get clear about what is involved in asking and answering it.

It is generally agreed that some normally wrong actions may be excused if there are extenuating circumstances, or they may even be justified if the alternatives to them would be worse. If they are excused or justified, then of course they should be forgiven. Part of the reason why the question is hard is that there are conflicting views about what excuses or justifications are reasonable.

The primary context of forgiveness is the relationship between the forgiving and the forgiven persons. Forgiveness is up to those who were harmed by the wrong actions, and it is directed toward the wrongdoers whose wrong actions harmed them. Since there are

53. Immanuel Kant, *The Metaphysics of Morals*, trans. Mary Gregor (Cambridge, UK: Cambridge University Press, 1797/1996), 182.

no wrong actions without wrongdoers, it is always wrongdoers who may or may not be forgiven for their wrong actions. I say that this is the primary context of forgiveness because there are also secondary contexts in which wrong actions may be those of governments, institutions, corporations, or authorities, not persons. And the possible forgivers may not be the victims, especially if they are dead, but those, if any, who are entitled to speak for them.

If normally wrong actions are not excusable or justifiable, then they are in fact wrong, and the reasonable response to them is to blame the wrongdoers. But it is always the wrongdoers of wrong actions who are blamed or forgiven for their supposedly wrong actions. "Supposedly" is an important qualification because actions may be mistakenly regarded as wrong.

Central cases of forgiveness or blame involve harm to others. The more serious the harm is, the more difficult it is to find good reasons for forgiving the wrongdoers for having done it. In cases that involve harm to others, the evaluation of reasons for and against forgiveness or blame, or for excuses and justifications, are from the moral point of view. It is important to recognize, however, that not all wrong actions are morally wrong, nor do they all involve harm to others. Actions may be wrong even if they harm no one, or only the wrongdoer. They may be wrong from economic, legal, medical, political, religious, or some other point of view. The widespread tendency to treat questions about forgiveness as moral, and then to treat forgiveness as a virtue and blame as a vice, should be resisted because it ignores the obvious fact that there are many reasons why actions may be wrong and why it may be reasonable to forgive or blame the wrongdoers for their wrong actions. Financial decisions, monetary policies, judicial rulings, jury verdicts, medical diagnoses, political compromises, international treaties, interpretations of works of art or religious texts, the award of prizes, and so on may be wrong, and they may be justifiable or excusable, blameworthy, or forgivable without morality having much to do with it. Bequests, bribery, fame, generosity, investments, nepotism, pity, and tax laws may be wrong even though they harm no one, and they may be right for some to enjoy, even though they do not deserve it.

Recognizing this will perhaps cool and certainly complicate the often passionate moralizing views about forgiveness and blame. The same action may be reasonably evaluated as wrong, or right, or neutral from different points of view, in different contexts. And that, of course, makes it an even harder question whether it is right to forgive actions that are taken to be wrong from some point of view and right or indifferent from another. This is especially so if we remember that it makes a great difference whether the actions in question are isolated episodes in the life of the wrongdoers or parts of a pattern characteristic of the wrongdoers who normally act that way in that sort of situation.

Bearing these complexities in mind, we can say that if a normally wrong action is justified or excused, then in that particular case it is not wrong, and need neither be forgiven nor blamed. But if there is no reasonable justification or excuse for it, then the action really is morally or otherwise wrong, its wrongdoer is reasonably blamed for doing it, and forgiveness is out of place. I stress once more that the wrong actions may be blamed even if they harm no one or only the wrongdoer.

A first approximation, which will be refined later, is that normally wrong action may be justified or excused and then forgiven if the following conditions are met: it is a single episode, not part of a pattern of like actions in the life of a wrongdoer; it is attributable to illness, ignorance of relevant considerations, understandably divided attention, fatigue, or the pressure of some genuine emergency; it conforms to moral, personal, political, religious, or other evaluations generally accepted in that context; no one could have been reasonably expected to foresee the bad consequences that followed from the action; the wrongdoer came to regret having done the action; made appropriate amends for having done it; and it was reasonable to believe that the available alternatives to the action were even worse than the action. Whether these conditions are met and whether normally wrong action are reasonably regarded as justified or excused and thus forgiven are routinely disputable.

These disputes cannot be settled in general terms and their complexities rule out a general answer to the hard question of whether it is right to forgive wrong actions. Nevertheless, I will endeavor to show that the reasons for and against forgiveness, blame, justification, and excuse can be reasonably evaluated. But it can be done only on a case-by-case basis by paying close attention to the particular context formed of the wrongdoer's character, the prevailing evaluative framework, the foreseeability of the relevant consequences, the wrongdoer's response to the realization that the action was wrong, and to the alternatives to the action that were actually available to the wrongdoer. I think that the source of the inconsistent views about forgiveness I have cited at the beginning is that their defenders mistakenly assume that there is a general answer to the hard question and that they have found it.

WHAT IS FORGIVENESS?

Much has been written about this. Instead of giving a long list, I refer to the full bibliography in Paul M. Hughes, "Forgiveness"[54]

Let us begin with Jeffrie Murphy's widely accepted definition:[55]

Forgiveness may be viewed as the principled overcoming of feelings of resentment that are naturally (and perhaps

---

54. http://Plato.stanford.edu/entries/forgiveness/.
55. Jeffrie G. Murphy, "Forgiveness" in *Encyclopedia of Ethics*, eds. Lawrence C. Becker and Charlotte B. Becker (New York: Routledge, 2001), 561.

properly) directed toward a person who has done one a moral injury. . . [and it] involves a change of heart—in how one feels about a wrongdoer.

There are several reasons for questioning it.

First, while blaming rather than forgiving the wrongdoer for a wrong action may involve overcoming resentment, it need not. Blaming may be motivated by sadness at the darker aspect of our evolutionary inheritance, or sympathy for victims, or melancholic acknowledgment of human ill-will, stupidity, weakness, or self-deception. These are usually quiet emotions, not shrill resentments, and they need not get out of hand, nor involve a change of heart. Even more telling against the definition is that reactions to wrong actions may be entirely free of emotion. Their source may be an impersonal sense of justice, or the belief that one should not be overly optimistic about human nature, or withdrawal from the turmoil of the world, or the cultivation of Stoic tranquility, or seeking consolation in works of art whose appreciation frees us from dwelling on the outbreaks of inhumanity that the media revel in depicting. Such reactions may be accompanied by resignation rather than resentment that needs to be overcome by forgiveness.

Second, there is a hoary strategy for combining forgiveness and blame, and thereby making it easy to answer the hard question of whether it is right to forgive wrong actions. The strategy has been mistakenly and anachronistically attributed to Augustine (among others by myself). It has become a much-used cliché favored by indiscriminate defenders of forgiveness, namely that one should hate the sin but not the sinner. Or, to put it in secular terms, one should blame and perhaps even resent the wrong action but forgive and overcome one's resentment of the wrongdoer.

As far as I can see, there is nothing that can be reasonably said in favor of this strategy, and there is much against it. Wrong actions are done by wrongdoers. If normally wrong actions are unjustified and unexcused, then the wrongdoers are reasonably blamed. This is true regardless of whether the wrong actions are isolated episodes in the life of the wrongdoers or form a characteristic pattern in their lives. It is also true, however, that isolated wrong actions reflect less badly on the wrongdoers than patterns of wrong actions. Premeditated murder of an innocent victim is undoubtedly wrong, but a pattern of such murders is even worse. And the worse the wrong actions are, the more reasonable it is to blame the wrongdoers for them. Wrong actions, especially patterns of wrong actions, unavoidably reflect on the wrongdoers. They are reasonably blamed, and then they should not be forgiven for their wrong actions.

Defenders of forgiveness will ask: what if the wrongdoers genuinely regret their wrong actions, make amends for them, and reform? Should they not be forgiven then? These questions rest on a confusion. Blaming or forgiving wrongdoers is for their wrong actions, not for what they may have done subsequent to their wrong actions. How we may evaluate what the wrongdoers have done or become after their actions is an entirely different matter.

It is a common experience for most of us to think well of some people in one respect and badly in another. Some of their actions may be justified, excused, forgiven, or blamed, and some of their other actions may be evaluated differently. The overall evaluation of wrongdoers is one thing, the evaluation of their actions subsequent to wrongdoing is quite another. They may be blamed for their wrong actions and praised for regretting, making amends, and reforming themselves. But such praise or blame has no bearing on it being reasonable to blame them for the unjustified, unexcused wrong actions they have done in the past. No amount of regret, compensation, and reform could undo or change their blameworthiness for their past action.

Third, blame should be distinguished from punishment. It may be reasonable to blame wrongdoers for their wrong actions and unreasonable to punish them. The more harm a wrong action caused, the stronger is the case for punishing it. But even the strongest case for punishment may be overridden by countervailing considerations. Think, for instance, of the aftermath of the collapse of a vicious regime. Its supporters may be reasonably blamed, but punishing them may endanger hard-won domestic peace, cause civil war, require the practically impossible identification and punishment of thousands of those who silently collaborated with the regime. Only a fanatical moralist would agree with Kant that

> Even if a civil society were to dissolve itself by common agreement of all its members ... the last murderer remaining in prison must be first executed, so that everyone will duly receive what his actions are worth and do the bloodguilt thereof will not be fixed on the people because they failed to insist on carrying out the punishment.[56]

In general, punishing reasonably blamed actions may have consequences that would be unreasonable to accept. Furthermore, wrong actions may harm no one but the wrongdoer, for instance by risky financial decisions, distrusting friendship, raging at the world, or in Hume's words

> celibacy, fasting, penance, mortification self-denial, humility, silence, solitude, and the whole train of monkish virtues ... [that] stupefy the understanding and harden the heart, obscure fancy and sour the temper.[57]

56. Immanuel Kant, *The Metaphysical Elements of Justice*, trans. John Ladd (Indianapolis: Bobbs-Merrill, 1797/1965), 102.
57. David Hume, *An Enquiry Concerning the Principles of Morals*, ed. Tom L. Beauchamp (Oxford: Oxford University Press, 1751/1998), 146.

Although such actions are wrong, they are not morally wrong, harm only the wrongdoer, and it would make matters worse if the wrongdoers were punished on top of the harm they are causing themselves.

The fourth consideration that counts against Murphy's definition is that even if there is no resentment that needs to be overcome, forgiveness may be motivated by compassion, generosity, and pity. These are fine sentiments that make life more endurable, more civilized, less fraught with strife and conflict, and may make forgiveness reasonable. All this may often be true. But just as blame may get out of hand and lead to resentment, so can forgiveness get out of hand and lead to forgiving the unforgivable, such as mass murders or the prostitution of Anna (as we have seen in the preceding chapter). It is never an easy question what emotions and in response to what events are too strong or too weak. Compassion, generosity, and pity, like other emotions, may be misguided if they are over or underdone. As Aristotle saw

> up to what point and to what extent a man must deviate before he becomes blameworthy it is not easy to determine by reasoning . . . such things depend on particular facts, and the decision rests with perception.[58]

What, then, are the particular facts and what is involved in their perception—by which I take Aristotle to mean their evaluation? Surely, the particular facts and their evaluation depend on the conditions that may justify or excuse normally wrong actions: namely, the character of the wrongdoers, the evaluative framework in their

58. Aristotle, *Nicomachean Ethics*, trans. W. D. Ross, rev. J. O. Urmson, in *The Complete Works of Aristotle*, ed. Jonathan Barnes (Princeton, NJ: Princeton University Press, 1984), 1109b20–23.

context, the foreseeable consequences of the actions, and the availability of alternative and better actions. Particularly important among these conditions is the evaluation of just how wrong the actions in question are. Do they involve broken promises or mass murder, financial hardship, misdiagnosed maladies, the denigration of fine works of art, the imposition of dogma on an entire population, or genocide? Do they involve schoolchildren stealing candy bars or con men defrauding old people of their savings? Were the wrongdoers forced, indoctrinated, ignorant, ambitious, greedy, or vindictive? Were they guided by political ideology, religious faith, scientific research, military discipline, or moral imperatives?

Reasonable evaluations of the appropriateness of forgiveness or blame must be based on answering these context-dependent questions and keeping in mind just how wrong the actions are in each question. These questions and answers are unavoidably particular. There can be no general answer to the hard question of whether it is right to forgive wrong actions. It is sometimes right, sometimes wrong, and often complicated. But it does not follow from the lack of a general answer that there are no reasonable particular answers to particular questions about whether particular wrongdoers in particular contexts should be forgiven or blamed for their wrong actions. I will now endeavor to show how this may be reasonably done by comparing two wrongdoers whose actions were undoubtedly morally wrong and caused harm to others.

VERE

Vere followed the law, ordered the hanging of Billy Budd, who, Vere knew, was morally innocent.[59] Billy's crime was to strike; and because

59. My account is based on Herman Melville, *Billy Budd, Sailor* in *Herman Melville*, ed. Harrison Hayford (New York: Library of America, 1843/1983). I have added a few remarks of my own that express what Melville left unwritten.

he was very strong he struck and killed an officer of the warship commanded by Vere. Naval law was clear: this was a capital crime. Vere's clear duty as the captain of a warship at the time of war was to enforce the law. This was especially important because England was in the midst of the Napoleonic War, the control of the seas was crucial for preventing the invasion of England, and naval discipline had to be strictly enforced. In actual fact, there had already been mutinies in which disaffected, press-ganged crews rose up against officers. The crew of Vere's ship was restive, their dissatisfactions were palpable, and armed Marines were needed to clamp down on the slightest indication of disobedience. All this was generally known both to the officers and the crew, and the context was fraught with tension.

Billy was an inarticulate, simple, saintly, powerful youth. The officer he struck and killed was vicious and regarded Billy's very existence and popularity as a daily affront to himself for being the hateful person he in fact was. In the presence of Captain Vere and other officers, he falsely accused Billy of fomenting mutiny. And that was when Billy, shocked by the malicious lie, struck his accuser and killed him. Given the context and naval law, Billy committed a capital crime, and for that the punishment was hanging.

Vere and the other officers who witnessed what happened knew that the accusing officer was vicious and the accusation was false. Nevertheless the law was clear, the threat of mutiny serious, and they had to condemn Billy to death. Following Vere's instruction, that is what they did. Vere might have found, or invented, extenuating circumstances, some way of circumventing naval law, but he did not. He had no doubt that Billy was morally innocent and legally guilty, and he knew that it was his duty to enforce the law. In a long private conversation during the night before the hanging he tried to explain all this to Billy. He was apparently successful because in the morning before Billy was hanged, he shouted his last words for all to hear: long live Captain Vere!

Vere was an intelligent, well read, thoughtful, and decent man. He knew exactly what he was doing and why. We can safely say that if in that context he had to do it again, he would have done the same thing. But he regretted what he thought he had to do, accepted responsibility for it, and for the rest of his life he was haunted by what his duty required him to do. He knew that he had faced a conflict between morality and the law, between his moral and legal responsibility; but he chose to act on his legal responsibility and knowingly violated what he knew was his moral responsibility. The last we hear of Vere is when he is dying of a wound he suffered in a naval battle. His dying words echoed Billy's: Billy Budd! Billy Budd! he said, and then he died.

Vere faced a conflict between moral and legal evaluations. Conflicts between different evaluations are familiar experiences to business executives, police officers, military commanders, parents with limited resources, physicians, politicians, and others. They are committed to different kinds of evaluation feel responsible for acting according to them, but they cannot because they conflict. Whatever they do in case of such conflicts they will act contrary to one of the conflicting evaluations, and then they must do what they recognize is wrong from the point of view of one the evaluations, even if it is right from the point of view of another. It is a hard question whether they should be forgiven or blamed, justified, or excused for their wrong actions. And the same is true about Vere. I will leave him for a moment and return to him later.

SPEER

Consider now another man, Albert Speer, who in real life also faced a conflict between evaluations but, unlike Vere, in Melville's story, did not think that there was a conflict.[60] Speer did what he thought was his duty. He was as close to a friend as Hitler ever had. He joined the Nazi Party in 1931 and was one of its earlier members. In the glorious early days of World War II when the Third Reich triumphantly occupied much of Europe, Speer was Hitler's architect, and they jointly formed grandiose architectural plans of transforming Berlin into the capital of the world. Later on while the murderous, aggressive, unjust war of Hitler was gradually being lost, the slaughter of millions had been going on, and fourteen million imported foreign laborers were forced to work under brutal conditions on a starvation diet—it was called "extermination by labor"—to produce the urgently needed weapons, planes, tanks, ammunition, and supplies.

Hitler put Speer in charge of the war production. He was an exceptionally intelligent man, a great organizer, amazingly efficient, and utterly devoted to Hitler, Nazism, and winning the war for the Third Reich. His efforts prolonged the war, the slaughter, and the continuation of extermination by labor for at least two years. He personally killed no one, but he produced the means that enabled the continuation of the war and the murder of millions in concentration camps and forced labor on starvation diet, and who had to endure long hours of very hard work under brutal conditions. Without Speer's efforts, the Third Reich would have collapsed years earlier, and millions of lives would not have been lost.

He was one of the Nazi leaders who were tried in Nuremberg. Most of them were hanged, a few were acquitted, and some were sentenced to long terms in jail. Speer was among the jailed ones. He

---

60. I rely mainly on Gitta Sereny, *Albert Speer: His Battle with Truth* (New York: Knopf, 1995); Albert Speer, *Inside the Third Reich* (London: Weidenfeld and Nicolson, 1970); Joachim Fest, *Speer*, trans. Ewald Osers and Alexandra Dring (New York: Harcourt, 1999/2001); Joachim C. Fest, *The Face of the Third Reich*, trans. Michael Bullock (New York: Pantheon, 1963/1970).

was forty-one, spent the next twenty years in jail, and was released at age sixty-one. He then published several best-selling memoirs, made a lot of money, gave interviews, and was becoming an icon for those who at once cherished and regretted the awful history of the Third Reich and had a gruesome fascination with those who perpetrated the horrors.

During the trial, throughout his imprisonment and the years after his release, he maintained that he was dedicated only to war production and that he had not known about the murder of millions of the Jews and prisoners of war, nor about the deliberately caused starvation and death of millions of forced laborers under his control. He invariably claimed that he first heard about the murder machinery of the Third Reich from the overwhelming filmed evidence and eyewitness testimony presented during the Nuremberg trials. He said that then and during his subsequent life he was and remained sickened by the evidence that, he claimed, was news to him. He said that he accepted that he was guilty of sustaining the regime, perpetuating the war, and protecting the Third Reich, but he claimed that he was doing his duty exactly as his American and British counterparts were doing in support of the war effort of their respective countries. His testimony was accepted and mostly believed by the prosecutors and judged, and that is why he was not hanged, but jailed.

Gitta Sereny, the trilingual, anti-Nazi author of the book I am relying on, extensively interviewed Speer over several years, had many hours of intimate conversations with him, and became a frequent and welcome visitor in Speer's home. She had asked Speer all the important questions that needed to be asked, and she was not reluctant to question Speer and express doubts about his answers. Throughout the years she continued to marvel at and try to understand how Speer, such an intelligent man of apparent decency and considerate manners, could have continued to defend the Third Reich and its evil Fuhrer when he knew that the war was lost and could not but know that millions of lives continued to be lost for no reason. Speer's invariable explanation was that he was bewitched by Hitler's charisma, his own patriotism, and his duty to meet the strategic and tactical problems of war production. He presented himself to Sereny, to his prosecutors and judges at the trial, to his family and friends, and to the rest of the world as an apolitical technocrat, a German patriot, who in exceptionally difficult circumstances, under the personal influence of Hitler, did what he thought was his duty. He adamantly denied that he knew of the awful conditions of the millions of forced laborers under his command, of the massacre of millions of Jews, of the reign of terror of the Gestapo, and the indiscriminate mass murders by the SS of millions of civilians, Jews, gypsies, homosexuals, in Germany, as well as in the Ukraine, Russia, and Europe occupied by the German army.

Speer's denials of knowledge of these facts were outright lies. There has emerged documentary evidence and eyewitness testimonies of several people that Speer was present at the notorious secret Poznan meeting in 1943, two years before the end of the war, at which Himmler, the head of the SS, instructed top SS officers about how to continue with the final solution meaning the murder of the Jews. He himself records that Hitler said at dinner in his presence: he wants to annihilate the Jews in Europe! This war is the decisive confrontation between National Socialism and world Jewry. One or the other will bit the dust, and it certainly won't be us.[61] Speer's own office memos show that he knew about the dreadful conditions under which millions of forced laborers were compelled to work, and he knew as well, years before Germany finally surrendered that the war was lost. Yet he continued to serve the Third Reich. Speer lied his way into saving his life, making a lot of money after his release, and maintaining the facade that he was a remorseful patriot seduced by the

61. Fest, *Speer*, 1988.

force of Hitler's personality and ignorant of the horrors perpetrated by the Third Reich he had so devotedly served until its very end.

At the end, Gitta Sereny finally confronted Speer with all the unimpeachable evidence she had accumulated over the years showing that Speer had systematically lied. She asked for Speer's reaction. What she got in response was Speer's reiterated phony remorse, protestation of ignorance of the murders, and the same lies told again as if the evidence he had just been presented were not in front of him. He continued to insist on his ignorance of what he had undoubtedly known was going on. He remained to his end utterly unwilling to acknowledge that his lies, incontrovertibly refuted by the evidence, were indeed lies.

The truth is that he knowingly helped sustain the Third Reich, was a faithful Nazi, his efforts prolonged the war by two years, and he enabled the pointless murder of millions of innocent people to continue as the war was being lost. When the war finally was lost, he saved his life through lies that he repeated until his own death. He died as a rich, respected, grand old man, beloved by his family. His lies were believed by many people who respected him as the remorseful survivor of the lamentable history of Germany in World War II.

I have discussed Vere and Speer in order to ask and look for the answer to the hard question of whether it is right to forgive them for their wrong actions. My view is that the reasons for forgiving Vere are stronger than the reasons against it, but the reasons against forgiving Speer are overwhelming. Interesting as I find their cases, I am not discussing them because our retrospective evaluations of them are important. What is important is that they help us understand in concrete terms the reasons on which forgiving or blaming wrongdoers for their wrong actions depends. It is important to bear in mind that forgiveness is of wrongdoers. Although it is for their wrong actions, nevertheless their actions must be understood in terms of the internal psychological and external social conditions of the wrongdoers. Reasons for and against forgiveness and blame depend on these conditions. And I stress once more that forgiveness or blame need not be for actions that are morally wrong but may also be for actions that are wrong from an economic, legal, political, religious, scientific or some other point of view.

CONDITIONS OF FORGIVENESS

I now return to the conditions of forgiveness. One of these conditions is the *character* of the wrongdoer. Is the wrong action an uncharacteristic single episode in the life of the wrongdoer, as it was for Vere, or is it part of a characteristic pattern, as it was for Speer? It requires explanation why a wrongdoer has acted in an uncharacteristic way, but it is a matter of course if the characteristic actions of a wrongdoer are wrong. Conscientious people, like Vere, tend to act conscientiously. Technocrats like Speer tend to act efficiently. The explanation of a single uncharacteristic wrong action is usually in terms some unexpected condition that requires the wrongdoer to act in some uncharacteristic way. An emergency, a conflict, the discovery of hitherto unknown crucial facts, serious threats, a political crisis, or some unignorable provocation may be such unexpected conditions. But the explanation of characteristic patterns of wrong actions is usually in terms of the combination of external social and internal psychological conditions that have formed the wrongdoer, for instance their upbringing and education, the hardship and injustice they have experienced, or having been indoctrinated or manipulated.

The explanation of Vere's uncharacteristic single wrong action of hanging the innocent Billy was the conflict between the requirements of naval law, preparedness for battle, and the threat of mutiny, on the one hand, and, on the other hand, a basic requirement of morality.

Vere understood this and gave priority to naval law, but he did it unwillingly, as it were against his nature. And for that he should be forgiven or blamed. Speer's pattern of wrong actions, however, followed from his character. Throughout his adult life he was a technocrat who excelled in finding the most efficient way of achieving whatever his aim happened to be. In World War II, his aim was war production. It required, among other things, a cheap labor force. And what mattered to Speer was cost, efficiency, and outcome. It did not matter to him that it involved the extermination through the slave labor of millions of forced workers.

The reasons for forgiving single uncharacteristic wrong actions may be that they are excused or justified if the wrongdoers were compelled to act that way by circumstances beyond their control. Characteristic patterns of wrong actions cannot be excused or justified in this way because wrongdoers typically act in that wrong way whatever their external circumstances happen to be. Given only this first condition, it seems obvious that there are reasons for forgiving Vere, rather than blaming him. But in Speer's case, the reasons for blaming him outweigh the reasons for forgiving him. But this is far from a final evaluation because the reasons for and against forgiveness and blame depend also on other conditions.

One of the other conditions has to do with the *aim* of the wrong actions. Vere and Speer acted as they did in pursuit of victory in the war their country waged. In Vere's case, the aim was the just defense of his country against Napoleon's unprovoked aggressive attempt to conquer England, Russia, and Europe. In Speer's case, the aim was to facilitate Hitler's remarkably similar unjust, unprovoked, aggressive attempt to succeed where Napoleon failed. (It is unclear, at least to me, whether Hitler was aware of the historical parallel.) The reasons for and against forgiveness and blame partly depend on whether the wrong actions had a good or a bad aim. The aim of Vere's single wrong action was the good one of defending his unjustly attacked country.

The aim of Speer's pattern of wrong actions was the bad one of furthering Hitler's unjust, aggressive, unprovoked war. The reasons for forgiving, rather than blaming, Vere's wrong action were stronger because they had a good aim. While the reasons for blaming, rather than forgiving, Speer's pattern of wrong actions were stronger because it had a bad aim. Of course, good aims do not, by themselves, excuse or justify the means, but reasons for forgiving or blaming wrong actions partly depend on whether their aim was good or bad.

Yet a further condition of forgiving wrong actions depends on what, if any, *realistic alternatives* were available to the wrong actions. It is difficult to specify in general terms what alternatives are realistic. It depends on the context and on what the wrongdoers can be reasonably expected to know about and be motivated by. But what expectations are reasonable varies with time, place, and persons. I discount life-threatening extreme and science-fictional situations, seriously handicapped or extraordinarily knowledgeable people, as well as saints and monsters. Realistic alternatives, then, are those that unexceptional people in their particular context can be expected to know about the alternatives available to them.

Both Vere and Speer had realistic alternatives to their wrong actions, and both had reasons for choosing to act on one rather than another of those alternatives. Vere's reason was his responsibility for having the ship ready for battle. He could have resigned his command, but it would have passed on to his first officer who was far less competent than he was, and he too would have had to hang Billy. As Vere saw it, the only realistic alternatives he had were to hang or not to hang Billy, and the reasons for hanging him were stronger. Vere thought hard about choosing between the battle-readiness of the ship he commanded and Billy's life, and he understandably found the reasons for the former stronger than the latter. We may disagree with the choice he made, but we cannot reasonably deny that he had reasons for it.

Speer did not see that there was a choice between conflicting alternatives. He thought that the importance of war production not only overrode but silenced all other alternatives. But for this there was hardly even a reason. In the first place, he knew when he accepted the position of directing production that the war was lost. And he need not have accepted it. There were others who clamored for it. He could have pleaded illness, inexperience, or the availability of other qualified candidates who were eager to accept the position. But he chose to accept it, even though he knew that his efforts merely prolonged the war at the cost of millions of lives, including German ones and the continued destruction of German cities. And yet he persevered because, being the technocrat he was, he was eager to accept the challenge of the difficult task although he knew that it was doomed, and its cost was staggering. Even if we evaluate the pattern of his wrong actions merely from his own technocratic point of view—laying aside the injustice of the war, the continued destruction of Germany, and millions of innocent lives lost—we cannot but conclude that his own cost-benefit analysis was a disastrous failure because the cost of war production was immense and the benefits nil.

There were reasons both for and against forgiving Vere, rather than blaming him. But, it seems to me, all the reasons were for blaming Speer, and none for forgiving him. The evaluation of reasons in both cases unavoidably depends on the context in which the wrong actions were done. That is why there is no reasonable general answer to the hard question of whether it is right to forgive wrong actions. If there were a general answer, the question would not be hard, but there is not, and it is hard. Yet there is a reasonable particular answer in both cases. It depends on the character of the wrongdoers, the aim of their wrong actions, and the alternatives available to them. But all these conditions depend on the context in which the wrong actions were done, and the context differs from case to case.

There are two other conditions of forgiveness. Unlike the previous ones, they are about what the wrongdoers do in retrospect, after the actions were done. One of these has to do with *regret*. Vere had no doubt that hanging Billy, while believing him to be morally innocent, was normally a wrong action. And for that he would normally have been reasonably blamed. But circumstances were not normal. There was a war, he commanded a warship that had to be battle-ready, the threat of mutiny hung over the entire navy, morality and naval law came into conflict, and the requirements of both were clear, and, in that context, clearly incompatible. Vere would have liked to do what he well knew normally should be done, but he thought that in that context he should not do it. He thought that, given the context, hanging Billy was regrettable but excusable. Whether or not he was right or wrong about this, he weighed the reasons for and against hanging Billy, and he made his decision on that basis. But for the rest of his life Vere regretted having had to do what he did. His dying words were "Billy Budd! Billy Budd!"

Speer did not think that the pattern of his actions was wrong. He assumed that it was justified, and he did not think that it needed to be excused. What justified his participation in the murder of millions of innocent people was the importance of winning the war. He assumed also that moral, personal, political, religious, and other evaluations were reasonable only insofar as they furthered, rather than hindered, the aim of winning the war. And the war itself was justified because it aimed at the domination of the world by superior racially pure Aryans. This was at heart of the Nazi ideology that Hitler formulated many years earlier in *Mein Kampf*, a book that few of his followers, or indeed opponents, actually read.

The Nazi ideology, of course, was indefensible: its factual assumptions were grotesquely false and the evaluations that followed from its indefensible premises lead to the crimes against humanity for which the most prominent Nazis were condemned at the Nuremberg trial after the war. Speer, however, accepted the ideology and did not regret doing the wrong actions that were dictated by it. When the war came to its predictable end, Germany finally surrendered, and the leading Nazis, including Speer, were tried in Nuremberg. Then Speer systematically lied about knowing about the horrors that those under his command inflicted on millions of innocent people in the name of the ideology. He continued to think that what he did was justified, and he did not regret what he did.

Vere's regret and Speer's lack of it are among the reasons for forgiving Vere and blaming Speer. There are also reasons against forgiving Vere. Vere's decision to hang Billy was based on his evaluation of the threat to the battle-readiness of the ship by the danger of mutiny. His evaluations can be questioned, and with it the reasons for forgiving him. But his regret for having hanged Billy is unquestionable. It seems to me, however, that the reasons against forgiving Speer—given his character, aim, and alternatives—are overwhelming and unquestionable.

The last condition I will mention concerns *responsibility*. Vere knew what he was doing, and he accepted the responsibility for hanging Billy. Speer blinded himself to what he was doing, did not accept responsibility for his collaboration that enabled the horrors of the Third Reich, and systematically lied about his knowledge of them before, during, and after the trial at Nuremberg. Vere was responsible for hanging a morally innocent but legally guilty person. Speer was responsible for enabling the murder of millions of innocent people. Vere realized, as he should have, that what he did was normally wrong, even though he thought it was excusable in that context. Speer justified and lied about what he knew he was doing, while mouthing the insincere acceptance of his responsibility for it, so as to save his life and maintain his self-respect. He was

incapable of comprehending guilt. It was like blind spot. He worked hard on the humble gestures that belonged to his role as a sinner, and he gravely repeated the formulas that the indulgence imposed on him. . . .He had only a superficial understanding of the fundamental norms against which he offended, why he incurred guilt, and how he could have emerged from those years differently and unblemished.[62]

Vere's wrong action may or may not be excusable and forgivable, but there can be no reasonable doubt that Speer's pattern of wrong actions were inexcusable and unforgivable.

COMPLEXITIES

I have tried to show that the application of these conditions to the wrong actions of Vere and Speer involves considerable complexities. This is generally the case when the reasons for and against forgiveness or blame are evaluated. One of these complexities is that it is the exception, not the rule, that there is a clear yes-or-no answer to the question of whether any one of these conditions has been met. It is not easy to say when an person's action is uncharacteristic because it is typically difficult to say how much an action is like or unlike another action. Are hasty, stupid, thoughtless, negligent actions like or unlike one another? How close is the resemblance between risky, ignorant, ill-considered, or short-sighted actions? The same is true of the other conditions. The aims of actions are usually neither clearly good, nor clearly bad. Aims, like motives, are often mixed. Is aiming at power, wealth, fame, or success good, bad, or mixed? Surely, the reasonable answer depends on what the particular aim is, in what context it is pursued, and what realistic alternatives there are to it.

62. Fest, *Speer*, 347–348.

Typically, each of these considerations has its own set of complexities. That is why there can be no general formula for deciding whether the pursuit of an aim is good or bad. There is a reasonable answer, but it depends on the careful consideration of the complexities. And whether a wrongdoer should be forgiven or blamed for a wrong action depends also on how strong were the wrongdoer's reasons for thinking that its aim was good or bad, for regarding some alternatives as available and others as unrealistic, for accepting the wrongdoer's regret and acceptance of responsibility as honest, as it was for Vere, or dishonest, as it was for Speer. Very often the reasonable answer to questions about whether or not these conditions have been met is equivocal: partly yes, partly no, and partly unclear. The reasons for forgiving or blaming the wrongdoer for a wrong action are usually mixed.

These complexities in the way of the unequivocal evaluation of the appropriateness of forgiveness or blame are frustrating. But the frustration is caused by a disappointed expectation that should not have been held in the first place. Its mistake is to suppose that there is a universally applicable and context-independent principle that could be appealed to for deciding whether any wrong action is forgivable or blameworthy. There are also other complexities that show, I think, that it is futile to try to formulate such a principle. And that, of course, is part of the reason why it is hard question whether it is right to forgive a wrong action.

Another complexity is that an action can be right or wrong from various points of view, which may be moral, personal, political, religious, or other. And the action may be wrong from one of these points of view and right or indifferent from another. From different points of view different evaluations may follow. So the claim that an action is wrong must be qualified in two ways: the point of view from which its wrongness follows needs to be specified; and reasons need to be given why in a particular context the action should be evaluated from that specific point of view, rather than from another. In some contexts, the moral point of view is clearly most important. But in other contexts other points of view may be more important. It often happens that a morally wrong action may be excused, justified, and thus forgiven because economic, legal, medical, moral, personal, political, religious, or scientific evaluations have overriding importance. And of course in some contexts and cases moral evaluations may override non-moral ones. It is impossible to specify in advance which evaluation is or should be the dominant one in a particular context. Whether a wrong action should be forgiven or blamed, then, depends on the context and the evaluation.

However, we have not reached the end of complexities. Let us assume for the moment that a wrong action clearly meets the conditions I have described and it is thus forgivable. That need not mean that it should be forgiven because there may be reasons against forgiving a forgivable wrong action that meets the conditions. One such reason may be that it would be unjust to forgive it. Justice essentially involves treating wrongdoers as they deserve. But forgiveness essentially involves treating them more generously, leniently, kindly, in a word compassionately than they deserve.

Compassion is a fine sentiments, but it may or may not be appropriate. And whether it is appropriate depends on just how wrong the action was, how characteristic it was of the wrongdoer, how good or bad was the aim to which the action was a means, how genuine is the wrongdoer's regret and acceptance of responsibility? It is one thing to treat Vere more compassionately than strict justice requires from the moral point of view, but quite another to treat Speer, mass murderers, or Anna's abusers compassionately.

The hard attitude of justice and the soft attitude of compassion may or may not be appropriate. They may have more to do with the worldview from which they follow than with the wrongdoers who may be forgiven or blamed. In the Old Testament, justice is generally regarded as primary; the New Testament generally gives priority to compassion. Conservatives tend to stress justice, while many liberals think that justice should be administered compassionately. Those who think that human beings are basically good, reasonable, and perfectible see that as a reason for compassion in preference to justice, while those who think that human beings are basically ambivalent, often bad and unreasonable, and some are and others are not perfectible think that as a reason for justice, rather than compassion. This is not the place for discussing the relative merits of these conflicting worldviews. I want merely to stress that the answer to the hard question of whether it is right to forgive wrong actions involves complexities that follow from deep assumptions about the human condition. And that is one of several reasons why being frustrated by the lack of a crisp answer ignores the deep sources of these complexities.

Hume's observation, I think, is right:

> [These] questions are infinitely complicated, and ... there scarcely ever occurs, in any deliberation, a choice which is either purely good, or purely ill. Consequences, mixed and varied, may be foreseen to flow from every measure: And many consequences, unforeseen, do always, in fact, result from everyone. Hesitation, and reserve are, therefore the only [appropriate] sentiments.[63]

THE ANSWER

My answer, then, to the hard question of "Is it right to forgive wrong actions?" is that it is right if it meets the following conditions: it is a

---

63. David Hume, "Of the Protestant Succession" in *Essays, Moral, Political and Literary*, ed. Eugene F. Miller (Indianapolis, IN: Liberty Press, 1741/1985), 507.

single uncharacteristic episode in the life of the wrongdoer, not part of a pattern of like actions; the aim of the action is good, rather than bad; the wrongdoer had considered the available realistic alternatives to the action and had reasons for choosing the action in preference to alternatives to it; the wrongdoer came retrospectively to regret having done the action and accepts responsibility for it. But whether these conditions are met depends on the case-by-case resolution of the complexities involved in the evaluation of whether or not these conditions have been met.

If they have been met and the complexities are resolved, then the wrongdoer should be forgiven for the wrong action. If they are not met, then the wrongdoer should be blamed. And if it is unclear whether or not the conditions have been met and the complexities are resolved, then it is unclear whether it is reasonable to forgive or blame the wrongdoer for the wrong action. Since it is often unclear whether the conditions are met and the complexities are resolved, in many cases it is unclear whether it is reasonable to forgive or blame the wrongdoer for the wrong action. All these unclarities leave us with one clear conclusion: there can be no reasonable general answer to the hard question of whether it is right to forgive wrong actions. That is just why the question is hard and the answer to it is context-dependent and particular. This is not a failure of reason but a consequence of often conflicting evaluations and of the forever-changing conditions in which we all live.

Chapter 8

Does Shame Make Life Better or Worse?

THE QUESTION

Shame is a painful emotion of self-condemnation. It arises from the realization that we have fallen short of our own evaluation. The hard question is whether a painful emotion that leads us to condemn ourselves could be good. One answer is that shame is good as a means of protecting the self-respect we all want to have. I will refer to this as the standard view, because it is widely held:

> [Shame] protects one from appearing to be an unworthy creature (Deigh, 151); focuses on failing to be a worthy person as one conceives it (Morris, 61); [in] shame . . . one has fallen so far below one's ideal of selfhood that life . . . is now less bearable (Murphy, 60); if someone has self-respect then under specifiable conditions he will be feeling shame . . . the close connection between these makes clear why shame is often thought to be valuable . . . [because] it protects the self from . . . corruption and ultimately extinction (Taylor 80–81).[64]

---

64. See, for example, John Deigh, "Shame and Self-Esteem," *Ethics and Personality*, ed. John Deigh (Chicago: University of Chicago Press, 1992/1983); Herbert Morris,

A contrary answer is that shame imposes on us a psychological double jeopardy. Our self-respect is damaged because we realize that we have acted in a way we deplore. If are honest enough to admit it, we condemn ourselves for it. Shame makes it worse by adding to it the painful emotion that further damages our self-respect. It is like being sick and making it worse by castigating ourselves for it. It is true that if we are committed to any evaluation at all, then there must be some limits we would not want to violate. But there are better ways of protecting our self-respect than having the threat of shame hanging over us.

Nietzsche writes:[65]

> *Whom do you call bad?*—Those who always want to put to shame. . . . *What do you consider most humane?*—To spare someone shame.

And that includes not putting ourselves to shame.

Isenberg says in agreement with Nietzsche that

> it is as unreasonable to tolerate the sear of shame upon the spirit as it is to permit a wound to fester on the body.[66]

"Guilt and Shame," in *On Guilt and Innocence* (Berkeley: University of California Press, 1976); Helen Merrell Lynd, *On Shame and the Search for Identity* (New York: Harcourt Brace, 1958); Herbert Morris, "Persons and Punishment" in *On Guilt and Innocence*, (Berkeley: University of California Press, 1976); Jeffrie G. Murphy, *Getting Even* (Oxford: Oxford University Press, 2003); John Rawls, *A Theory of Justice* (Cambridge, MA: Harvard University Press, 1971), 442–446; Michael Stocker, *Valuing Emotions* (New York: Cambridge University Press, 1996), 217–230; Gabrielle Taylor, *Pride, Shame and Guilt* (Oxford: Oxford University Press, 1985); J. David Velleman, "The Genesis of Shame," *Philosophy and Public Affairs* 30 (2001): 27–52; and Bernard Williams, *Shame and Necessity* (Berkeley: University of California Press, 1993).

65. Friedrich Nietzsche, *The Gay Science*, trans. Walter Kaufmann (New York: Vintage, 1882/ 1974), par. 275.

66. Arnold Isenberg, "Natural Pride and Natural Shame" in *Explaining Emotions*, ed. Amelie Rorty (Berkeley: University of California Press, 1980), 369.

Although shamelessness is bad, that does not make it good to be ashamed.[67] This, I think is the right view, and the standard view is mistaken. Defenders of the standard view need to explain how a painful emotion of self-condemnation could protect, rather than weaken, self-respect. And their opponents owe an explanation of what better ways than shame are there for the protection of self-respect.

The dispute between these two views is not trivial. How we think and feel about ourselves depends on our self-respect and it matters a great deal whether shame strengthens or weakens it. It matters whether shame is an internalized form of social condemnation, or whether it is a way in which we condemn ourselves and make ourselves ashamed. Being shamed by others and feeling ashamed of ourselves may coincide or diverge. Whether we identify with or are estranged from the evaluative framework in our context partly depends on whether we are shamed by the condemnation of others or we feel ashamed because we condemn ourselves regardless of what others think.

It would be helpful at this point to have a definition of what exactly shame is and how it differs from other bad feelings, but I cannot provide it, and I doubt that one could be provided. All attempts to define what shame must always be and what it can never involve sooner or later become arbitrary. There is no clear distinction between shame and other more or less overlapping emotions such as chagrin, disgrace, dishonor, embarrassment, guilt, humiliation, prudishness, regret, remorse, self-contempt, and so on. A sharp distinction between shame and these other emotions unavoidably simplifies the complexities of our reaction to what we recognize as a failure to be or to act as we think we should.

---

67. Aristotle, *Nicomachean Ethics*, trans. W.D. Ross, rev. J.O. Urmson, in *The Complete Works of Aristotle*, ed. Jonathan Barnes (Princeton, NJ: Princeton University Press, 1984), 1128b32–33.

A rough indication of what I mean by shame is that it is a painful emotion caused by our violation of some evaluation we regard as important for living as we think we should. We feel ashamed when we have failed in some important way. Shame makes us feel badly about ourselves because of that failure. But what we think is important may not be, and our sense of failure may be misplaced if we set an unreasonably high standard to which we cannot live up.

One of the complexities involved in deciding whether and why shame is good is that we are committed to various often conflicting moral, personal, political, religious, and other evaluations, and some of them are more and others less important for living as we think we should. Any of these evaluations may be mistaken even if we do not realize it, and it is not easy to say whether we should be ashamed if we fail to live up to an evaluation that unknown to us is mistaken. Is it reasonable to be ashamed of not being as affluent or powerful as we think we should be? And even if the evaluation in question is not mistaken, we may be mistaken about the importance we attribute to it. Is it a matter of shame if we are not as physically fit as we think we should be?

Another of the complexities is that we are committed to an evaluation and are ashamed of violating it, because we have been manipulated by propaganda, bullying, charismatic ideologues, false prophets, fashion, or the threat of eternal damnation. Is it reasonable to be ashamed of violating an evaluation if we came to hold it under such duress? Moreover, our evaluations often conflict, and it is not our fault if we cannot honor all of them. Should we be ashamed of not being able to do what we cannot, like not meeting conflicting obligations or not being able to help someone who needs it?

Finally, sometimes it may actually be to our credit if we fail to act as some evaluation of ours demands. Say that honesty requires us to tell a very painful truth, or justice demands that we condemn someone's wrongdoing, but we cannot bring ourselves to do it because love or pity gets the better of us. Is it reasonable then to be ashamed of what we then have failed to do? When our beliefs and emotions conflict, there is often no simple way of telling which should override which. Should we then be ashamed if we act against one of them?

These complexities make it a hard question whether shame is good. Sometimes it is instrumentally good, and that is a reason for the standard view. Sometimes it is self-lacerating and prevents us from thinking clearly about the nature and importance of the evaluations that we perhaps mistakenly follow, and that is a reason for rejecting the standard view. Its critics and defenders agree that having no sense of shame at all makes us despicable. But the alternative to shamelessness need not be shame. It may be to cultivate a sense of duty that leads us to act according to our evaluations even when it is difficult; or to be understanding and forgiving of the failures not just of others but also of our own; or to keep firmly in mind how we think we should live and cope with obstacles to it as they arise. None of these and other complexities are simple matters of definition. They cannot be resolved by consulting usage or dictionaries.

Nor can there be a general answer to the question of whether shame is good. Reasonable answers must be particular and context-dependent. They must take into account what the evaluation is that we are ashamed of violating, why we have violated it, whether we could have avoided its violation, what the circumstances were in which acted as we did, and so on. Such complexities make it a hard question whether and when shame is good and what alternative there is to it. The answer depends on how we think we should live, given our experiences, personal attitude, and the evaluative framework and the conditions of the context in which we live. As I will show, the standard view takes no account of these complexities, but its critics are centrally concerned with them.

I will now consider first one and later another woman who had to answer this hard question. They did it differently in different contexts, relying on different evaluative frameworks and for different reasons. By thinking about the reasons each had, we can perhaps learn from them to do better than they did.

THE QUEEN

One of the remarkable stories Herodotus tells concerns Candaules, King of ancient Lydia, his wife, the Queen, and Gyges, the King's guard, confidant and advisor.[68] The King was so besotted by his wife's charms that he could not keep his great good fortune to himself. He bragged to Gyges about his marital bliss and bullied him to hide in their bedroom so that Gyges could have direct evidence of the Queen's superior graces. Gyges was horrified: What an improper suggestion! he said. But the King persisted: You know what they say: off with her skirt, off with her shame. Gyges pleaded: Do not ask me to behave like that. Kings however have a way of prevailing, and Gyges finally did as he was told and hid in the bedroom. The Queen saw him and realized what her husband had done. But she did not betray the shame she felt. She silently resolved to have her revenge because Lydians thought that it is shameful even for a man to be seen naked by those who had no right to it.

Next day the Queen summoned Gyges and said to him: You have two options, and you may choose between them. Kill the King, seize the throne, and marry me, or die here and now so that never again may your blind obedience to the King tempt you to see what you have no right to see. One of you must die: my husband, who hatched this shameful plot; or you who have outraged propriety by seeing me naked. Gyges chose to live; the next night he once again hid in the

---

68. Herodotus, *The Histories*, trans. Robin Waterfield (Oxford: Oxford University Press, 440 BC/1999), 7–13.

bedroom, and killed the King. He succeeded him, married the Queen, no doubt enjoying her charms, and reigned for thirty-eight years.

This story could be considered from the point of view of each participant, and shame would figure prominently in each. The King was shameless; Gyges had a sense of shame, but it was too weak to make him act on it; and the Queen was overpowered by shame. I will concentrate on the Queen's point of view. Her outrage was majestic. If we are to understand why it was so extreme, we need to understand the evaluative framework of her context.

Viewed from our context, arranging the murder of her husband was a disproportionately violent reaction to his vulgar plot. She was badly used, but was it so bad as to call for murder? We can understand that Lydian women were ashamed of being seen naked except by their husband, the Queen was so seen, and she was ashamed. We think that it would have been right for her to resent her husband, he certainly deserved censure, but in arranging his murder, the Queen had overreacted.

The inadequacy of this line of thought comes from a simplistic view of shame and of the nature of the Queen's shame. It assumes that she overreacted because the King violated merely a superficial custom that concerns minor matters of modesty, prudishness, or seemliness. It is understandable if those who live in that context are ashamed if they act contrary to the prevailing evaluations, but they are of no great importance. We think that propriety matters but not very much. It is one of a class of lesser important concerns, like amiability, cheerfulness, or tact. They concern manners, not morals. Moral, personal, political, or religious evaluations are not normally relevant to them. We may think that the Queen's mistake was to inflate the importance of the relatively unimportant evaluation of propriety. If she had a better sense of proportion about the importance of being seen naked, she would not have been driven by her justified indignation to unjustified murder.

The Queen's reaction will seem less excessive, however, if we understand that the Lydian evaluative framework was very different from ours. She was not a superficial person who cared too much about unimportant matters. In the Lydian evaluative framework propriety and being treated accordingly were crucial matters of self-respect. The Queen was formed by and was committed to that evaluative framework. Her self-respect was inseparably connected with acting and being respected as it was proper given her status as Queen, wife, and whatever other status she had. In that context, people were expected to act and to be respected in a way that is appropriate to their recognized status. The Queen was through and through what was proper for her to be, and her actions and expectations reflected the Lydian evaluative framework. She was enraged by what her husband did, because, although she was acting as she was expected to act, her husband failed to respect her as he should have done, and that violated her self-respect and shamed her.

If her husband's plot is understood in these terms, it will no longer seem as a violation of the Queen's inflated sense of propriety but as serious blow to her self-respect. As Queen and wife, she was not to be seen as naked by Gyges or others, except by her husband, but Gyges saw her thus, and that shamed her. The King deliberately put her in that situation: she was shamed in her own eyes, even though it was the King who wronged her, and she herself did nothing blameworthy. Her husband's plot shamed her by violating her self-respect—remember his "off with her skirt, off with her shame"—and that explains her passionate reaction.

If we understand this about her evaluative framework, her reaction will no longer seem excessive, especially not if we realize that it is cast in the heroic mold familiar to us from the myths and literature of ancient Greece. The reactions for instance of Achilles, Ajax, Medea, and Hecuba come from the same mold. Each was shamed, felt the sear of damaged self-respect, and reacted with rage. The expression of that kind of shame in dramatic action does not remove the shame, but it does makes it easier to bear it by allowing the expression of the outrage felt by those who are shamed.

However, our response to the Queen's action may still remain as it first was, even if understand why the Queen had acted as she did. We may continue to think that there is something wrong with the Lydian evaluative framework if it leads to such disproportionate reactions as the Queen's was. Being seen naked is just not serious enough to warrant murder, and it is a mistake to make propriety into a matter of self-respect. The Queen should have been more critical of the Lydian evaluative framework. She should not have identified with it so thoroughly as to be unable to question it.

This response makes good sense to us, but it would not have made sense to the Queen or to other Lydians. There are deep differences between the Lydian and our evaluative framework. We do and Lydians do not distinguish between feeling ashamed and being shamed and between personal and social evaluations. These differences lead us and had led them to the see the possibilities and limits of life very differently.

If a politician in our context is caught taking a bribe, as was for example Agnew, Vice President under Nixon, then he is publicly shamed. But he may not feel privately ashamed, as apparently Agnew did not. He may have believed that politicians routinely take bribes and that there is no real difference between accepting cash in a white envelope, as he did, and accepting a check for a so-called campaign contribution, which most politicians do. Or, I may feel ashamed for losing my temper with a persistently inquisitive neighbor, but few would find it shameful if I do not to live up to the unusually great importance I ascribe to politeness. For us, being shamed and feeling ashamed may or may not coincide.

For the Lydians, however, they did coincide. In their evaluative framework, there could be no difference between feeling shame and being shamed. If they were shamed, as the Queen was by the King's plot, they, like she, would have felt ashamed. There was for her and for Lydians in general no difference between how they were evaluated by others and how they evaluated themselves. Their personal evaluation of what was shameful was the same as the moral, political, or religious evaluation of it. Being seen naked was shameful, and the Queen felt ashamed because Gyges saw her naked. There was a relentless objectivity about what the Lydians thought was shameful: the mere fact that she was seen naked was shameful. It made no difference that the King caused her to be so seen. Only the fact mattered, not how it came about.

If we ask "Was the Queen's shame good?" it is clear, I think, that the answer cannot be a simple yes or no. A reasonable answer must take into account the Lydian evaluative framework, the Queen's place in it, and whether their evaluative framework was reasonable, unreasonable, or a mixture of both at that time in their circumstances. The answer that follows from the standard view is a simple yes. Critics of it take these complications into account and look deeper into the differences between how the Lydians and we think about shame.

PERSONAL AND SOCIAL EVALUATIONS

One source of these differences between the Lydian and our own ways of thinking about shame is that we do and the Lydians do not distinguish between personal and social evaluations. When we feel ashamed, it is because we have failed to act according to our personal evaluation. We may also be shamed by others for having acted contrary to some social evaluation, but we need not feel ashamed because of that. Our personal and social evaluations may or may not coincide. Of course, none of us wants to be publicly shamed, but that makes us feel ashamed only for actions that violate some of our own personal evaluation. This was not so for the Lydians. Their personal evaluations were the same as their social evaluations. If they were publicly shamed, they felt ashamed, and they felt ashamed because they acted contrary to some evaluation that was at once personal and social. Being seen naked outside of marriage was shameful—period.

They simply did not think that their personal and social evaluations were different. They did not have the conceptual tools to distinguish between them. It was as impossible a thought for them as it is impossible for us to think that we have no past. We could not be who we are without a past, not even if we do not remember much of it. And the Lydians could not be who they were if they did not identify themselves with the evaluations that were for them indistinguishably social and personal.

As I expressed this difference between the Lydians and us, it needs to be qualified. Individual Lydians did not share all their social evaluations. Many of them were connected with their status, gender, age, power, occupation, and so forth, and the evaluations differed as these conditions differed. But that did not make these different evaluations personal. They were still social evaluations because all Lydians whose conditions were the same were committed to the same social evaluations. They had to meet the same expectations. If they met them, they were respected for it. If they failed to meet them, they were shamed and either felt ashamed or were condemned for being shameless.

This is not so for us. We may prize personal evaluations that no one else in our context has, such as love for a person, gratitude for kindness, nostalgia for a recollected past, or seeing the world and our place in it with detached irony. Perhaps the Lydians could have had these experiences—Herodotus is silent about that—but their social evaluations did dictate how they should act on the experiences they had. Our social evaluations do not dictate whether and how we should act on our personal evaluations, nor whether we should regard them as more, less, or equally important as we do the social evaluations.

It is possible for us to have personal evaluations independently of the social evaluations because in our evaluative framework the development of individuality, privacy, autonomy, independence, and the like are encouraged. Good parents raise their children so as to enable them to be autonomous. Of course we recognize that personal evaluations can be abused and misused. They may not just be different from but contrary to social evaluations. But, unlike the Lydians, we have them. And it is because we have them that we can be shamed for acting contrary to a social evaluation and yet not feel shame if it is a personal evaluation that leads us to act contrary to it.

It is clear, I think, that in this respect our evaluative framework is better. It is possible for us to be critical our entire evaluative framework, but it was not possible for the Lydians. They could not have had any reason against it because anything they could have recognized as a reason was derived from that evaluative framework. They could, of course, be critical of some of their evaluations but only by appealing to other evaluations to which they were committed. Their criticisms of their evaluations were all internal to their evaluative framework. If they had rejected their entire evaluative framework, they would have been left without any evaluations from which they could derive reasons.

We, however, can appeal to evaluations that are outside of our evaluative framework: namely the evaluations of other evaluative frameworks we know about from anthropology, history, and literature. We can travel to and live in very different contexts. And even if we do not travel, we have access to the accounts of those who have traveled to and observed life in other contexts. This makes it possible for us to compare our own with other evaluative frameworks. We may find that some of their evaluations are better than ours, and that enables us to be critical of some of the ones to which we are committed. And then we may become critical of and even reject our entire evaluative framework and resolve to live according to a different one.

We thus have possibilities that the Lydians did not have because they had no access to anthropology, history, or literature. And if they traveled, which they rarely did or if they had visitors, which rarely happened, they regarded the alien contexts and visitors as contemptible precisely because their way of life was contrary to the Lydian evaluative framework. Some Greeks, like Herodotus, were exceptional in the ancient world in having observed evaluative frameworks other than their own. The Lydians had not acted on this possibility, if, indeed, they were aware of it. They were without a possibility we have. And it is that possibility that enables us to compare our evaluative framework with others and perhaps become critical of it. The Lydians could not do this.

The point of these comparisons between the Lydians and us is not that they show that our evaluative framework is better than theirs. It is better in one respect but may not be so in others. The distinction between social and personal evaluations and the possibility of comparing our evaluative framework with others leads to conflicting reasons for and against how we should answer the hard questions in general, and the particular hard question about whether shame is good. It is a possible thought for us that there are better ways than shame of protecting our self-respect, but it was not for the Lydians.

The Lydians faced no hard questions because they did not have to resolve conflicts between social and personal evaluations, since they did not distinguish between them. Nor did they have to decide whether other evaluative frameworks were better or worse than their own, since they did not compare them. This made their lives much simpler than our lives are. Their evaluative framework made it clear to them how they should live, but it left them with a conception of shame that befell on individuals even though they have done nothing to deserve it.

Their evaluative framework had the advantage of simplicity. Ours is enriched by possibilities they did not have, but they saddle us with complexities and conflicts. They knew what was and was not shameful and which actions were which. We are unclear and often ambivalent about that. Who could tell with certainty what is and what is not shameful in the prevailing economic, medical, sexual, political, or religious practices?

We have no simple way of resolving conflicts between personal and social evaluations, partly because we have learned to question both. It is for us a hard question whether or when shame is good. And it is hard also to resolve conflicts between our personal and social evaluations. We know from personal experience that such conflicts are frequent. Yet this hard question has what seems to me a reasonable answer. I now consider another woman to see what we can learn from her about facing the hard question.

HESTER

Hester Prynne is the main protagonist in Nathaniel Hawthorne's novel, *The Scarlet Letter*.[69] The events described take place in Puritan Boston of the seventeenth century. She is married, but her husband, who was many years older than she, had been absent for years. He finally returns only to find Hester pilloried, with a young baby in her arms. She is shamed for being an adulteress and sentenced to wearing the scarlet letter "A" for adulteress on her dress for the rest of her life. She refuses to name the baby's father, even when she is promised

---

69. Nathaniel Hawthorne, *The Scarlet Letter* (New York: Dover, 1840/1994).

amnesty in return. Adultery is regarded as shameful by everyone, and, in the long years to come, everyone around her makes her feel it daily. She lives alone with her child in a shack just outside of Boston, which was then a small town. The husband, the father of the child, and the child are also important for the story Hawthorne tells, but I will concentrate on Hester, on her being shamed, and on her feeling ashamed.

She is a young beautiful woman, full of life, earning a living through her skilled needlework. The father of the child is in fact the highly respected minister, the moral and religious authority in the Puritan context. They encountered each other by accident on a forest path, and sudden passion and years of pent up frustration overtook them: they made love, and that is how she becomes pregnant. But the minister, that moral and religious paragon, not only remained silent but took part in shaming her. The story of Hester is the story of her growing defiance. At first she identified herself with the prevailing evaluative framework. Its social evaluations were also her personal evaluations. When she was shamed by the prevailing evaluations for being an adulteress, she felt ashamed.

Her first act of defiance was to refuse to name the father of the child. She just could not bring herself to do it, although she does not know why. She was young, inexperienced, had no self-knowledge, and was not at all thoughtful. But she was also strong, loved her child, and rejoiced in her existence. During the long years in isolation she slowly began to suspect that what she felt was

> half a truth, and half a self-delusion ... [and that] the torture of her daily shame would at length purge her soul, and work out another purity than that which she had lost (55) ... [she felt] no genuine and steadfast penitence, but something doubtful, something that might be deeply wrong, beneath (57).

She realized that

> the truth was that the little Puritans, being of the most intolerant
> brood that ever lives, had got a vague idea of something . . . at
> variance with ordinary fashions, in the mother and child; and
> therefore scorned them in their hearts. . . .Mother and daughter
> stood together in the same circle of seclusion from human so-
> ciety (64–65).

She gradually grew much more thoughtful, defiant, and refused

> to measure her ideas of right and wrong by any standard external
> to herself . . . [she] did not now occupy precisely the same po-
> sition in which they beheld her during the earlier periods of her
> ignominy (109–110). [She was] standing alone in the world—
> alone as to any dependence on society . . . she cast away the
> fragments of a broken chain. The world's law was no law for her
> mind (112–113). . . . [The] long years, under the torture of the
> scarlet letter, inflicted so much of misery, and wrought out no
> repentance (121).

And Hawthorne summed up her resulting frame of mind:

> She had wandered, without rule or guidance, in a moral wil-
> derness. . . . Her intellect and heart had their home, as it were,
> in desert places. . . . For years past she had looked from this
> estranged point of view at human institutions, and whatever
> priests and legislators had established. . . .The tendency of her
> fate and fortunes had been to set her free. The scarlet letter was
> her passport into regions were other women dared not tread.
> Shame, Despair, Solitude! These had been her teachers – stern

and wild ones – and they made her strong but taught her much amiss (137).

Hawthorne left unanswered several questions that attentive readers will ask: What exactly did Hester learn? What remained much amiss? Why did she return to live in Puritan Boston after all that had happened to her? It is a fault of the novel that although these questions are suggested, the answers are not given. I now go on to answer them, but I do not know whether Hawthorne, if he were alive, would accept these answers.

What, then, did she learn? It was to free herself from the shame of adultery. She no longer accepted the Puritan social evaluations that at the beginning made her ashamed. She no longer judged her adultery and her daughter's illegitimacy by those evaluations. The world's law was no longer law for her (113). She had grown to have personal evaluations other than the social ones: love of her daughter, strength to resist ignominy, independence, and self-sufficiency. And, perhaps most remarkable of all, she became kind and forgiving.

As Hawthorne says (111), she transformed the scarlet letter "A" from meaning "adultery" to meaning "able." She learned to become her own person. But she was not shameless. She gained self-respect by rising above her suffering. With her self-respect came the possibility of shame. But that shame would not have been for the violation of social evaluations but for the violation of her personal evaluations from which she derived her self-respect.

We may say that nevertheless something remained amiss. What was it? The obvious answer is only part of the answer. What was obviously amiss was the moralistic, intrusive, authoritarian Puritan evaluative framework in which she lived. It was pervaded by sanctimonious hypocrisy and sexual repression enforced by the threat of eternal perdition. But there was also something else amiss that was much less obvious.

The clue to it is that Hester, who eventually realized this, remained in Puritan Boston although she could have moved elsewhere. She was unexpectedly left enough money, briefly visited England where she was born, and yet returned from there to live in the same shack, even if this time without her daughter. She remained in the same context with which she knew so much was amiss. Why? Because her self-respect demanded it. She wanted to show the Puritans what she had become and how the suffering they had inflicted on her had transformed her in a way they had not intended. She wanted to show them a possibility of life for which their narrow, repressive, intolerant evaluative framework left no room. This may seem like a noble endeavor, but there is reason to doubt it.

The unobvious thing that remained amiss is what led Hester to return to and live there. It was her ambivalence. She continued to regard herself as part of that context and judge herself partly by its evaluative framework. She had also grown to have personal evaluations, and she followed them when they conflicted with the social evaluations. Yet there still remained her other personal evaluations that coincided with the Puritan social evaluations. She continued to feel that she belonged to that context, that she was formed by it. And although she rejected many of its social evaluations, enough of them remained for her to want to follow them. After all, they were not all mistaken. Conscientiousness, a sense of obligation, practical savvy, self-reliance, and personal responsibility are important for living as she thought she should. Her self-respect, derived from her personal evaluations and from those social evaluations she shared with the Puritans, made her feel that she belonged to that context. She saw what was amiss with its evaluative framework, and that made her ambivalent toward it

She wanted to show Puritans the possibility of a life that she thought was freer and more tolerant than theirs. After long years, the Puritans came to accept and forgive her, but they continued to be committed to the social evaluations she rejected. They were quite unwilling to follow the possibility she came to represent by living among them and showing them the kind of person she became. Yet she lived there.

This was and continues to be the situation of those, like Hawthorne's own, who are clear sighted about what is amiss with their evaluative framework but having been formed by it, continue to evaluate themselves, others, and actions by many, if not all, of its standards. Yet they cannot help but condemn their evaluative framework. They have liberated themselves enough to reject many of its evaluations but not enough to free themselves from the entire evaluative framework. They can neither love nor leave their context; they want to do both but are unable to do either. So they continue to live in it, even though their personal evaluations are contrary to many of its social evaluations. This is the answer, I believe, to the questions that were left unanswered by Hawthorne's book.

If they temporarily leave and live for a while elsewhere, they nevertheless return, like revenants, and sorrowfully, unhappily, indignantly criticize the evaluative framework they can neither wholeheartedly accept nor reject. Rejecting them would be to reject part of themselves. Few people can bring themselves to do that, and Hester was not one of them. Those who remain are ashamed of themselves for living according to what they think is the deeply flawed evaluative framework in their context. The hard question for them is whether that shame is good. And the hard question forces them to struggle with the conflict between accepting the shame they feel and rejecting it and thereby condemning part of themselves.

Is there a reasonable answer to the hard question: Is shame good? There is. It depends on two reasons against the standard view of shame. These reasons are also reasons for the contrary view, according to which there are better ways than shame of protecting our self-respect.

SELF-RESPECT AND SHAME

As we have seen, the standard view is that shame is good because it protects our self-respect. This cannot be right. We feel shame *after* we have done something that damages our self-respect and for which we are ashamed. So shame is a reaction to what has already happened. It cannot protect self-respect from the damage that has been done to it. Perhaps the *fear* of shame can protect it in the future. But fear of shame is not shame any more than fear of falling is falling. This is much more than a quibble. Fear of shame is, at most, one among several ways of protecting our self-respect. There is no reason to suppose that it is always the best or even a good way. In any case, there are often much better ways: ways that are less painful, more effective, and less damaging to our self-respect.

The connection between self-respect and shame is like the connection between the heart and a heart attack. A heart attack assails us, but it is much better to avoid it than to have it. And so it is with shame. There are better ways of protecting our heart than fearing a heart attack. And there are better ways of protecting our self-respect than fearing shame.

What are these better ways? They are obvious. One way is to focus on how we think we should live, act accordingly, and not act in ways that are contrary to it. Another is to examine and question our motives and do what we can to avoid acting on false beliefs, misguided emotions, or unwise desires. Yet another is to cultivate self-knowledge and self-control. We thereby prevent ourselves from succumbing to short-term satisfactions that are contrary to the long-term ones derived from living as we think we should. A further one is to resist self-deception, fantasy, and wishful thinking that disguise from us our unworthy motives such as envy, jealousy, prejudice, pride, rage, and so forth. We can remind ourselves of our moral, personal, political, religious, and other evaluations and do not act contrary to them.

Nor should we forget that a sense of duty and responsibility, concern for others, solidarity, conscience, or just simple socially ingrained habit may keep us from acting in ways that may damage our self-respect. These ways protect our self-respect, strengthen rather than weaken it in the way the painful emotion of shame does. Shame tends to damage our self-respect by exacerbating the blame we already accept for being or acting in ways contrary to how we think we should. These considerations, I repeat, are obvious and familiar. They are reminders of what most of us know anyway. But, it seems to me, defenders of the standard view have forgotten them.

Let us return for a moment to the Queen and Hester. Did the shame, or the fear of it protect their self-respect? It certainly did not protect the Queen's self-respect. So long as the Queen accepted the Lydian evaluative framework, there was virtually nothing she could do to protect her self-respect, since she had no control over the actions of others, like those of the King and Gyges, that shamed her and damaged her self-respect. Given the Lydian evaluative framework, she derived her self-respect from others who treated her as was appropriate to her social status. She had little control over whether others did or did not do this. Whether she felt shame and had self-respect depended on others, not on her, so her shame could not possibly protect her self-respect. It was reactive, not proactive.

What about Hester? Did shame protect her self-respect? It did not. It led her to endure long years of suffering and daily humiliation inflicted on her by others with whom she had only brief contacts because she was for many years despised and shunned. Shame almost destroyed her. What protected her was the strength she had found in herself to resist the shaming to which she was subjected. Her slow development of critical reflection eventually led her to question and abandon just those Puritan evaluations that led to her shame. Contrary to the standard view, she protected her self-respect by rejecting the shame that was intended by the Puritans to damage it.

The Lydian and Puritan evaluative frameworks were, of course, very different from ours. But shame may be as damaging to our self-respect as it was for the Queen and Hester. Think of the experience of many people here and now who have been shamed by others for falling short of the evaluation of what they came to regard as the right accent, address, clothing, manners, taste, and so forth. Such shaming is not just on account of class but also for race, religion, education, and ethnicity that may lead some to see others as inferior. If such attitudes are prevalent in a context, then its victims are shamed by them, although they have done nothing shameful. They are not shamed for something they did, but for what they have become as a result of conditions beyond their control. There is little they could have or could now do about that, and the shame they may come to feel damages rather than protects their self-respect.

The rejection of the standard view does not lead to the indefensible alternative to it that shame could never be good and that it must always be destructive. We sometimes are and should be ashamed and are the better for it. We may realize that we should not have done that, should have been more thoughtful, tried harder, been more helpful, not have dismissed an idea, person, or possibility hastily, and so on. My point is that shame is no more than one of several ways of protecting our self-respect, but it is often not the best way, and it makes failure even harder to endure than other responses to it. The standard view is at best only partly true. But partly true views are partly not true, and that is why I think that the standard view is mistaken.

Its mistake, as Hume had noted, is a common one made by philosophers:

> They confine too much their principles, and make no account of that vast variety, which nature has so much affected in all her operations. When philosopher has once laid hold of a favourite principle, he extends the same principle over the whole creation, and reduces to it every phaenomenon, though by the most violent and absurd reasoning. Our own mind being narrow and contracted, we cannot extend our conception to the variety and extent of nature; but imagine, that she is as much bounded in her operations, as we are in our speculation.[70]

Or, in Wittgenstein's only slightly exaggerated words,

> a main cause of philosophical disease—a one-sided diet: one nourishes one's thinking with only one kind of example.[71]

One way in which defenders of the standard view make this mistake is that they focus on a one-sided diet of examples: they view shame as a moral emotion. They think that because it is moral, it is more important than any non-moral response to failure. But this is no more than an unjustifiable prejudice. Failure of foresight, imagination, self-knowledge, sympathy, taste, understanding, and so on may make us non-morally ashamed and we may find that as painful as moral failure. We can avoid failing and we can protect our self-respect by improving ourselves just in those non-moral and moral respects in which we have failed.

---

70. David Hume, "The Sceptic" in *Essays, Moral, Political, and Literary* (Indianapolis: Liberty Press, 1741/1985), 159–160.
71. Ludwig Wittgenstein, *Philosophical Investigations*, trans. G.E.M. Anscombe (Oxford: Blackwell, 1968), 593.

SHAME AND CONFORMITY

Another reason for doubting that shame is good is that if we have accepted mistaken social evaluations, then shame may obstruct our efforts to free ourselves from them. This is not a rare occurrence. We all accept some social evaluations, and few of them are free of mistakes. Our own situation is not all that different from the one that became Hester's after she became critical of the Puritan social evaluations. Our evaluative framework is far more tolerant than the Puritan one was. The consequences of being shamed by our violation of the prevailing social evaluations are not nearly as drastic as they were for Hester.

Nevertheless, we might see our own violation of them as shameful and that damages our self-respect. It, then, becomes natural to ask: is shame on that account good? The question compels us to face the conflict between blaming the social evaluations for the shame our violation of them makes us feel or blaming ourselves for having violated them.

Consider us facing this conflict in the ordinary course of life. We may not be deep thinkers, social critics, or reformers. We have a way of life, job, family, the usual satisfactions and burdens. We live as well as we can, guided by our upbringing, experiences, preferences, and the resulting personal attitude, all of which are at least partly formed by and permeated with the prevailing evaluative framework in our context. Some of the evaluations that follow do not concern important matters, but others are moral, personal, political, or religious, and they are not only said to be important, but we also feel that they are. They are not just social but have become personal through our identification with them. We rely on them to tell the difference between what is good and bad, better and worse, noble and base, permissible and forbidden, and so on. If we act in a way that violates one of the important evaluations, then we and everyone else we know regard that as shameful.

For the Queen, it was seen naked outside of marriage; for Hester it was adulterous pregnancy; for us it would be to violate our deep commitment to a moral, personal, political, or religious social and personal evaluation. Then we are ashamed. We have to respond to it in some way, and we face a conflict between accepting the shame or rejecting the evaluation from which the shame follows.

The Queen accepted the shame. Hester eventually rejected the evaluations whose violation at first shamed her. We can learn from her, but it is difficult to act on it. We can accept shame and damage to our self-respect, feel terrible, and try to reform. Or we can deflect the shame, protect our self-respect, and disown the evaluations we have violated. The consequences of disowning important ones are more damaging than accepting shame for their violation. If we disown them, we become estranged from our evaluative framework. Our intimate relationships with others will sooner or later suffer from our rejection of the evaluations by which they continue to live. Our way of life would have to alter basically, and we would probably lose our livelihood if it depends on the good opinion others have of us.

It might be thought that the evaluations we disowned were only the social ones that became our personal evaluations as well, but we would still have some personal evaluations left that we have not disowned and which could sustain us. However, apart from our commitment to them, there would be nothing else we could rely on to sustain our personal evaluations. It is difficult to live in this way. It takes exceptional strength, self-confidence, pride, or some combination of all three to live in isolation from the most important social evaluations in our context. We would be sentencing ourselves to internal or external exile and would be as isolated as Hester was.

We are all social beings and it is close to psychologically impossible for us to remain a fully functioning person if we live long in isolation from everyone who might share or at least respect, the evaluations by which we live. If we isolate ourselves, we will begin to question the personal evaluations that led to our isolation, and we will have no resources left beyond the personal evaluations we are questioning. We will come to doubt the personal evaluations on which alone we base our self-respect. That will be as painful an experience as it would be if we had accepted the mistaken social evaluations whose violation shamed us and damaged our self-respect. Both the acceptance and the rejection of the mistaken social evaluations will damage our self-respect: the first by conformity; the second by isolation. It may be thought then that neither accepting blame nor rejecting our evaluative framework from which shame follows is an acceptable alternative. But this would be a mistake.

There is another way of resolving the conflict between accepting and rejecting the mistaken social evaluations that shame us. It is to deny that shame should play a significant role in how we think we should live. This alternative, I think, is implied by the recognition that there are better ways than shame of protecting our self-respect and that we are social beings who cannot remain long estranged from some social context, even if we think that some of its social evaluations are mistaken. In conclusion, I indicate how, if we reject the standard view, we should answer the hard question about shame.

THE ANSWER

The main conclusion is that there is no simple answer to the hard question of "Is shame good?" I have dwelled at some length on comparing the situations of the Queen, Hester, and our own to show just how complex, varied, and context-dependent are the reasons for and against thinking of shame as good. That is why the question is hard. In rare cases, shame is good, but most often it is not. There are numerous context-dependent reasons for and against the conflicting answers to the question of whether a particular experience of shame by a particular person in a particular context is good. And the reasonable answer in one context cannot be carried over to another, very different context. Hard questions in general and the one about shame in particular are evaluative. The evaluations depend on who and why we are feeling shame and on the time, place, and circumstances involved; on our experiences, preferences, and the available alternatives; on the prevailing evaluative framework; on the importance of the violated evaluation; on how we think we should live; and on whether our evaluations in question are reasonable. The complexities and conflicts involved in the evaluation of the relevant reasons are what makes the question about shame hard.

If we acknowledge the hardness of the question and the difficulty of resolving the conflicts, then we must acknowledge as well the complexity of finding a reasonable answer to it. Those who favor the standard view want simplicity. They say that self-respect and shame go together. But they often do not go together, especially not when there are better ways of protecting self-respect than shame. And even when they do go together, there are significant differences between how self-respect and shame are understood in different contexts. The hardness of the question, however, does not mean that a reasonable answer cannot be found. It means that there are no reasonable and final answers. There are reasonable answers, but they depend on the complexities involved. No matter how reasonable the answers are in one context, they cannot be generalized and applied to another context.

This is the view I have been defending. Opposed to it is the standard view that takes no account of the complexities and conflicts involved. Its defenders focus on cases in which the shame in question is moral and clearly good, but they ignore cases in which the shame is non-moral, when there are better alternatives to it, and when the self-respect that shame supposedly protects should not be protected.

Chapter 9

Is It Always Good to Be
True to Who We Are?

THE QUESTION

Who we are depends on the combination of our personal attitude, the evaluative framework of the context in which we live, and the prevailing personal and social circumstances. Our personal attitude has been formed by our experiences, history, family, formal and informal education; by our beliefs, emotions, and desires; and by our native and acquired capacities and incapacities, talents, and weaknesses. The evaluative framework includes the moral, political, religious, and other evaluations of the non-evaluative circumstances of life as good or bad, better or worse. We evaluate all this from the point of view of how we think we should live. Each of these evaluations may be mistaken. And even if none of them is mistaken, they may still conflict and make us uncertain about how we should live. If we are free of such mistakes and conflicts, if we think that we are living as we should, and if we are satisfied with how our life is going, then we have good reasons to be true to who we are.

The main reason against it is that virtually all of us find that how we live is not how we think we should live. We are more or less seriously dissatisfied, uncertain about how to come closer to living as we think we should, and how to resolve conflicts between our various evaluations. Such dissatisfactions are widely felt. If in doubt, consider how many of us could honestly say that we do not regret any of the important choices we have made, and that our children, finances, friendships, health, housing, marriage, sex life, work, and so on are as we wish them to be? We know better than anyone that for whatever reason our life is not going as we think we should. That is why we are dissatisfied. And then we should not be true to who we are. We should be better, less mistaken, less conflicted, and less uncertain than we are.

Our dissatisfactions are caused by the combination of the conditions in our context and our mistaken evaluations of the possibilities open to us. If we are fortunate and live in a peaceful, stable, civilized society governed by the rule of law, then we can evaluate the relative importance of the available possibilities and choose between them. This is a routine part of life, a familiar experience to most of us, when we do not face dire emergencies. The resulting evaluations vary from person to person because many of the available possibilities vary with age, gender, health, motives, relationships, religion, social position, wealth, and so on.

If we are dissatisfied, we may suspect that our evaluations are mistaken and that we should not be true to who our mistaken evaluations have led us to be. We may think that we have been manipulated or bullied by parental, moral, political, or religious authorities to accept their evaluations. Or we may think that our personal evaluations are conflicting, impractical, prejudiced, too demanding or much too timid, overly rigid, or fickle and changing as our moods do, and so on. It is reasonable to question our evaluations if we think that they prevent us from living as we think we should. And the more we question them, the more dissatisfied we will be.

Not all dissatisfactions are caused by mistaken evaluations. They may be caused by economic crises, scarcity, social unrest, widespread criminality, and other social ills. However, I will be concerned only with dissatisfactions that are caused by mistaken moral, political, religious, and other evaluations of our society, or by our false beliefs, misdirected emotions, and misguided desires that are parts of our personal attitude. And even if our evaluations are not mistaken, they may conflict with one another, and then how we think we should live could not be reasonably guided by both of the conflicting evaluations. If we think that our evaluations of the possibilities of life are mistaken or conflicting, then we have good reasons not be true to who we became as a result of them.

Who we are depends on a great variety of interconnected evaluations. They influence and have implications for one another. They are weakened or strengthened by these reciprocal influences, and we routinely have reasons for or against some of them on the basis of some of our other evaluations. We at once rely on and question them, and then we become uncertain about which of the evaluations of our possibilities should or should not guide how we think we should live. There are no easy answers to the question of how we should resolve such familiar conflicts. When should one of them have priority to the others? And why should any one of them have priority? Our conflicts add to our uncertainty about whether we should or should not be true to who we are. Our dissatisfactions are the consequences of these conflicts and uncertainties.

Our predicament is that the only way we could distinguish between the mistaken and unmistaken evaluations is by relying on yet other evaluations. But we do not know whether they are also mistaken. If we follow the advice of others, we still have to rely on our evaluations to choose whose advice we follow. And their advice may also be based on their own possibly mistaken evaluations. Trying to distinguish between our mistaken and unmistaken evaluations is like doing surgery on ourselves, and it is no less painful. We are thus left with the hard question: should we be true to who we are? The question is hard and pressing because we are dissatisfied with who we are and are uncertain about how to become less so.

In contemporary thought, being true to who we are is valued for being autonomous, authentic, self-directed, or self-governing. It is widely assumed that it is good to be in these ways and that a good society creates and protects the conditions in which we can achieve it. This assumption is at best only half true, and the other half of it is false. For how could it be good to be true to who we are if we are conflicted, confused, cruel, dishonest, dogmatic, fearful, foolish, prejudiced, or unreasonable? Weighing the conflicting reasons for and against being true to who we are leads to the hard question this chapter is about.

I turn now to the Colonel and Peter who faced and answered this hard question. The Colonel was true to who he was and died because of it. Peter, after years of anguish, was untrue to it, and that liberated him from the burden he carried for years. Each made mistakes in their evaluations of the possibilities of life they had. I will discuss who each was and the very different mistakes they made. By comparing their predicaments with our less acute problems, we can learn from their mistakes how we could give a more reasonable answer to the hard question of whether we should be true to who we are.

THE COLONEL

The facts of the Colonel's life are a matter of public record, but the reconstructions of his frame of mind are mine. He came from a military family and followed the family tradition. At the age of eighteen he was accepted to West Point and went through four years of rigorous and demanding physical, military, and academic training. Upon graduation he was commissioned as a junior officer, married his childhood sweetheart, and had two children. He loved his family, but the marriage was difficult because his duties required frequent and prolonged absences, and he returned from them physically and emotionally drained. But he was wholeheartedly committed to the Army's evaluative framework in which duty, honor, and country overrode conflicting considerations. Throughout his life he had been guided, without realizing it, by Hume's precept:[72]

> Let a man propose to himself the model of a character, which he approves: Let him be well acquainted with those particulars, in which his character deviates from the model: Let him keep a constant watch over himself, and bend his mind, by a continual effort, from vices, towards virtues; and I doubt not but in time, he will find in his temper an alteration for the better.

But following this precept prevented him from being as good a husband and father as he thought he should be, and that was part of his dissatisfactions. At the time I am writing about, he was over forty and has been in active service for almost twenty years. He was an experienced and dedicated Army officer who led the troops under his command on numerous combat missions. He was respected and valued, but he was not thought to be outstanding, and the recognition he received was not commensurate with his efforts. This added to his dissatisfactions, but they were not serious enough to make him question his commitment to duty, honor, and country.

He was stationed in Iraq, commanding a mixed unit composed of American soldiers, remnants of the Iraqi army, and battle-hardened mercenaries recruited from all over the world, euphemistically called civilian contractors. The unit was in charge of protecting the security of civilian population in a segment of Baghdad. There was

---

72. David Hume, "The Sceptic" in *Essays, Moral, Political and Literary*, ed. Eugene F. Miller (Indianapolis: Liberty Press, 1741/1985), 170.

considerable reciprocal resentment between the three groups under his command. The civilian contractors and the Iraqi ex-soldiers had no conception of or commitment to duty, honor, country. The American soldiers thought that it was all right for officers to be hardnosed about adhering to it, but the soldiers were not officers. Drugs were ubiquitous, danger constant, prostitution rampant, the native population distrusted everyone who carried arms, and they were equally hostile to foreigners, ex-Iraqi soldiers, and American occupiers.

Corruption, bribery, theft, and extortion from the civilians were widespread and well known to everyone, including the Colonel and the entire hierarchy of higher-ranking officers who commanded the American forces in Iraq. The civilian contractors and the ex-Iraqi soldiers wanted to enrich themselves, and the GIs wanted to survive until their tour of duty came to an end. All through this were the ever-present roadside bombs, snipers, mines, booby-trapped facilities, the impossibility of distinguishing between civilians who wanted security and enemies who wanted to kill or at least maim as many of the occupying forces as they could.

It was the Colonel's duty to protect the security of the civilian population, control the troops under his command, and prevent them from extorting money, sex, drugs, or goods from the civilian population. He soon realized that he could not do his duty. In that context, and with those troops, no one could. The task was impossible. And that added to his dissatisfactions. He was dedicated to serving his country, but he did not know how he could do it then and there with the troops he had. Nor did he know who was friendly, neutral, or hostile in that country divided by centuries old hatred between religious, ethnic, and regional factions. He nevertheless tried to do as well as he could but came to realize that his efforts were useless, and his troops were unreliable and corrupt.

He laid out to his commanding officer the impossibility of the situation. This was not news to him, nor to those higher up in the chain of command. The American forces in general faced a fraught situation in the aftermath of a war when they had to act as a police force rather than an Army. They had been trained to fight battles: not to establish and enforce law and order, or to pacify the deeply divided population. His superior told the Colonel to do as well as he could in the circumstances. But the Colonel realized that his best was not good enough to enable him to live up to his commitment to duty, honor, and country.

He gave himself time to think about what he should do. He thought about the pressures, dangers, and uncertainties under which he had to function; the worsening corruption of his troops; about his parents, wife, and children whom he loved; and about what his friends and fellow officers would have him do in that situation. He thought about his own life and responsibilities; and about what could be the purpose of the occupation of Iraq.

The only answer he could find was that his commitment to duty, honor, and country came first, and his love of life, of his family, and of what others would think of him came second. After as serious reflection as he was capable of, in the face of all the reasons he had against it, he chose to remain true to his commitment to the military evaluative framework to which he had been dedicated throughout his life. He thought that those he cared about would eventually understand that he was compelled by who he was to do what he decided to do. He saw that the day of reckoning had come for him, as it had come to some others he had read about and discussed during his training and afterward with is fellow officers:

> when they have to declare the great Yes
> or the great No. It's clear at once who has the Yes
> ready within him; and saying it,
> he goes from honor to honor strong in his conviction.
> He who refuses does not repent. Asked again,

he'd still say no. Yet that no—the right no—
drags him down all his life.[73]

He then said the great Yes to remaining true and killed himself, rather than say No to it and live on in a desultory way that would have dragged him down all his life.

Before that day of reckoning, the Colonel was only moderately dissatisfied. He accepted that he was responsible for his marital problems and for being only a good but not an outstanding officer. He told himself that he did as well as he could and did not see how he could do more. His dissatisfactions, however, were more than counterbalanced by the conviction that he was meeting his commitment to duty, honor, and country. He had good reason to think that he lived as he thought he should and that he was being true to himself. He acknowledged his dissatisfactions, but he had good reasons also to say to himself that everyone has dissatisfactions, and he should not allow them to get out hand and interfere with his being true to who he was. But when the day came, and he found himself in a situation in which, through no fault of his own, he could not be true to who he was, his moderate dissatisfaction turned into an extreme one, and it was then that he killed himself. He had a good reason for that as well. Was he mistaken?

PERSONAL ATTITUDES AND EVALUATIVE FRAMEWORKS

Our reasons for our evaluations are guided by our personal attitude and evaluative framework. The difference between them is not

73. C. P. Cavafy, *Collected Poems*, trans. Edmund Keeley (Princeton, NJ: Princeton University Press, 1975), 12.

that our personal attitude is subjective and the prevailing evaluative framework is objective. Both are subjective, if by that we mean our own evaluations of the available possibilities of how we might live.

The crucial difference between them is that our personal attitude focuses on the strongly felt immediacy and force of how we think we should live, while the evaluative framework makes us decenter what we believe, feel, and desire and concentrate instead on articulating and evaluating them from an moral, political, religious, or some other point of view. But, I repeat, both are our own evaluations, although they follow from two different yet overlapping points of view. If the two kinds of evaluation conflict, which they often do as we know from our own experience, then each gives us reason for questioning and being critical of the other.

The evaluations that follow from our personal attitude do not give us an impartial, disinterested, universal point of view of that mythical entity, the ideal observer or a fully rational agent who acts, as the phrase goes, from the point of view of the universe—as if it could have a point of view. Nor do they follow from that other mythical entity, an ideal theory that all who understand it would accept and follow. The evaluations that follow from our personal attitude are practical, not theoretical, and guide our efforts to find a fit between our beliefs, emotions, and desires and the evaluative framework of our context. Both are inescapably personal evaluations of how we think we should live, not how anyone else should live. Both may be mistaken because we may be misled by our ignorance or misinterpretation of the available possibilities, or by the various subterfuges by which we disguise from ourselves that our dissatisfactions are our fault. And sometimes they really are not because conditions beyond our control may frustrate our reasonable endeavors. But in civilized societies and fortunate circumstances usually we are to blame if we are dissatisfied because it is our fault that how we live is not how we think we should live.

Lastly, I stress that our personal attitude and evaluative framework are both context-dependent. They are our evaluations of our possibilities, but what the possibilities actually are depends on a great plurality of physical, physiological, psychological, social, and international conditions that often change and affect us in different ways. This plurality and these changes are part of the reason why there cannot be an impersonal, impartial, universal theory of how each of us should evaluate whatever our possibilities in life may happen to be.

Returning now to the Colonel, we can see that the evaluations of his situation that followed from his personal attitude was identical with the evaluations that followed from the military evaluative framework. There were possibilities and reasons in addition to those that the Colonel had regarded as his own, but the Colonel did not see them as possibilities and reasons for him. He thought that he had to choose between the two possibilities: either act as his commitment to duty, honor, country required, or kill himself. Since he could not act as the first possibility required, he thought that he had no alternative but to act on the second, and he so acted. Killing himself was his way in that wretched situation of being true to himself.

Anything else was unthinkable for the Colonel. But it would not have been unthinkable for others. They were unthinkable only for him because of his personal attitude and evaluative framework to which he was so deeply committed. He could not think that there were also other possibilities for him because his entire life, training, experiences, and evaluations were formed by the Army's evaluative framework, which became also his personal attitude. He was attached to them as ineluctably as he was to his body and could no more live without one as without the other. Given his commitment, honorable death was incomparably better than dishonorable life. These reciprocally reinforcing reasons derived from his personal attitude and evaluative framework left him no room for other alternatives. That is why it was unthinkable for him to do anything else but what he did.

Evaluations that did not take into account the centrality of his commitment were utterly irrelevant to his being true to who he was.

We can perhaps understand this about the Colonel and still go on to question both his commitment to duty, honor, and country that overrode all other considerations. Duty is to act as his superiors in the chain of command ordered, but their orders may have been strategically or tactically mistaken. Honor may require disobeying illegal or badly mistaken orders that endanger the lives of hundreds of soldiers and non-combatants. Country may be ruled by politicians who pursue policies contrary to the interest of the citizens and who care more about staying in power than about those who put them there. How could that be the overriding evaluation? And even if we recognize the importance for someone like the Colonel to be guided by his evaluative framework, why should he think that it overrode all conflicting considerations, such as the common good, justice, liberty, kindness, peace, or love of family? Should the Colonel not have asked these questions? Should he not have considered that he might be mistaken in seeing his choice as a stark one between two alternatives that excluded all other possibilities?

Should he not have considered whether or not the occupation of Iraq was a futile attempt to rule a country divided by deep ethnic, religious, and political hatreds, a country that has been ruled throughout its history only by dictators who repressed dissent and ruled by fiat? Should he not have been aware of what happened in Afghanistan, Algeria, the Congo, Indonesia, Kashmir, Rwanda, Sudan, Vietnam, Yugoslavia, and many other places when the collapse of a bad regime led to even worse mass murders motivated by the centuries-old tribal, ethnic, regional, and religious hatreds. Should he not have asked whether the same might not be true in Iraq, where American occupation merely injected another element that exacerbated an already fraught situation. Did duty, honor, country really require him to do or die for that?

The point of these questions is not to suggest that the answer the Colonel gave to the hard question he faced was mistaken. The point is rather that he was mistaken in not recognizing that the question was more complex than he supposed. Could the Colonel have avoided making this mistake, recognize the complexities he faced, consider more possibilities than he had done, and only then give his answer to the hard question he faced? Perhaps if he had been an exceptional and very unusual officer, he could have been sufficiently thoughtful and historically and politically informed to recognize the complexities of the question and find a reasonable answer to it. But the Colonel was not such an officer.

Well, then, what could he or should he have done that he did not do? Given his personal attitude, evaluative framework, and the situation in Iraq, there was nothing he could have done then and there. What he could have done lies far back in the past when he made the series of choices that eventually led to who he was and what he did in Iraq in his forties. In the past, he had a choice about following his family's military tradition, going to West Point, being commissioned after his training there, and opting to be an officer in infantry with combat responsibilities, rather than serving in some other branch of the Army. He chose to become who he was. One of the consequences of that choice was that he became the kind of person who could not but be true to who he was. Another consequence was that he had to face situations in which he had to be prepared to die if duty, honor, and country required it.

A country needs such soldiers, as well as police officers and firefighters, and they could not very well do what they are responsible for doing if they ask complex questions about history, international relations, morality, politics, and perhaps religion as well. The Colonel's choice was a consequence of his evaluations of who he was and of his commitment to being true to it. But a different person might have chosen differently.

I hope to have made clear that the Colonel derived his reasons for and against being true to who he was from his evaluations of the possibilities open to him. There also were other evaluations available, but, given his commitment, they were not for him realistic possibilities. I now turn to Peter whose mistaken evaluations made him deeply and wrongly dissatisfied with who he was and who had no reason to be true to who he thought he was.

PETER

When it all began Peter was ten and Paul, his brother, was nine.[74] They were carefree children who went on a familiar hike near their house up a hill overlooking a lake. They sat down, looked at the lake, and chatted about this and that. Paul stood up to pee from the top of the hill into the lake below when an unusually strong gust of wind made him lose his balance. He fell, but Peter grabbed his hand and held it. Paul hung on, scrambled but found no footing. Peter tried but he was not strong enough to pull him up, there was no one else around, Peter's grip weakened, Paul's hand slipped out, and he fell, bouncing down the rock-strewn slope toward the lake as Peter watched him helplessly roll into and sink in the water. He ran home as fast as he could and alerted his parents who rushed to the lake, but it was too late. When they finally pulled Paul out, his body was battered, face disfigured, and he was dead. Peter saw all this and was in shock. He repeated again and again to his parents and the authorities what happened. No one blamed him. But he and his parents were devastated.

---

74. My account of Peter is loosely based on Arthur Koestler's novel, *Arrival and Departure* (London: Hutchinson, 1943). I have changed details of the story.

After this a miasma had descended on the family. The parents were assailed by guilt. Peter was haunted by nightmares. The happy boy he used to be turned into a dense miserable lump. In a few months, the nightmares eventually dissipated, his memory of the events faded, but his misery persisted. As the years passed, he became a sullen, slovenly adolescent. He was a poor student and had no interests. He was uncommunicative, unreachable, often unwashed, distracted, lethargic, forgot the simplest things, and unreachable by the affection of his parents or by the overtures of others. He was indifferent to food, clothes, and how he appeared. He was friendless, lonely, withdrawn, and felt awful about himself and everyone else. He was deeply dissatisfied with himself. If he had been articulate, which he certainly was not, he would have said that he had good reasons not to want to be true to the wretched person he believed he was.

Then the world intruded. An awful dictator grabbed power in his country and held it by terror. A feeble resistance movement was formed and Peter, now eighteen, was asked to join the few who dared to do something. This was the first time in years he was asked anything. He agreed and was given the task of distributing leaflets at night denouncing the dictator. He was soon caught, imprisoned in a notorious camp for political opponents, interrogated, and tortured when he refused to give any information about others in the resistance. This happened to all those who were arrested, but sooner or later they all broke under torture and told all they knew. Peter, however, did not. To everyone's amazement, not the least his own, he did not break. The torture went on, but Peter did not weaken. The word got around. His fame spread. The resistance movement was revitalized. And breaking him became especially important for the dictatorship. Yet Peter still did not break. He became a symbol of heroic resistance.

A daring rescue freed him. He was smuggled to a neighboring country. There Peter was looked after by a psychologist who had tried to counsel him years ago when he was a miserable child. She had left the old country a long time ago and established a practice in the new one. Peter arrived there alone, had no money, and knew no one else. The psychologist took him in, gave him a room in her house, fed and looked after him. Peter had much to recover from both physically and psychologically. He slowly opened up to her, and he and she talked. Their relationship evolved into an affectionate friendship. Peter told her bit by bit what he endured in the prison camp. He found that his memories came flooding back, and with great relief he talked and talked to her about his life and childhood miseries. She listened, encouraged him, and eventually asked why he did not confess. All Peter could say was that he would have minded confessing even more than being tortured.

After all this, Peter slowly became a changed person, but he still had no idea why he minded the torture less than confession, nor why he had been so miserable. He eventually mentioned Paul's death to the psychologist, but, he said, it happened many years ago, no one talked about it anymore, and he did not think about it. It seemed to him just another hateful episode in his life. The psychologist nudged him gently, and he began to recall Paul's fall and how terrible he looked when he was pulled from the lake. The bare facts then slowly, over time, became infused with his gradually remembered traumatic emotional reactions to them, and he started to reexperience them vividly. Only then, with the psychologist's help, did he realize that he blamed himself for what happened. He remembered that after the event he was haunted by the thought that he could have held on to Paul's hand, or pulled him up, or broken his fall, or did something else. He came to understand that he had been miserable because he felt guilty for failing to prevent Paul's death.

He then saw his whole past in a new light. The facts have not changed, but his personal attitude to them has. He has understood that the cause of his miseries was guilt and that he was mistaken to feel guilty because there was nothing more he could have done than what he did. And then, in the light of his reevaluated past, it dawned on him that he did not break under torture because he regarded the pain inflicted on him as deserved punishment for letting Paul die. He also realized that his heroic resistance was a misguided reaction to a mistakenly evaluated past. For the first time since Paul's death, Peter had a realistic view of himself.

However, that view enabled him only to recognize that his evaluations of the possibilities he had in the past, and his view of what happened had been mistaken. He had no reason to feel guilty, no reason to be dissatisfied with who he was and what he did. He realized that he should not have been true to the guilty person who he mistakenly supposed himself to be. But to have realized that about his past evaluation of himself did not tell him what he should do with himself in the future. It is a metaphor, but not a farfetched one, to say that he was, in William James's redolent phrase, twice-born who

> must die to an unreal life before he can be born into the real life . . . the psychological basis of the twice-born character seems to be a certain discordancy or heterogeneity in . . . an incompletely unified moral and intellectual constitution.[75]

His second birth was certainly painful, but it freed him from his misinterpreted past and brought his unrealistic evaluations of the possibilities of life closer to the realistic evaluations of them. But that left him with the burden of his newfound liberation. He was faced with having to reexamine his beliefs, emotions, and desires, and with them his personal attitude to the possibilities of life now open to him.

---

75. William James, *The Varieties of Religious Experience*, in *William James: Writings 1902–1910)* (New York: Library of America, 1987), 154, 156.

Being free of his misinterpretation of his past did not free him from all of it. Many of the beliefs, emotion, and desires that motivated him in the past have persisted in a corrected form, and his evaluations of how he thought he should live were, of course, influenced by them. One of these possibilities was to act on his justified hatred of his torturers and of the dictatorship they served. This possibility was reinforced when a representative of the resistance movement contacted him and asked for his help. At the same time, the psychologist offered to pay for and support him in other ways through university education in the new country. So Peter had a choice between two possibilities: rejoining the resistance and beginning to build a better future for himself.

His awful experiences, however, were not utterly wasted. For after much travail they enabled him to evaluate realistically, no longer obstructed by misinterpretations, of the relative importance of these two possibilities. He could and did ask himself what he should do, what kind of person he should want to become, and to which of these two kinds of life he would want to be true in the years to come. He was asking the right questions and was trying to find reasonable answers to them. And there I leave him. Koestler, writing in the midst of World War II, had no patience with uncertainty and has Peter rejoin the resistance, but we, from a safe distance, can be more thoughtful.

THE BURDEN OF THE PAST

In different ways and for different reasons, the burden of their past made the lives of the Colonel and Peter very difficult. They were alike in having to struggle with the adverse circumstances that understandably made them deeply dissatisfied with who they were. This happened to them because the burden they bore of their past prevented them from recognizing possibilities that were in fact available to them. The Colonel's commitment to the military evaluative framework and Peter's guilt had locked them into a personal attitude they had formed in the past. The reasons they thought they had and the beliefs, emotions, and desires that motivated their action were derived from their personal attitudes. It was unthinkable for them to abandon or even to question them because they were essential components of who they were. They recognized no other guide to how they could or should evaluate anything. And the sovereignty of their personal attitudes prevented them from considering, let alone realizing, that they were in fact mistaken.

The Colonel was trained to be a combat leader, to remain cool, think quickly, and assess dangerous situations when his troops depended on him to make the right decisions. It would have been debilitating for him to question the evaluative framework because it would have prevented him from doing what duty, honor, and country required. Peter, for very different reasons, was in the same situation. He was at first just a child and later an adolescent who was a black hole of misery. The guilt he did not even know he felt possessed him and left him no psychological space for considering that his personal attitude may be mistaken. The burden of the past they labored under excluded the possibility of the Colonel of questioning his commitment and Peter questioning the guilt he did not know he felt. And they both suffered the consequences of it.

We fortunate ones, however, are not doomed as they were to bear the burden of our past. Living in a civilized society, we rarely have to face the sort of crises the Colonel and Peter did. We can evaluate our personal attitude to how we think we should live and how the way we actually live seems from the point of view of the moral, political, religious, and other evaluations we derive from the evaluative framework of the context in which we live. Unlike the Colonel and Peter, we have the possibility of both kinds of evaluation. We could do what they in their situation could not. If they had done it and embarked on the evaluation of the possibilities open to them, it would have enabled them to question what motivated them. They were true to who they were, and it led to suicide in one case and misery in another.

Although we could question the evaluations that follow from our personal attitude and evaluative framework, we do not normally do so. Most of us question them only when we are seriously dissatisfied with the gap between who we are and who we think we should be. And then we may suspect that we are dissatisfied because our evaluations are mistaken. We may suspect that our personal attitude is based on false beliefs, misdirected emotions, and unwise desires; and the moral, political, religious, or other evaluations of our evaluative framework are faulty in being too demanding, or irrelevant to changed circumstances, or impoverished, dogmatic, or unrealistic about human motivation. And our dissatisfactions are often exacerbated by the frequent conflicts between our evaluations. "Should we be true to who we are?" is a hard question because the complexities, mistakes, and conflicts involved in our evaluations and the temptations of self-deception, wishful thinking, fantasy, self-aggrandizement, and other ways of hiding from ourselves the facts make it difficult to find a reasonable answer it.

When we are assailed by deeply felt experiences, for instance of evil, despair, failure, grief, guilt, loss of meaning, or shame, we are forced to ask and to try to answer the hard questions this book is about. And we may not know then and there how we should answer them because we are overwhelmed by the immediacy of the experience. But even then we can realize that we have come to a dangerous pass, and we can guard against coming to it again in the future. This is difficult to do. If we do it, it can become an impetus to cultivating the habit of looking at ourselves from the outside and thus becoming able to be more critical than we have been of our possibly mistaken evaluation of these experiences.

Many of us are much too busy living and have no interest in the critical questioning our evaluations by our other evaluations. But our dissatisfactions with how we live are reasons for cultivating such critical evaluation of our evaluations. If all goes well, we can then correct the mistaken ones. But all rarely goes well because our critical evaluations are as liable to be mistaken as the evaluations of which we are critical. Both are based on our possibly mistaken beliefs, emotions, and desires.

The Colonel in Iraq and Peter before being tortured could not distance themselves from their situation by cultivating evaluations of the immediacy of their experiences. Given their situation and the stage they have reached in their lives, I doubt that there was anything they could have done. The Colonel at over forty was committed to being who he was. And Peter, first as a child and later as a teenager, could not see beyond the years of guilt that—unknown to him—permeated his life. There were other possibilities, but the joint influence of their past and present situation prevented them from distancing themselves sufficiently from their own evaluations in order to question them.

We, however, are in a better position. From their predicaments we can learn the importance of cultivating the critical evaluation of our evaluations. The reason why I discussed the Colonel and Peter is to show in concrete terms why such comparative cases are important for us. They enable us to think better about how we think we should live, how to cope with our dissatisfactions, and how to become the kind of person to whom we should want to be true. Although our critical evaluations may also conflict and be mistaken, the burden of our past does not exclude the possibility of reciprocal criticism and correction, and thus the improvement, of our fallible and often mistaken evaluations. We cannot be free of our past, but we can question it and be critical of the evaluations we derive from it.

RESPONDING TO DISSATISFACTIONS

The more dissatisfied we are, the more reasons we have to want to change who we are. But the contrary is also true. If our dissatisfactions are counterbalanced by satisfactions, we may say to ourselves that on the whole we are living as we think we should, and our dissatisfactions are no more than familiar and unavoidable frustrations caused by not having all we think we deserve. This is a reasonable and realistic attitude that avoids both starry-eyed optimism and debilitating pessimism. It is in fact the attitude many of us eventually arrive at in civilized societies when we leave childish things behind.

We know, or should know, that life is not an uninterrupted picnic on a cloudless yet cool sunny summer afternoon spent in the company of our family, friends, undisturbed by mosquitoes, as our children and dogs cavort on the grass we never have to mow. Yet our dissatisfactions may be serious and far outweigh the satisfactions we have. And then we may realize that we are dissatisfied because our evaluations of how we should live have been mistaken. If we have reached this point, we will see that the importance widely attributed to who we are, under the names of autonomy, authenticity, second-order evaluations, self-governance, strong evaluation, and their cognates, may perpetuate rather than correct our mistakes.[76] The fine philosophers listed below who attribute crucial importance to being true to who we are have not recognized that we may be true to the fanatical, greedy, irrational, power-hungry, stupid, or vicious person

---

76. See, for example, Harry G. Frankfurt, *The Importance of What We Care About* (New York: Cambridge University Press, 1988); Christine M. Korsgaard, *Self-Constitution*, (Oxford: Oxford University Press, 2009); J. M. Schneewind, *The Invention of Autonomy*, (New York: Cambridge University Press, 1998), Charles Taylor, *The Ethics of Authenticity* (Cambridge, MA: Harvard University Press, 1992); and Bernard Williams, *Truth and Truthfulness* (Princeton, NJ: Princeton University Press, 2002).

we are, and it would be much better not to be true to who we are if this is who we are.

Standing in the long tradition of Thucydides, Machiavelli, Hobbes, and Nietzsche, among others, Freud recognizes it in a work that many of his followers disown:[77]

> The inclination to aggression is an original, self-subsisting disposition in man, and . . .it constitutes the greatest impediment to civilization. . . . Man's natural aggressive instinct, the hostility of each against all and of all against each, opposes . . . civilization. . . .The evolution of civilization is . . . the struggle between . . . the instinct of life and the instinct of destruction, as it works itself out in the human species. This struggle is what all life essentially consists of.

If we see this struggle in ourselves and we are dissatisfied with who we are, then we have reason to try to change who we are, rather than remain true to it.[78] How can we do that?

The obvious answer is that we can do it by correcting our mistaken evaluations. This is easy to say and hard to do. The evaluations in question are not matters of taste, passing preferences, or responses to situations that are unlikely to recur. They have continuous influence on how we live. They concern our marriage, children, work, how we think about aging, death, God, health, justice, money, morality, politics, and so forth. Such evaluations have formed our lasting attitudes to how we should live. And it is important to consider whether they may be mistaken. It is far easier to attribute our dissatisfactions to

---

77. Sigmund Freud, *Civilization and Its Discontents*, trans. James Strachey (New York: Norton, 1961/1930), 81–82.
78. I have written about this in *The Roots of Evil* (Ithaca, NY: Cornell University Press, 2005) and *How Should We Live?* (Chicago: University of Chicago Press, 2014).

adverse circumstances than to our mistakes. Blaming the world rather than ourselves makes us feel much better than taking a hard look at our own faults.

Suppose, however, that we are honest and critical enough to acknowledge that we are dissatisfied because our evaluations have been or are mistaken. The question is then whether the mistakes follow from our personal attitude or from the evaluative framework. If the former, then the evaluations are mistaken because they are based on our false beliefs, misdirected emotions, or misguided desires. If the latter, then they are mistaken because they follow from mistaken moral, political, religious, and other evaluations we derive from the evaluative framework of our context. And then we can examine and be critical of our personal attitude from the point of view of our evaluative framework, and vice versa. The best case is when our personal attitude and evaluative framework coincide. How we believe, feel, and desire that we should live would be how our moral, personal, political, religious, and other evaluations motivate us to live. We would then be perfectly adjusted to the context in which we live. This, of course, rarely happens, because both kinds of evaluation are often mistaken. We are dissatisfied then and can become less so if we manage to correct the evaluations that we think are mistaken.

Part of the reason why this is difficult is that our personal attitude and evaluative framework overlap. Our beliefs, emotions, and desires have been partly formed by the evaluative framework in our context. And we accept or reject, partially or entirely, the moral, political, religious, and other evaluations of our evaluative framework on which our personal attitude depends by relying on the beliefs, emotions, and desires of our personal attitude. In trying to correct one kind of evaluation by relying on the other kind, we in fact rely on the one we are trying to correct. Are we then simply stuck with our personal attitude and evaluative framework of our context? If so, it would be useless to try to correct one by relying on the other, since both are in need of correction. Is there something else we can then rely on in order to correct our mistaken evaluations?

Yes there is. We can compare our lives and evaluative framework with the lives and evaluative frameworks of others whose contexts are different from our own. The respects in which we compare ours with theirs are the evaluations of the possibilities of life. The basis of these comparisons is not that we and they have entirely different evaluations. It is very unlikely that there might be complex societies that do not have moral, personal, political, and religious evaluations of some kind. The differences have to do with the content of the kinds of evaluation both have, with what is included in and excluded from them, and with the relative importance we and they attribute to what is included. We have to rely for such comparisons mainly on anthropology, history, literature, psychology, and to a lesser extent on our much more limited personal experience of different societies and different ways of life.

These remarks about the possibility of comparisons are much too abstract and general. They can be telling only if they are expressed in concrete and particular terms. We can compare personal attitudes and evaluative frameworks on the basis of how they respond, for instance, to adversity, conflict, crime, death, illness, poverty, and strangers; what they treat as a predominantly moral, personal, political, or religious matter; who is recognized as having legitimate authority, expertise, or power to make reasonable evaluations in various areas of life; how traditional or changing they are; and so on. On the basis of such specific and context-dependent evaluations, we can compare our personal attitude and evaluative framework with theirs. If we think that ours are mistaken, we can ask whether theirs are likely to be less or more mistaken than ours, and that may strengthen or weaken the reasons we have for or against our own evaluations. We are then no more locked into our evaluations than we are into our past. We have the means to question and be critical of them. And that enables us to respond reasonably to our dissatisfactions and decide on that basis of whether we should be true to who we are. The comparative cases in the preceding and following chapters are one of the important ways in which we can arrive at reasonable responses.

This, however, is no more than a possibility we might explore. We are often much too busy living to spend much time examining how we live. Or we are willing to put up with our dissatisfactions. Or we are ambivalent about asking the hard questions to which the exploration of this possibility unavoidably leads. We may prefer letting sleeping dogs lie. And even if we seriously consider embarking on such an inward exploration of our evaluations, we may be daunted by our fallibility and the lack of any universal and context-independent theory, principle, or value on which we could rely to prevent us from making the same sort of mistake in evaluating our evaluations as we have made in forming the evaluations that we now suspect may be mistaken. That seems to me to be the source of our uncertainties, dissatisfactions, and of the hard questions with which we are saddled.

The fact is that our evaluations depend on our beliefs, emotions, and desires, as well as on the prevailing moral, political, religious, and other evaluations. Each may be mistaken. Each varies with persons, contexts, times, and a multitude of conditions. And even if a particular evaluation is the right one once, it will have to be made again differently in response to the forever changing contingencies of life. We all face and have to respond to this predicament whether or not we are aware of it. There is no way out of it, not even if we are as reasonable as we can possibly be. The hope for a way out has motivated enduring religions and metaphysical worldviews; lastingly influential moral, political, and religious evaluative frameworks; as well as many great works of art. But, as I have been trying to show, it is an unfulfillable hope.

THE ANSWER

Whether we should be true to who we are depends on how dissatisfied we are with who we are. Most of us are at least somewhat dissatisfied and try to change who we are by correcting our mistaken evaluations that have led to our dissatisfactions. Our efforts to do this are, in Mill's lastingly influential words, experiments in living.[79]

> As it is useful that while mankind are imperfect there should be different opinions, so it is that there should be different experiments of living; that free scope should be given to varieties of character, short of injury to others; and that the worth of different modes of life should be proved practically, when anyone thinks fit to try them.

He rightly stresses the importance of experiments in living, but he does not say much about the risks involved in conducting our own experiment, nor about the lamentable fact that our own experiment may fail, not just succeed. One of the main causes of dissatisfactions are failed experiments of living. And the prevalence of dissatisfactions indicates the prevalence of failed experiments.

Should we take the risk? Or should we live a conventional life, do as well as we can, put up with our dissatisfactions, enjoy what we can, and keep out of deep waters? There are reasons for and against both alternatives. Thoughtfully or otherwise, we evaluate the relative weight of these reasons, the extent of our dissatisfactions, and our willingness to experiment and risk failure. There is no universal and context-independent guide to how we should make such evaluations. We have to make them as well as we can for ourselves and take the consequences.

79. John Stuart Mill, *On Liberty* (Indianapolis: Hackett, 1859/1978), 54.

As Oakeshott, alluding to Montaigne's view, writes:[80]

The human condition . . . understood as an adventure in personal self-enactment. Here there was no promise of salvation
for the race or prevision that it would soon be gathered into
one fold, no anticipation of a near or distant reassemblage of a
'truth' fragmented at the creation of the world or expectation
that if the human race were to go on researching long enough
it will discover 'the truth', and no prospect of a redemption in
a technological break-through providing a more complete satisfaction of contingent wants; there was only a prompting not to
be dismayed at our own imperfections and a recognition that 'it
is something divine for a man to know how to belong to himself
'and live by that understanding.

80. Michael Oakeshott, *On Human Conduct* (Oxford: Clarendon Press, 1975), 241. The allu-
sion is to the last paragraph of Montaigne's *Essays*.

Chapter 10

Do Good Intentions Justify Bad Actions?

THE QUESTION

During the intermission of Rossini's *Guillaume Tell* in the Met a man was observed scattering white powder in the orchestra pit. Witnesses reported it to security, terrorism was suspected, the performance was canceled, fear spread, the Met was evacuated, and biological warfare experts quickly appeared on the scene. The highly embarrassed man explained that what he scattered were the ashes of his recently deceased friend. They were both ardent opera lovers, and when his friend was dying, he asked to be cremated and his ashes scattered in his beloved opera house. And that is what his faithful friend did. The security staff cleaned up, he profusely apologized, the authorities graciously excused him, and that was the end of the episode.[81]

The opera lover's intention was the clearly good one of honoring his dead friend's wish. But his action was bad because it inconvenienced a lot of opera lovers, caused the Met the loss of much-needed revenue, and it needlessly alarmed security forces. Good intentions can obviously lead to bad actions. No doubt I am

---

81. See *The New York Times*, November 3, 2016.

frivolous in not being able to take this episode very seriously. Still, it suggests that even if good intentions were to justify bad actions, they would not do so by themselves. Whether the actions prompted by good intentions are good or bad depends on the answers to several complex questions: Are the intentions merely believed to be good, or are they really good? How does the context affect the goodness of badness of an action? Are the consequences that follow from the actions good or bad, and how good or bad are they? These questions and the answers to them introduce complexities that make it far from simple to give a reasonable answer to the question of whether good intentions justify bad actions.

Even if this episode verges on the farcical, there are contexts in which the question I am concerned with becomes hard and serious indeed. History and contemporary life abound in supposedly good intentions that lead to unquestionably bad actions that cause grievous harm to innocent victims. Ideological mass murderers typically believe that their intentions are good and their actions benefit humanity. Some psychopaths and crazed malefactors may knowingly nurture bad intentions and act very badly indeed, but such people are fortunately rare.

The perpetrators of most bad actions, however, are neither psychopaths nor crazed. Many of them genuinely believe that their intentions are good and that justifies their bad actions. They may even acknowledge that, although their actions would normally be bad, in the prevailing circumstances they are justified because they aim to defeat enemies of the good. Their normally bad actions are justified by their good intentions to bring about good consequences.

Their beliefs, however, may or may not be true depending on what their intentions actually are, whether they are really good or mistakenly believed to be so, whether those they regard as enemies are really enemies of the good, what the consequences of their actions are, and whether those who are harmed by their actions deserve to be harmed. These complexities must be resolved before the hard question can be reasonably answered. It makes the question even harder that there are different and often conflicting evaluations we rely on to evaluate whether our own or other people's intentions are really good and whether the circumstances, the consequences, and those who are harmed by the actions are as we or others believe them to be.

As I have stressed throughout the book, evaluations may be moral, personal, political, religious, and so on. And intentions and actions may be evaluated as good or bad in terms of one of these evaluations and often quite differently in terms of a conflicting one. One reason why the answer to the hard question: "Do good intentions justify bad actions?" is complex is that it often depends on balancing the reasons for and against conflicting evaluations of the goodness and badness of intentions and actions. I will explore these complexities and conflicts by considering Fyodor Vasilevich Mochulsky and Kurt Gerstein who believed that their good intentions did justify their bad actions, although they acknowledged that in normal circumstances their actions would be bad.

MOCHULSKY

Mochulsky (1918–1999) was a minor officer in the NKVD, as the secret police was called in the Soviet Union.[82] It was in charge of enforcing the priority of political evaluations that took the form of so-called communist ideology. It was supposed to clear the way to making the world safe for the human good. Those who were opposed

---

82. I rely on Fyodor Vasilevich Mochulsky, *Gulag Boss: A Soviet Memoir*, trans. Deborah Kaple (New York: Oxford University Press, 1990/2012); Robert Conquest, *The Great Terror: A Reassessment* (New York: Oxford University Press, 1990); Anne Applebaum, *The Gulag: A History* (New York: Doubleday, 2003).

to the ideology were deemed enemies of the human good, and the role of the NKVD was to expose and crush them.

One of the means by which this was done was the Gulag. It was the name given to 478 forced labor camps. In them an estimated 25 million prisoners who had been sentenced to hard labor lived, suffered, and died. They were forced at gunpoint to work in twelve-hour shifts, much of the year in arctic temperatures, inadequate clothing, and a diet of 300 grams of bread and a bowl of soup. Their quantity could be proportionally increased if they exceeded the already backbreaking daily norm of work set for them. It is estimated that about seven million of them were executed, often for no particular reason, many perished slowly from starvation and the cold, and an untold number died on the long trip to one of the camps. The casualty rate was about 40 percent.

The Gulag existed between 1928 and 1953. The prisoners were a mixed group of intellectuals, artists, and officials all of whom were convicted of questionable loyalty to the Soviet Union, often on the basis of the uncorroborated testimony of malicious informers. There were also a smaller number of hardened criminals who were sentenced for serious offenses. The camps were in Siberia, most of them situated above the Arctic Circle. They were under the jurisdiction of the NKVD.

Mochulsky was one of about a million NKVD officials who ran the camps. He was an engineering student, appointed to the Gulag in 1940 at the age of twenty-two. His job was to supervise the prisoners while they built a railway. He was told that the railway was part of the war effort against the coming German invasion and that it was essential for the defense of the Soviet Union that the 500 miles of the railway, crossing rivers and undulating permafrost terrain, be built at all costs across the uninhabited land stretching across the vast territory between the Urals and the sea. He was a patriot and a committed communist who wholeheartedly accepted what he was told by the party, the newspapers, the radio, his teachers, and the officials he had encountered throughout his life. He knew of no alternative to the ideology that gave absolute priority to political evaluation, even and especially when it conflicted with moral, personal, and religious evaluations. Mochulsky was indoctrinated throughout his life to follow this ideology, and he knew of no other.

He was an intelligent, ambitious young man who rose through the ranks of Gulag officials. He was proud of the good work he was doing and of the recognition he received. He saw the conditions of the prisoners and the way in which the strong and hardened criminals among the prisoners dominated and exploited the much weaker intellectuals and artists. But he knew as well that the work had to be done at all costs. He tried to improve the prisoners' living conditions in small ways and he knew that their death rate was high. Still, the work had to be done, and he saw to it that it was done.

As far as I know, Mochulsky's memoir is a unique document: the only work published by an official of the Gulag. There are many works written by survivors, but the point of view of this book is from the other side. It was written by the author many years after the time he spent in the living hell of the Gulag, reflecting on his experiences there. The author shows how his younger self—intelligent, ambitious, ignorant, inexperienced, and indoctrinated—could for years play an increasingly leading part in the enslavement and mass murder of millions of innocent people whose starvation, suffering, and death he experienced daily. The author understood his younger self, as it were, from the inside. I want to understand it from the outside.

The key to this understanding, I think, is to recognize that he mistakenly but genuinely believed that his intentions were good. They aimed to do what the political authorities he accepted told him he should do in order to defend his country against the German aggressors and against internal enemies who opposed the communist ideology that guided the way to the human good. Mochulsky saw himself as playing a small part in defending his country when its entire way of life that was under attack. It was one in which he flourished, and which encouraged and rewarded him.

Being intelligent, he must have known that what was done in the Gulag to the prisoners would normally have been unquestionably bad. However, he believed that the circumstances were not normal. The war effort, combined with his supposedly good intentions, patriotism, the crimes for which the prisoners were convicted, and the guidance of the Communist Party, justified the treatment of the prisoners. And that is why he willingly and diligently participated in it and was well rewarded for it. He had reasons for doing what he did. But, of course, he also had reasons against it: namely, coming face to face daily with starving, half-frozen prisoners, many of them dying or fallen dead from the backbreaking work that they were forced at gunpoint to do and often summarily shot if failed to fulfill the norm set for them. On balance, however, he acted on the reasons for doing what he did and not for the reasons against it.

He followed the ideology he genuinely believed in and with dedication served. It informed his intentions and actions, and he believed that they were justified and good. But his belief was false, and his intentions and actions were very bad indeed. Yet his indoctrination prevented him from knowing any of that. He knew of no alternative to the ideology and political evaluation that permeated his entire life and whose propaganda he regarded as the truth.

It complicated matters that the propaganda was not entirely false. The Germans were indeed vicious aggressors and the real criminals in the Gulag were indeed internal enemies of the prevailing system. Falsehoods that contain elements of the truth are harder to see through than complete falsehoods. Still, juxtaposed to all the putative justifications and the endlessly repeated propaganda, there was the palpable suffering and deaths he witnessed for years. Ideology and its slogans are abstractions, but witnessing daily the suffering and deaths he was instrumental in inflicting had an immediacy that normally sensitive people could not and should not ignore. Nevertheless, Mochulsky ignored them and avoided questioning what he participated in doing. After the initial shock at the conditions he found, the prisoners' lives, suffering, and death became for him routine. He stopped thinking about it. In his memoir, published after the demise of the Soviet Union, he questions his actions, but that came only many years later.

His bad intentions and actions were certainly not justified. The communist ideology, with which Mochulsky was imbued, instituted and maintained the Gulag, doomed innocent victims to work and die in inhuman conditions, and was as bad as any in history. It had long endured because the ideologues who governed the Soviet Union made the people subject to them subservient by fear of the NKVD and propaganda. They convinced their subjects like Mochulsky that they were acting for the human good and that their awful actions were necessary for defeating its enemies. Their beliefs were grotesquely false, but those whom they duped did not know that. Their humane impulses were extinguished by fear and the relentless propaganda that permeated their lives.

GERSTEIN

Kurt Gerstein (1905–1945) was an officer of the Waffen-SS, the elite of the elite of the security forces that were in the vanguard of enforcing the racist ideology of the Nazis in Germany and the territories they occupied.[83] They functioned just as the NKVD did in the

83. I rely on the biography of Saul Friedlander, *Kurt Gerstein: The Ambiguity of Good*, trans. Charles Fullman (New York: Knopf, 1967/1969). I must say that this is an awful translation that disgraces its publisher.

Soviet Union, only their ideologies differed. The Waffen-SS was in charge, among other things, of the extermination and forced labor camps in which many millions of Jews, gypsies, homosexuals, and prisoners of war were gassed or died as a result of the practice rightly called extermination by labor. Gerstein was a chemist by training, and one of his tasks was to obtain and deliver Zyklon B, the chemical that generated the gas in the gas chambers. After the collapse of the Nazi regime when in French custody, he committed suicide by hanging himself. But there is much more than this to the story of his life, and that is what makes it remarkable.

Throughout his life up to 1943, Gerstein was deeply conflicted. On the one hand, he was a militarist, nationalist, anti-Semite who accepted the Nazi ideology and joined the Nazi Party as early as 1933. On the other hand, he was a devout Lutheran who was inspired by the New Testament. His rigid religiosity made him a self-righteous, narrowly moralistic, meddlesome prude, but he yearned for warm human contacts. He respected the authority of his father who was an even stricter Lutheran than he, but he kept rebelling against it. He always did what he regarded as his duty, but he was haunted by guilt throughout his life. He was nothing if not conscientious, but he was also unpleasant, unhappy, and conflicted.

In 1943 he reached a point in his life after which he was no longer conflicted. He discovered the Nazi murders, largely done by the Waffen-SS. Then his rigidity, sense of duty, and religiosity led him to form the adamantine resolve to do something to stop the murders. That is why he joined the Waffen-SS. He was welcomed because he looked like the blond, tall Aryan ideal and was a long-standing member of the Nazi Party. He thought that by being inside that vicious force that regarded the cruel treatment of supposedly inferior races as a virtue, he could become familiar with the facts and inform the world of the details of what was done. He also thought that he might find a way of saving at least some lives.

He knew that by being part of the Waffen-SS he would unavoidably have to collude in the murders, but he regarded the terrible guilt he would knowingly bring upon himself as a sacrifice that it was his duty to make. He hoped that he could at least save some lives by alerting public opinion both inside and outside Germany to what was being done. He knew the personal risks he himself was taking, but he accepted them as well.

After he learned the facts he took action. He began by informing the Lutheran and Catholic religious leaders and all the foreigners and diplomats his dreaded uniform enabled him to reach of how and where the murders were done and how numerous the victims were. He sabotaged the delivery of Zyklon B whenever he could. He buried the canisters and denied that he received them or claimed that they were defective and could not be used. He did what he could, but as we now know his efforts came to nothing, apart from the great guilt he felt for colluding in the murders. That is why he surrendered after the war to the first authorities he came across, who happened to be French, and why he committed suicide in custody.

Gerstein, then, was driven by good intentions to accept guilt for the bad actions he did in order to prevent the bad actions of others. He knowingly violated the Pauline principle (Romans 3:1) that hitherto had been one of his main guides in life: Do no evil so that good may come of it. The principle that guided him instead was to do evil in order to lessen the evil done by others. Of course, he failed, knew it, and that made his feeling of guilt even more devastating.

Thinking about him, we can reasonably say that once he resolved the conflict between Nazism and Lutheranism in favor of the latter and committed himself to opposing the murders, his intentions were good. His self-righteous rigidity informed his intentions and led him to oppose the crimes of the Nazis. Some of the actions that followed from his good intentions were also good. Nevertheless, others were clearly bad. He was right to feel guilty about his participation in the Waffen-SS, aiding mass murders, even as he ineffectually tried to hinder them because sometimes he actually did deliver Zyklon B and thereby enabled the gassing of many people. Moreover, by having been anti-Semitic, militarist, nationalist, and an early member of the Nazi Party, he did help in a small way the vicious regime to attain power, wield it, start World War II, that caused the deaths of tens of millions of people, and, incidentally, also the devastation of large parts of his beloved Germany and the death of many of its citizens.

Given this complicated story, did his good intentions justify his bad actions? I do not think this question has a simple answer. But it does have a complex one. The source of its complexity is that intentions and actions are often partly good and partly bad, as were Gerstein's. This is because their goodness or badness can be evaluated in terms of different and often conflicting moral, personal, political, religious, and other points of view. The reasons for and against the evaluations that follow from them need to be balanced, and the agents, whose intentions and actions they are may culpably or otherwise not be aware of all these conflicts and reasons. These complexities make the question hard.

Take his intentions first. Certainly, his intention was to save innocent lives. But it was also to act as a Lutheran should, and as a German patriot, and as one his father would be proud of, and as morality demanded, and as a man who could look at himself without regret for what he did, and as someone driven by conscience, and so on. Such complex, often undistinguished elements were jumbled together, partly overlapped and partly diverged, in many of his intentions even when their contexts were not as dramatic, or tragic, as they became for Gerstein. Novelists such as Trollope, Proust, and James show their readers such complexities again and again. It is the stock in trade of psychoanalysts. Elizabeth Anscombe's *Intention* is a classic philosophical treatment of it. And it is tediously familiar to patiently enduring parents of rebellious teenagers.[84]

The same is true of actions. Most actions most of the time can be described in many different ways. Are we to say that Gerstein's actions were Christian, patriotic, moral, self-exculpating, self-sacrificing, compassionate, courageous, useless, futile, or impractical? And how could anyone sort out the precise importance each of these elements played in the most reasonable description of the variety of his actions. Should it be stressed that he informed the church leaders of what was going on, spoke to foreign diplomats, lied to his superior officers, negotiated with the manufacturer of Zyklon B, thought about what he was doing during his many sleepless nights, used the uniform of the feared Waffen-SS to gain access to usually inaccessible diplomats and church leaders? and so on.

The point of stressing the multiplicity of elements that jointly form intentions and actions is to make clear that there are reasons for and against the conflicting evaluations of these elements. How are we to weigh the reasons on which the evaluations of intentions and actions are based? From which of the evaluations involved do these reasons follow? The difficulty of finding the optimum balance of reasons for and against these often-conflicting reasons and evaluations explains why giving a reasonable answer to the hard question "Do good intentions justify bad actions?" is a complex matter.

COMPARISON

Bringing out the complexities involved in the evaluation of Mochulsky's and Gerstein's intentions and actions is only a first

---

84. G. E. M. Anscombe, *Intention* (Oxford: Blackwell, 1957).

step toward actually evaluating them. The next step is to compare and contrast the intentions and actions involved in their very different responses to the awful circumstances in which they had found themselves.

Thinking about complexities, we should bear in mind several crucial considerations. One is that intentions can be based on propaganda, indoctrination, self-deception, and ignorance or misinterpretation of relevant facts. This is what happened to Mochulsky's intentions and actions in the Gulag and to Gerstein's before he knew about the murders. Another is that intentions mistakenly believed to be good may lead to bad actions, as did Mochulsky's, and good actions may follow from intentions that were believed to be bad from the Nazi point of view, as in Gerstein's case. And yet a further consideration is that the goodness or badness of intentions actions may be evaluated from often conflicting moral, personal, political, religious, and other points of view. This Mochulsky could not do, but Gerstein could.

These considerations seem to me to vitiate both of the most widely accepted principles that guide many contemporary moral and political evaluations. The first is Kant's principle that

It is impossible to think of anything at all in the world . . . that could be considered good without limitation except *good will* (49). . . . A good will is not good because of what it effects or accomplishes, because of its fitness to attain some proposed good, but only because of its volition, that is, it is good in itself, and regarded for itself, it is to be valued incomparably higher than all that could merely be brought about by it (50).[85]

85. Immanuel Kant, *Groundwork of the Metaphysics of Moral*, trans. Mary J. Gregor, in *Immanuel Kant: Practical Philosophy* (Cambridge, UK: Cambridge University Press, 1785/1966).

It follows from it that since Mochulsky's and Gerstein's intentions were motivated by good will, they were good regardless of what actions followed from them. No reasonable person can believe that. The other principle is Mill's according to whom

> the Greatest Happiness Principle [states] the ultimate end, with reference to and for the sake of which all other things are desirable (214) ... [which] holds that actions are right in proportion as they tend to promote happiness, wrong as they tend to produce the reverse of happiness (210).[86]

And that, of course, is just what both the communist and the Nazi ideologues aimed at by murdering the enemies of what they took to be the greatest happiness.

What has gone wrong with both of these principles is that they do not take into account that beliefs—both about the goodness of an act of will and about what promotes the greatest happiness—are often misled by ideological or personal falsifications. Nor do they recognize that there is a plurality of conflicting and often false and conflicting moral, personal, political, and religious evaluations of what makes the will good and what the greatest happiness requires in different contexts. The principles are empty formulas that offer vacuous advice to be guided by the human good. If the beliefs about it were not often false or conflicting, then we would already know what the human good is and would not need a principle to tell us to aim at it. But since beliefs about the human good are often false and conflicts about it are frequent, the principles cannot help us, nor could they have helped Mochulsky or Gerstein.

---

86. John Stuart Mill, *Utilitarianism* in *Collected Works of John Stuart Mill*, ed. J. M. Robson (Indianapolis: Liberty Press, 1861/2006).

They lived in a society dominated by an ideal of the human good. It was dictated by a vicious political ideology that suppressed conflicting moral, personal, political, religious, and other evaluations. Mochulsky and Gerstein were both exposed to pervasive propaganda, reinforced by the sinister, lawless, secret police, telling them that they have to choose between those who were said to aim at the human good and those who were enemies of it. They were told again and again that the prevailing regime aimed to bring the world ever closer to the human good. That was the supposed justification of the grievous harm the ideologues inflicted on those who were deemed enemies of the ideology and the human good. In this respect, Mochulsky and Gerstein were in much the same situation. But in another respect, there was a crucial difference between them, and that makes a difference to how we evaluate their intentions and actions, and to how we answer the hard question as it pertains to them. Did their good intentions justify their bad actions?

EVALUATION

Mochulsky knew of no alternative to the ideology that dominated life in the Soviet Union. He was born, raised, and educated in it. He saw life in terms of it, and the propaganda daily reinforced his way of seeing. Gerstein knew of an alternative to Nazism. He was in his mid-thirties when the Nazis took power. Until then he was guided by the strict Lutheranism of his family and upbringing, and he unthinkingly shared the prevalent anti-Semitism, militarism, and patriotism that made so many in Germany receptive to the Nazi ideology. But Gerstein was conflicted throughout his life. He was never wholehearted in accepting any authority. This doomed him to feel guilty throughout his life for falling short of what the authority he then accepted regarded as the human good. But his half-hearted early allegiance to both a religion and an ideology enabled him later to realize that they aimed at conflicting ideals of the human good. He tried to combine them, and for a while he thought he had succeeded. But then came his knowledge of the murders, and he realized that his religion and ideology were incompatible and that he had to choose between them. He then made a choice in favor of religion.

Mochulsky was not conflicted. Although he was intelligent, he knew of only one ideal of the human good, he had no reason to question it, and he lacked the will and evaluative resources to resist it. Gerstein's conflicting allegiances made resistance possible. Mochulsky did not see the viciousness of the ideology for what it was, not even when he came face to face with the daily suffering and murder of countless people. He knew the ideological justification that was offered of it. Yet these justifications were abstract, while his experiences of the suffering and death of countless people were immediate.

Being normally intelligent, he had to know that the horrors he witnessed were contrary to minimum requirements of the human good. He had to know that no ideology genuinely committed to human good could reasonably be in favor of doing what he participated in doing for years. The ideological rhetoric and propaganda claiming that what was done was justified because it aimed at the human good was only verbiage that disguised the real aim of the ideology, which was to kill those who opposed it and force the rest by persuasion, threat, or force to do what they were told.

Mochulsky was not a monster, psychopath, or crazed. At first he had normal humane reactions to the horrors he had witnessed. But he allowed himself to be blinded by the ideology to the significance of the facts he experienced, and he became callous. He should have known that no defensible ideal of the human good could be compatible with the prolonged cruelty that preceded mass murder in the Gulag. And even if he had accepted the ideological justification of all this, he need not have been as diligent and efficient an officer as to merit the approval and promotion after promotion in the NKVD, that purveyor of terror.

In marked contrast with Mochulsky, Gerstein knew the significance of what was done in his context. His religion enabled him to see that the victims of the ideology were not enemies of the human good but innocent people persecuted by racist ideologues. Both had normal humane impulses, but Mochulsky's were silenced by ideology, while Gerstein's were not. When they came face to face with cruelty and mass murders, Gerstein's intentions and actions led him to resist it, and he rightly believed that his intentions were good. Mochulsky's were bad, although he believed otherwise.

Gerstein tried to save lives because he gave priority to his religious beliefs when it conflicted with the Nazi ideology he was also committed to until he encountered the cruelty and murders to which the ideology led. Mochulsky did not. He participated in the cruelty and murders even though they undeniably violated minimum requirements of the human good to which the ideology claimed to be aiming. Gerstein's familiarity with an alternative ideal of the human good enabled him to see that the Nazi ideology led to the horrors he witnessed. And then, in difficult circumstances, he did what he could to resist it. Mochulsky, knowing of no alternative ideals, refused to see what was happening in the Gulag for what it was: mass murder preceded by great suffering in inhuman conditions. The Soviet Gulag and the Nazi concentration camps were among the most shameful events in human history. In the midst of these terrible circumstances, Gerstein proved to be a better, if flawed, human being than Mochulsky.

But what about their intentions and actions? Mochulsky's intentions and actions followed from his belief that the prisoners were enemies of the human good. The belief, however, was false. It is doubtful that he could have known it because indoctrination, propaganda, and the authorities whom he trusted prevented it. He had access only to information the authorities deemed acceptable. If by accident he encountered anything contrary to the received viewed, he was taught to regard it as misinformation spread by enemies of the human good. If his belief had been true, it would have explained his intentions and actions, but it would still not have justified them.

The explanation of the causes intentions and actions is one thing; their evaluation is quite another. And if we grant the patent absurdity that the mass murder of falsely believed enemies of the good had been justified, the great cruelty of prolonged starvation, brutality, and inhuman conditions that were inflicted on them prior to their murder could not possible be instrumental to the human good. They would have to be condemned by all reasonable people who knew the facts. Although Mochulsky's intentions and actions were based on a false belief, he could and should have known that it was false, and that is why his intentions and actions were bad, regardless of what he believed about them.

There comes a point at which evaluations, intentions, and actions are inseparable from and depend on the facts. That point is at which the minimum requirements of the human good are either met or violated. These requirements are not controversial. They are the satisfaction of physiological, psychological, and social needs that are so basic that human beings cannot function unless they are met. If at that point, the violations are not isolated episodes in extraordinary circumstances but form a pattern and affect many people, then no moral, personal, political, religious, or any other kind of evaluation can reasonably regard their violations as anything but bad.

This, of course, is not to say that the minimum requirements cannot be violated. They can be and often are violated, as we know from the lamentable facts of life. But their violations cannot be justified by any principle, theory, ideology, or evaluation. All reasonable ideals of the human good must begin with and do justice to these minimum requirements. Controversies, conflicts, and reasons for and against evaluations are, of course, many but, if reasonable, they must all acknowledge the minimum requirements of the human good. The Nazi and communist ideologies, among others, did not, and that is why they cannot be reasonably accepted.

Mochulsky and Gerstein came face to face with the point at which they encountered the lasting pattern of violation of these minimum requirements. Mochulsky violated them, Gerstein did what he could to oppose their violation. What people do at that point is the ultimate test of whether their good intentions can justify their bad actions.

Gerstein's intentions and action, after he found out what was going on, followed from his belief that murder was wrong. That was the most basic evaluation that guided him. His intentions and action were informed by that belief. And unlike the belief that guided Mochulsky, Gerstein's belief was true. The intentions and actions that followed from it were good. However, those intentions were not the only ones he had. He was an early supporter of the ideology from which the mass murders followed, and his anti-Semitic, militarist, and nationalist beliefs also motivated his intentions and actions and led him to support the ideology that later led to the mass murders that he rightly came to resist. It seems reasonable, then, to say that his intentions and actions were mixed, some good, some bad. The good ones were justified, the bad ones were not.

How, then, are we to answer the hard question as it arises about Mochulsky and Gerstein? Did their good intentions justify their bad actions? Mochulsky believed that his bad intentions were good because they aimed at the human good. The belief was false and his intentions and actions that were based on them were bad and unjustified. Yet the belief from which they followed was dictated by the ideological justification that what was done aimed at the human good. He could and should have known that his belief was false because the violation of minimum requirements of the human good he witnessed for years contradicted the belief that the ideology aimed at the human good. His supposedly good intentions and actions were in fact bad, and they were certainly not justified.

The reasonable overall evaluation of Gerstein seems to be that the balance of blame and justification strongly, but not entirely, tilts in favor of justification. When it mattered a great deal, he finally did the right thing. Whereas Mochulsky persevered in holding false beliefs to form what he mistakenly took to be good intentions followed, and they led to his bad actions. He should be blamed for that.

This overall evaluation of Mochulsky and Gerstein, however, needs to be qualified. In proposing it, I have proceeded from the victims' point of view. I had uppermost in mind the great undeserved harm the victims had suffered through the ideologies of their society. That seems to me by far the most important evaluative consideration. There is, however, also another point of view that proceeds from the point of view of the agents, such as Mochulsky and Gerstein. Each had the misfortune of living in a society that was dominated by a vicious ideology and their intentions and actions were inescapably influenced by it. They should be blamed for their bad intentions, but they should not be blamed as harshly as the ideologues. The ideologues knew the truth about what they were doing, nevertheless did it, while systematically lying about it through the elaborate propaganda and terror apparatus they have constructed. It is very difficult to resist long-term exposure to relentless propaganda and the threat of terror. Mochulsky could not, Gerstein eventually could resist it.

Neither was a good person, but Gerstein was not as bad as Mochulsky, yet neither was evil. Those were evil who created and maintained the propaganda and terror apparatus that imposed their noxious ideology on tens of millions of people.

THE HUMAN GOOD?

Appeal to the human good is intended to resolve conflicts between the evaluations of intentions and actions. If one evaluation always took priority over any that conflicted with it, then the conflicts could be resolved by giving priority to whatever evaluation is more likely to lead to the human good.

It is a matter of historical record that some particular moral, personal, political, and religious evaluations have been supposed, at one time or another, to take priority over all conflicting evaluations. Kantian, consequentialist, and natural law moralists think that the moral evaluation based on the categorical imperative, the common good, or the providential order should override all other evaluations that may conflict with them. Libertarians, egoists, and individualists think that personal evaluations should take precedence over all conflicting evaluations. Liberal, conservative, socialist, Nazi, and communist ideologues think that the political evaluations should have priority. And orthodox Jewish, Muslim, Catholic, Lutheran, Calvinist, and Hindu thinkers give priority to the religious evaluations.

Conflicts between evaluations, therefore, could be reasonably as opposed to arbitrarily resolved provided the reasons for giving priority to one evaluation overwhelmingly favor one of the conflicting evaluations. And, of course, defenders of each evaluation claim that the one they favor should take priority over the others. The question, therefore, remains to be unanswered: how could conflicts between evaluations be reasonably resolved? Only by answering it could intentions and actions be evaluated in a way that would be acceptable to reasonable people who know the facts and the alternatives and understand why a particular evaluation should have priority over others that conflict with it.

The usual strategy of defenders of the priority of an evaluation is to claim that the one they favor is presupposed by all the conflicting ones because it is a more basic requirement of the human good, which is the ultimate aim of all the various evaluations. They might say that the human good obviously depends on generally accepted moral evaluations of how people living together should treat one another; or on some personal evaluation of how we should live; or on a political evaluation of the conditions that enable us to coexist and cooperate in peace; or on some religious evaluation that can console us for misfortune, give us hope for the future, and make life meaningful. Plausible as these claims may seem, they cannot deliver what they promise.

Let us assume, if only for the moment, that each of these evaluations captures a basic requirement of the human good. That would not help to resolve conflicts between them because the others are also basic requirements of it. The conflicts between these evaluations could be resolved only if one of them were shown to be so basic that the others presuppose it. That requirement *should* have priority over the others. I stress the *should* because the crucial question is: Why should a particular moral, personal, political, religious, or any other evaluation of the human good always have priority over all conflicting evaluation in aiming at the human good? If we consider the reasons for and against all the conflicting evaluations, then the balance of reason will favor one of them, and that is the one that should have priority over the others. This *should* follows from our deliberation about the best way of going about approximating the human good.

Sensible as this appeal to reason is, it does not explain why one evaluation should always have priority over the conflicting ones. This is because even if the balance of reasons in a particular context favors the priority of one of the evaluations, it would not follow that whatever that evaluation is should have priority over the others in other contexts and in resolving other conflicts. It is no doubt true that in some circumstances a particular moral, personal, political, or religious evaluation is obviously more important than any of the others. But in other contexts, another evaluation will be more important. A moral evaluation should have priority if it involves, say, putting an end to the mass murder of innocent victims. A personal evaluation should have priority if the very meaning of one's life depends on it. If a society faces anarchy, chaos, or enemies that threaten its survival, then political evaluations should have priority. And if a society is debilitated by adversity, disenchantment, and a sense of the pointlessness of human endeavors, then perhaps the religious evaluation should have priority over conflicting evaluations.

However, even if this were true in a particular context at a particular time, it would not follow that it should also have priority in other contexts. Circumstances, places, and times change, conflicts between evaluations will recur, and the reasons for and against the goodness or badness of intentions and actions will have to be evaluated again and again as contexts change. The answer to the general question: Which evaluation should have priority over the others? and the particular one: What makes intentions and actions good or bad? are both unavoidably context-dependent and particular. And the evaluation that has priority in a particular context may not have priority in different contexts.

Is there, then, something on which we could reasonably rely to resolve conflicts between the evaluations in general, and of the goodness or badness of intentions and actions in particular? It might be supposed that there is, namely making life better by approximating whatever the human good may be. It will be accepted by reasonable people that there are deep and serious conflicts between evaluations of what the human good is. Nevertheless, it may be said that whatever it is, that is the evaluation that should have priority, and we should rely on it to resolve conflicts between evaluations of what intentions and actions are good or bad. And then we could reasonably answer the hard question: Do good intentions justify bad actions?

The problem with this supposition is that views about what the human good is and how it should be pursued are as controversial as the relative priority of evaluations. The awful history of morally, personally, politically, and religiously motivated wars and massacres followed from the clash between conflicting views of the human good. And those who waged them supposed that their intentions and actions were good because they aimed at what they thought was the human good. Normally bad actions would then be justified because the defense of the human good depended on them. The defeat of enemies is one crucial step toward achieving that. And so the familiar horrors followed whose perpetrators believed that their intentions were good and, although their actions would normally be bad, in their circumstances they were justified means to removing obstacles from the way of the human good.

There can be no reasonable doubt that the human good requires the satisfaction of basic physiological, psychological, and social needs for nutrition and rest, for human contacts and being able to make some choices, for living in secure, orderly society, and so on. But that is only a minimum requirement of the human good. All reasonable views about what it is must go far beyond the minimum. And then great differences emerge between societies and historical periods about which of the moral, personal, political, religious, and other evaluations should have priority over the conflicting ones in the pursuit of the human good.

These differences cannot be glossed over by appealing to an abstract view of the human good, such as to be motivated by good will, or aiming at the greatest happiness, or following God's law. Unless it is specified what the good will comes to in case of a particular conflict between two evaluations, which of two conflicting evaluations is more likely to lead to the greatest happiness, and how is God's law to be applied when we face a particular situation in a particular context, we would not how to resolve their conflicts. Any reasonable appeal to the human good must specify what it is supposed to be beyond the minimum requirements. As soon as that is done, however, all the conflicts between evaluations reemerge. The appeal to the human good is no more than an empty slogan unless it specifies what the human good involves in particular cases.

THE ANSWER

Good intentions can justify bad actions, provided the following conditions are met. First, the intentions are really good and the actions really bad, not mistakenly believed to be good and bad. Second, the intentions and actions are based on true beliefs about the relevant facts in the context. Third, the actions are bad, but not evil, because they do not involve a pattern of violation of the minimum requirements of the human good that affect many people. Fourth, the priority given to the evaluation of the goodness of intentions and the badness of the actions is justified by showing that the balance of reasons favors it.

These conditions are not easily met. It is very difficult to evaluate whether they have in fact been met. It often involves virtually unavoidable complexities, conflicts, the fallibility of the evaluators, uncertainties about what alternatives are actually available, and the permanent possibility of deliberate or inadvertent falsifications on which the proposed justifications rest.

I have endeavored to show in concrete terms throughout this chapter what some of these difficulties are. The fact remains, however, that most answers to the question of whether particular good intentions can justify particular bad actions are not as simple as the unserious case of the opera lover at one extreme and the deadly serious one of Mochulsky at the other extreme. In most cases, as in Gerstein's, intentions are mixed; some relevant beliefs are true, others are false; what bad actions are and are not parts of a pattern is contestable; and the reasonable resolution of conflicts between evaluations depends on the balance of reasons that can often be reasonably interpreted as tilting both ways. That is just why the question is hard. These complexities seem to me unavoidable in most cases in which intentions and actions are not indisputably good or bad. Accepting that will yield the benefit of avoiding simple answers that rely on good will, or the greatest good, or God's law, as if that could avoid the complexities and context-dependence of reasonable answers. Hard questions do have reasonable answers, but it is difficult to find them.

There is, however, one way of avoiding these complexities that seems to me simply mistaken: the appeal to the human good. For above the level of the violation of its minimum requirements, there is a great plurality of ideals of the human good, and even the same ideal changes and takes different concrete forms in different contexts. The search for *the* ideal of the human good has led to intolerant and dogmatic moral, personal, political, and religious evaluations, to the persecution of critics, and to rigidity that made it impossible to change them in response to changing circumstances.

I have tried to show in this chapter how political ideology is one way in which the appeal to the human good can lead to disastrous consequences. I used the examples of the communist and Nazi ideologies, but unfortunately there are many others. Ideologies can also be theocratic, nationalist, xenophobic, tribal, ethnic, and so on. I am not claiming that all ideologies are as bad as these two were. But all of them aim at an ideal of the human good by political means. They resolve conflicts by appealing to it, and construct and maintain the political order of the society they rule as the means to its pursuit. I repeat: I do not think that all ideologies are guilty of cruelly and murderously pursuing whatever happens to be their ideal of the human good. They may not have to do that if persuasion and indoctrination suffice.

However, all ideologues face a dilemma they cannot avoid. Either they do all that needs to be done to pursue their ideal of the human good, or they violate their commitment to it. If they really think that their ideal should have priority to all evaluations that conflict with it, then they cannot consistently allow such fainthearted considerations as toleration, compromise, or humane impulses that stand in the way of the pursuit of the ideal. They may temporize for tactical reasons but only because it is instrumental to the pursuit of the ideal of the good. If they are consistent, they must evaluate everything that interferes with its pursuit as contrary to the human good. And then they must do whatever needs to be done to overcome the interference: persuasion if it works, threat of force if need be, and its actual force if necessary. If, however, they allow interference, then they cannot consistently hold that their ideal of the human good overrides all that conflicts with it. The ideologue who had seen this with great clarity was Lenin.

The dilemma ideologues face, then, is that if they are consistent, then they must not allow moral, personal, religious, or contrary political evaluations to set limits to their pursuit of the ideal. If they are not consistent, then they violate their commitment to the pursuit of the human good. And so it comes about that if ideologues resort to the use of force, as communists and Nazis did, then they inflict grievous harm on those whom they regard as enemies of the human good, while claiming that their intentions are good and their bad actions are justified.

The way out of this dilemma is to abandon the hankering after *the* ideal of the human good, recognize that there is a plurality of reasonable ideals of the human good, give up the dangerous commitment to ideologies, and aim at a society in which the plurality of reasonable ideals of the human good can flourish.

Chapter 11

Are Moral Values the Highest
of All Values?

THE QUESTION

The distinction between morality and the evaluative framework is crucial for understanding the hard question this chapter is about. The evaluative framework includes all evaluation. Some of them are moral, personal, political, religious, but there are also others. In different contexts and at different times, the various evaluations that jointly comprise the evaluative framework overlap in some ways and diverge in others.

Moral evaluations are one of the evaluations within the evaluative framework. The hard question is: Should moral evaluations always override conflicting non-moral evaluations? There can be no reasonable doubt that in some contexts a moral evaluation should be overriding. But in other contexts, it is not at all obvious. It is certainly true that generally we should be kind, pay our debts, keep our promises, do the work we are paid to do, and do not lie, cheat, or betray confidences. But if these obvious moral evaluations prevent us from coping with economic collapse that threatens starvation, or with medical emergencies, or with saving our children from predators, or with protecting the political system that defends us from domestic crimes and foreign aggression, or with following the dictates of religious faith that makes life meaningful, gives hope, and the strength to face adversities, then which should override which becomes a complex question. Why should moral evaluations *always* override *all* the various personal, political, or religious evaluations if they come into conflict?

The answers to such questions are complex. The answer cannot be simply that the overriding evaluation should be one that is more important from the point of view of the human good. It needs to be explained why the overriding requirement of the human good must always be moral. Why should conflicts between the various requirements of the human good in different contexts *always* be resolved in favor of any one of the conflicting evaluations? If we recognize the need for such explanations, we are led back to the hard question: Should moral evaluations always override conflicting non-moral evaluations? It is arbitrary simply to assume this. It needs a reasonable answer.

If the reasonable answer is "yes," then moral evaluations are indeed be the most important among different kinds of evaluations. If the reasonable answer is "no," then moral evaluations are only one of the plurality of evaluations, and they might or might not override conflicting non-moral evaluations. The question is not whether moral evaluations should *sometimes* override conflicting non-moral evaluations, but whether they should *always* do so.

YES OR NO?

Two exceptionally influential approaches to answering "yes" have been proposed by Kant and Mill. They and the reasons for and against them have been extensively argued both by others and myself. I will not repeat these arguments here. In chapter 2 I gave some reasons against accepting their answers, here I give some more.[87]

> Kant wrote that his aim is (the italics are in the original) the search for and establishment of the *supreme principle of morality* (47)

which he called the categorical imperative, and claimed that

> it must hold ... for all *rational beings as such,* not merely under contingent conditions and with exceptions but with *absolute necessity* (62)

and the categorical imperative is:

> act only in accordance with that maxim through which you can at the same time will that it becomes a universal law (73)

There are, it seems to me, several reasons for rejecting this supposedly supreme principle of morality. To begin with, there is nothing in the principle that makes it specifically moral, rather than personal, political, or religious. Kant proposes the principle and simply assumes that it is moral. Why must it be moral? Defenders of each of the nonmoral evaluations can, and often have, claimed that all rational beings should to follow their evaluations and override other evaluations if they conflict with the ones they favor.

Another reason for rejecting the Kantian supreme principle is that many of the protagonists whose predicaments I have described in the preceding chapters can be characterized as having followed the categorical imperative of acting in a way which they could will

---

87. Immanuel Kant, *Groundwork of the Metaphysics of Morals* in *Practical Philosophy,* trans. Mary. J. Gregor (Cambridge, UK: Cambridge University Press, 1785/1999).

that it should become a universal law. Yet they knew and accepted the consequences that followed from it, even though no reasonable person could accept that the way they have acted should become a universal law.

Eleazar thought that the supreme principle was to follow God's law, and he chose to be tortured to death rather than violate what he took it to be. The Kamikaze believed that the supreme principle was to do their duty to their country, and they flew to their pointless death to honor it in a war they opposed. Creon thought that it was his duty to uphold human justice, and he devastated his family and city whose protection was his responsibility. Antigone believed that it was the unwritten law of natural justice, and she accepted doom rather than violate it. The Queen thought that the universal law was to be an honorable occupier of her station in life, and it led her to arrange the murder of her husband who failed to honor it. Vere regarded it as embodied in naval law, and he knowingly killed a morally innocent good man for violating it. For Mochulsky, the supreme principle was to follow communist ideology, and it led him to participate in the mass murder of falsely accused people. For Gerstein it was the kind of Lutheranism that doomed the faithful to lifelong guilt and the faithless to eternal perdition.

All these people could have said that they are following the Kantian supreme principle embodied in what they were convinced should be the universal law, namely

act only in accordance with that maxim through which you can at the same time will that it becomes a universal law (73)

The Kantian supreme principle should be rejected because there are conflicting moral and non-moral evaluations of what the universal law would require everyone to do, and because following it often leads to disastrous consequences that no reasonable person could accept.

Mill also thought that there is a supreme principle. He wrote that

there must be some standard by which to determine the goodness or badness, absolute and comparative, of ends, or objects of
desire. And whatever that standard is, there can be but one: for
if there were several ultimate principles of conduct, the same
conduct might be approved by one of those principles and
condemned by another; and there would be needed some more
general principle, as umpire between them.[88]

Mill was certainly right in supposing that principles may conflict and
some way of resolving their conflicts is needed. But why should we
suppose, as Mill does, that we need yet another principle for that?
Why could we not resolve conflicts between principles on the basis of
evaluating their relative importance in the circumstances of the context in which the conflicts occur or whether their consequences were
acceptable or whether they took account of all the relevant facts or
whether and why they conform to or deviate from accepted practices
in the context or whether the balance of reasons favors one or the
other of the conflicting principles? Such evaluations are by their nature particular and context dependent, and there cannot be a principle that is at once supreme and applicable to all conflicts regardless
of the differences in contexts, circumstances, and the relevant facts.

Mill, however, did what Kant did not, and made clear what he
supposed was the content of the supreme principle:

I regard utility as the ultimate appeal on all ethical questions; but
it must be utility in the largest sense, grounded on the permanent interests of man as progressive being.[89]

88. John Stuart Mill, *A System of Logic* in *The Collected Works of John Stuart Mill*, ed. J.M.
   Robson, vol. 8 (Indianapolis: Liberty Fund, 1843/2006), 951.
89. John Stuart Mill, *On Liberty* (Indianapolis: Hackett, 1859/1978), 10.

He meant by utility the pursuit of the greatest happiness. However, further on in the same work he defended the conflicting claim that

> there is no reasons that all human existence should be constructed on some one or small number of patterns. If a person possesses any tolerable amount of common sense and experience, his own mode of laying out his existence is the best, not because it is the best in itself, but because it is his own mode (64).

A tolerable amount of common sense and experience may lead people to reject what Mill supposes is the supreme moral principle on the ground that there is no reason why all human existence should be constructed on that pattern. If we follow our own mode of existence, then we may well think that the pursuit of justice, truth, or understanding, or the protection of our country, family, or liberty is more important than the greatest happiness.

As Nietzsche[90] wickedly put it:

> Man does *not* strive for happiness, only the Englishman does.

Nietzsche did not challenge merely Mill's supreme principle. He challenged the very search for any supreme moral principle:[91]

> In all 'science of morals' so far one thing was *lacking*, strange as it may sound: the problem of morality itself; what was lacking was any suspicion that there was something problematic here. What the philosophers called 'a rational foundation for morality'

90. Friedrich Nietzsche, *Twilight of the Idols* in *The Portable Nietzsche*, trans. Walter Kaufmann (New York: Viking Press, 1954), 12.
91. Friedrich Nietzsche, *Beyond Good and Evil* in *Basic Writings of Nietzsche*, trans. Walter Kaufmann (New York: Modern Library, 1885/1966), 38.

and tried to supply it was, seen in the right light, merely a scholarly variation of the common *faith* in the prevalent morality; a new means of *expression* for this faith; and thus just another fact within a particular morality; indeed, in the last analysis a kind of denial that this morality might ever be considered problematic.

We may disagree with Nietzsche about many things, I certainly do, but his criticism of the search for a supreme moral principle deserves a response.

These doubts about a moral principle make it natural to ask: Why search for it at all? Why suppose that conflicts between evaluations are bad rather than instrumental to the critical examination of the evaluations that guide how we should live? Why not recognize that conflicts between evaluations can be reasonably resolved without relying on any principle, by considering the reasons for and against them, by taking into account the context, the nature of the conflicting evaluations, and the foreseeable consequences that are likely to follow from them?

THE MINIMUM REQUIREMENTS

Even if we dispense with a supreme principle, there is another reason often given for claiming that at least some moral evaluations should be always overriding. This "should" follows from the need to set limits to all evaluations. Acting on a moral, personal, political, or religious evaluation does not make it reasonable to do just anything. To think otherwise leads to the great evils done throughout history in the name of some ideological, nationalist, or religious ideal of the human good. The claim then is that the limits are set by the minimum requirements of the human good and that these limits are moral. Moral evaluations are overriding, provided they concern these minimum requirements.

To meet them is morally good. To violate them is morally bad. (These minimum requirements are often called human rights, but I avoid the label because it raises more questions than it answers.)

There are, of course, great many different ideals of the human good, but if they are reasonable, they will recognize that there are minimum physical, physiological, and social requirements that all reasonable ideals of the human good should meet. The failure to meet them leads to life-threatening harm and eventually to death. It is well-known to torturers that prolonged starvation, extreme pain, sleeplessness, constant deafening noise, humiliation, and terror sooner or later break everybody. This is not a sign of weakness but a fact about all members of our species.

The question is why we should think of these minimum requirements as moral. Meeting them is certainly good and violating them is no doubt bad, but why would that be morally good or bad? It is useless to say that it is good or bad from the point of view of the human good, because the human good is not just moral but also personal, political, and religious. There is no more reason to identify the human good and bad with the morally good and bad than to identify it with what is good or bad from a personal, political, or religious point of view, or from a cultural, economic, educational, medical, scientific point of view. The minimum requirements of the human good must surely include some personal view of how we should live, a secure political system that provides protection from domestic and foreign aggression, and a sense, often religious, from which meaning, hope, and consolation may be derived.

There is no doubt that meeting these minimum requirements is good. However, even if we agree about calling such evaluations moral, it does not follow that they should *always* be overriding, nor that *only* moral evaluations are overriding. Personal, political, religious, and evaluations may also be concerned with the minimum requirements of the human good. And from these non-moral evaluations different and often conflicting actions follow about how the agreed upon minimum requirements of the human good should or should not be aimed at. All of them have the same aim, but they are often pursued in conflicting ways.

Furthermore, the claim that moral evaluations should always be overriding cannot be reasonably restricted to meeting the minimum requirements of the human good. As soon as soon as the minimum requirements are met, we need to go beyond them for communication, education, enjoyment, family, friendship, human contacts, justice, meaning, understanding, work, and so forth. And then we will encounter the familiar conflicts between happiness and duty, private life and social responsibility, integrity and prudence, law and liberty, self-knowledge and spontaneity, comfort and discipline, faith and doubt, and so on and on. These conflicts cannot be resolved by stressing the importance of the minimum requirements, because if the conflicting evaluations are reasonable, then they presuppose that the minimum requirements have been met.

And, of course, beyond the minimum requirements, the conflicts will not only be between moral evaluations but also between moral and non-moral evaluations, as well as between contrary moral, personal, political, and religious evaluations. If moral evaluations go beyond the minimum requirements and concern such matters as keeping promises, paying debts, being honest, kind, and just, then it will often happen that in particular contexts non-moral evaluations, such as medical or national emergencies, economic collapse, war, or the dictates of religious faith, will conflict with moral ones, and the prevailing circumstances may sometimes reasonably require overriding moral evaluations.

It adds to the complexity of conflicts between evaluations that even the acknowledged good of meeting the minimum requirements of the human good may be overridden. Heroes, martyrs, explorers, soldiers, police officers, firefighters, construction workers, researchers, and athletes may knowingly accept the possibility of injury and death in the line of duty, or for the sake of their ideal, or to save or protect the lives of others. When they do that, they put the minimum requirements of their own good at risk, and they may be rightly honored for acting on some evaluation that leads them to override the minimum requirements. Their reason for doing this need not be moral. They may be guided by a personal, political, or religious ideal, or by physical challenge that tests their courage and endurance, or by curiosity about the unknown, or by boredom, a sense of adventure, a desire to extend the reach of their imagination, or to probe the limits of human possibilities.

Such derring-do of course endangers the minimum requirements of their own good, but if they do it knowingly, aware of the risks, and accept that they may fail and seriously or fatally incapacitate themselves, then they have reasons for it. If they have weighed the contrary reasons against it, and in a cool moment decided that the reason for it are stronger than the reasons against it, then they may reasonably accept evaluations that override the evaluations that favor meeting the minimum requirements of their own good.

These reasons may extend also to endangering the minimum requirements of the human good of others, such as those of physicians and surgeons, rock climbers, spelunkers, and deep-sea divers who routinely and often reasonably put at risk the lives, health, and security of others who depend on them. And, of course, the same is reasonably done to enemy soldiers, violent criminals, terrorists, and other aggressors.

I conclude that moral evaluations may or may not be overriding, not even when the minimum requirements of the human good are at stake because there is a plurality of reasonable ideals of the human good that may involve risking and possibly violating these requirements. Reason may allow, although not require, us to accept any of these reasonable ideals. Whether or not we accept them depends on who we are, on what personal attitude motivates how we think we should live, on the various evaluations that have formed us, and on the circumstances and the evaluative framework of the context in which we live.

This assumes that the ideals are reasonable, but of course they may not be. They may fail to take into account readily available facts, or the predictable consequences, or how their pursuit is likely to affect the agent and others, or their acceptance and pursuit may be motivated by self-deception, stupidity, fantasy, or malignant or cynical destructiveness. And then they should not be accepted. Nevertheless, many of them are reasonable, and they may be reasonable even if they involve the pursuit of a moral, personal, political, or religious ideals that endanger the minimum requirements of the human good. Ideals of the human good can go wrong in countless ways and for countless reasons. The reasons for protecting the minimum requirements of the human good are in most cases strong, but not always conclusive.

I turn now to considering conflicts between moral and non-moral evaluations that meet the minimum requirements. If they conflict, should moral evaluation always override non-moral evaluations? Cato's answer is that they should; Montaigne's is that they sometimes should but at other times should not. Cato was a moralist; Montaigne a realist. I find their lives fascinating, but the main reason for discussing them is not that, but that thinking about the kind of persons they were and what they did can help us reflect critically on our own answers to the hard question, when it arises in our context, of whether moral evaluations should always be overriding.

CATO: THE MORALIST

Marcus Porcius Cato was born in 95 BC and died in 46 BC.[92] His years coincide with the last years of the Roman Republic, which came to an end when Julius Caesar seized power. Cato was born into one of the lesser ruling families, whose most prominent member was his great-grandfather, also named Cato. The older Cato was an exceptional figure in Roman politics, an exemplar of civic virtue in a corrupt society. The younger Cato, our present concern, admired the elder and modeled his entire life on him. From childhood on he was of

> inflexible temper, unmoved by any passion, and firm in every-
> thing. He was resolute in his purposes. . . . He was rough and
> ungentle toward those who flattered him, and still more un-
> yielding to those who threatened him. . . . He was dull, and slow
> to apprehend . . . but he would also ask the reason, and inquire the
> cause of everything (918). He . . . devoted himself to the study,
> above everything, of moral and political doctrine . . . [led] by a
> kind of inspiration for the pursuit of every virtue, yet . . . most
> of all . . . [for] that steady and inflexible justice which is not to
> be wrought by favour or compassion (920) . . . [He] habituated
> himself to go bareheaded in the hottest and the coldest weather,
> and to walk on foot at all seasons . . . the customs and manners
> manners of men at that time so corrupt, and reformation in them
> so necessary, that he thought it requisite, in many things, to go
> contrary to the ordinary way of the world (921).

92. I have discussed Cato before in *Enjoyment* (Oxford: Clarendon Press, 2008), chapter 10. I draw on but go much beyond of what I say there. The cited passages are from Plutarch, "Cato the Younger" in *The Lives of the Noble Grecians and Romans*, trans. John Dryden, rev. Arthur Hugh Clough (New York: Random House, c.100 AD/1932).

Cato was first elected tribune and later appointed to command troops. He showed great bravery in the fighting. In clothing, diet, and mode of travel he was like a common soldier, not as the ranking officer he in fact was. Cato was well on his way to becoming a Stoic saint: severe, formidable, and feared rather than liked.

> Cato's virtue looked like a kind of ecstasy . . . in the cause of what was good and just (932).

He was elected quaestor, which put him in charge of Rome's treasury. It was an office with even greater than the usual scope for corruption, but Cato alone in public life was scrupulously honest. He was unintimidated by threats of physical violence. He was neither bribable nor would he bribe others, both of which were accepted standard practices in Rome, generally regarded as we do fees, rather than as bribes. He was tireless and eloquent in defending the laws of Rome, even though others paid only lip service to them. And he was indifferent to how powerful were those whose interests would have been served by violating them.

In this manner, he pitted himself against the centuries-old political arrangements that made Rome great, and against Caesar, Crassus, and Pompey, the most powerful and richest men in Rome. They were the ones who came later to form the Triumvirate, whose disintegration led first to the civil war and later to the fall of the Republic and the reign of Caesar. Cato had only eloquence and uncompromising moral certainty on his side. At every opportunity, Cato was led as it were by inspiration [and] foretold all the miseries that afterwards befell the state (942).

But his warnings were not heeded. When it became clear that Caesar could be stopped only by civil war, if at all,

> from that day he never cut his hair, nor shaved his beard, nor wore a garland, but was always full of sadness, grief, and dejectedness for the calamities of his country (948).

Nor did he hesitate to tell his countrymen that he told them so:

> If you had believed me, or regarded my advice, you would not
> now have been reduced to stand in fear of one man (947).

His defense of the laws of Rome failed, and the old political system
was replaced by the rule of men who struggled for power and waged
civil war in order to attain it.

Cato was forced to take side, and he chose the side of Pompey
against Caesar because he believed that the interests of the Republic
and the laws were less threatened by Pompey than by Caesar.
Nevertheless Caesar prevailed, and Cato, in charge of the remnant of
an army loyal to the Republic, made his last stand in Africa. Caesar's
military genius and superior forces led to victory, and Cato knew that
the Republic was lost. Caesar's generosity to his defeated enemies
was well known by everyone, but Cato

> resolved on his own death (955) ... I would not be beholden to
> a tyrant for his acts of tyranny. For it is usurpation in him to save,
> as their rightful lord, the lives of men over whom he has no title
> to reign (956) ... he did not confess to any defeat in all his life,
> but rather ... he had got the victory, and had conquered Caesar
> in all points of justice and honesty (955).

And so we come to the gruesome end of his life. He stabbed himself with his sword, but his hand was injured in the last battle and he
could not aim properly, cut himself open, and in fact disemboweled
himself, much as the samurai did in committing hara-kiri. He

> lay weltering in his blood, great part of his bowels out of his body,
> but himself still alive and able to look at them. . . . [A] physician
> went to him . . . put in his bowels . . . and sewed up the wound.

... [But Cato] thrust away the physician, plucked his bowels, and tearing open the wound ... expired (777).

Cato died as he had lived, intransigently, willfully pitting himself against the world he regarded as corrupt, and uncompromisingly committed to living and acting in the way he regarded as right. He was immoderate in everything, including in virtue.

Extramarital sex and adultery were customary but not for Cato. When he married his first wife, she was his first sexual contact, and after their two children were born, he put her away (we are not told how) for misconduct. Then he married his second wife but gave her away to a man who needed her more than he, but the man died, and Cato took his ex-wife back to keep his house (921, 931). He suspected the rectitude of his wives, acquaintances, and all public figures. Not surprisingly, he had no lovers or friends. His personal relationships were at best frigid.

In public life, he was a scourge of bribery, but he did not hesitate to approve of bribery for the sake of enacting laws he regarded as good. He used lesser illegality in order to oppose what he regarded as greater, and he violated his own avowed principle not to break the laws which he sought to defend (945, 951). Whatever he did publicly or privately, he overdid. He was not content with being virtuous; he went to extremes, as he did in his austerity. He always dressed in black, wore the same clothes in heat and cold, and walked barefooted. He ate simply and drank hardly at all. It was not enough for him to cultivate excessive self-denial. He thought that everyone should do the same, and he was contemptuous of those who did not.

He absolutely refused to support political compromises that might have avoided the civil war. And he ignored the plain fact that the corruption he feared had for centuries permeated the political system he had fought to defend in the civil war that destroyed the very system he was concerned with defending. Nor did he acknowledge that Caesar, whose rule he adamantly opposed, was a kinder and far more prudent ruler than any of the alternatives, as well as an incomparable military genius whose services Rome badly needed.

Cato was blinded to all these considerations and to his own inconsistency by dogmatic moralism. It led him to scorn the reasonable personal, political, and religious evaluations on which everything he claimed to value depended. He was a fanatic, and fanaticism is never a virtue. He thought that what he regarded as the right moral evaluations should always override all non-moral evaluations that conflict with them, regardless of what the facts happened to be and what consequences were likely to follow. He had the absolute conviction that his moral evaluations were right and all conflicting moral and non-moral evaluations were wrong.

I am not alone in having an equivocal attitude to Cato's life and actions. Plutarch writing about the politics of Rome concluded that

Cato ... was by nature unfit for the business (946).

Cicero complained that

Cato speaks as if he was dealing with the ideal commonwealth of Plato, not with our corrupt and decadent Rome.[93]

Montaigne wrote that

it would perhaps be more wisely done to lower your head and give a little ... to make the laws will what they can do, since they cannot do what they will . . . there is much more fortitude in wearing out the chain that binds us than in breaking it, and more proof of strength. . . . It is lack of judgment and patience that

93. Quoted in Charles Oman, *Seven Roman Statesmen* (New York: Longmans, 1902), 216.

hastens our pace . . . [Cato's] inimitable straining for virtue that astounds us [was] severe to the point of being troublesome.[94]

We can learn from reflecting on Cato's life and actions the importance of recognizing our own fallibility and questioning both our own evaluations and the ones that are generally accepted in the context in which we live. The resulting personal attitude need not be one of dithering uncertainty, although even that is better than the sort of fanatical certainty that motivated Cato and other ideological, nationalist, and religious dogmatists who knew what the human good was and were convinced that they must pursue it at all costs. A reasonable alternative to hesitant uncertainty and dogmatic certainty is the realistic attitude. Montaigne is one of its notable representatives.

MONTAIGNE: THE REALIST

Montaigne is one of my favorite writers.[95] I have discussed him several times before in other books and I cannot avoid repeating here some of what I wrote before. He was born in 1533 into a Gascon Catholic family of lesser nobility. He was trained in the law, and, at the age of twenty-four (not unusual for that time) became a councilor in the Parlement of Bordeaux and acted as a magistrate. After thirteen years of service, Montaigne retired to his estate where he intended to read and reflect. He began to record his thoughts in a form that eventually became the *Essays*. Two years later he was called out of retirement to act as a mediator between the warring Catholics and Protestants of France. As a moderate Catholic and an experienced

94. Michel Montaigne, *Essays* in *The Complete Works of Montaigne*, trans. Donald M. Frame (Stanford, CA: Stanford University Press, 1588/1943), 89, 253, 851.
95. All quoted passages are from Montaigne's *Essays*.

man of affairs, he was acceptable to both parties. He was intermit-tently engaged in this for four years. When he was forty-seven, the first edition of the *Essays*, containing Books 1 and 2, appeared. It was well received. Montaigne then traveled for almost two years. In his absence, he was elected Mayor of Bordeaux, a prestigious office he did not seek and accepted only reluctantly. When his two-year term came to an end, he was given the rare honor of a second term. After which he once again took up residence on his estate, finished Book 3 of the *Essays* and kept revising the first two books.

The three books were first published together when he was fifty-one. He continued to revise them until he died a few months before his sixtieth birthday. He was regarded as a wise and learned man, an eminent scholar, and a distinguished public servant. French society was just as corrupt as Cato's Rome, and it, too, was riven by civil war. He, like Cato, often had to choose between conflicting moral and non-moral evaluations. But unlike Cato, he did it prudently and set an example that inspired many throughout the ages.

Montaigne had no illusions about the context in which he lived.

> In every government there are necessary offices which are not only abject but also vicious. Vices find their place in it and are employed for sewing our society together ... The public welfare requires that a man betray and lie and massacre (600)....Whoever escapes with clean breeches from handling the affairs of this world, escapes by miracle.... Whoever boasts, in a sick age like this, that he employs a pure and sincere virtue in the service of the world, either does not know what virtue is ... or, if he does know, he boasts wrongly, and, say what he will, does a thousand things of which his con-science accuses him (759). Consider the form of this justice that governs us: it is a true testimony of human imbecility, so full it is of contradiction and error.... How many condemnations I have seen more criminal than the crime! (819–820).

This was then and remains still a realistic view of what politics is like in a sick society. And we may reflect on whether ours is very different from it. Montaigne faced the truth about his society, obfuscated nothing, and pretended to no great virtue. He saw that conflicts between virtues and vices, pure and corrupt motives, good and bad reasons occur between and within all the various modes of evaluation, and that conflicts between moral and political evaluations may sometimes in some circumstances be reasonably resolved in favor of the political ones. This is because, as Montaigne said about his own society,

> our morals are extremely corrupt, and lean with a remarkable inclination toward the worse; of our laws and customs, many are barbarous and monstrous; however, because of the difficulty of improving our condition and the danger of everything crumbling into bits . . . the worst thing I find in our state is instability. . . . It is very easy to accuse the government of imperfections, for all mortal things are full of it. . . . But as for establishing a better state in place of the one they ruined, many of those who have attempted it have achieved nothing for their pains (497–498).

Why have they failed? Because supposing, as Cato did, that moral evaluations should always override conflicting non-moral evaluations relies on moral evaluations that may also be a mixture of virtues and vices, purity and corruption, good and bad reasons. Relying on them may just exacerbate the mistakes of the already mistaken moral evaluations. Montaigne regretted that this was so, but he saw no alternative to it. Cato railed against immorality, but he made matters worse by hastening the disintegration of the society he was concerned with defending, fomenting the instability caused by the civil war, and, incidentally, resulting in his own hideous death. If he had at least tried to be as realistic as Montaigne was, he might have ameliorated some of the worst that ensued.

What alternative, then, does the realistic view of Montaigne suggest? It suggests that if we live in a society many of whose evaluations are mistaken—and which society is entirely exempt from such mistakes?—we should understand that

the justest party is still a member of a worm-eaten maggoty body. But in such a body the least diseased member is called healthy; and quite rightly, since our qualities have no title except by comparison. Civic innocence is measured according to the places and the times (760).

If we manage to arrive at such understanding of the evaluative framework of our own context, the framework that has partly made us who we are, what can we do then? Montaigne answered that question as well. Such understanding, he thought, involved the realization that

things in themselves have their own weights and measures and qualities; but once inside . . . health, conscience, authority, knowledge, riches, beauty, and their opposites—all are stripped on entry and receive . . . new clothing, and coloring . . . and which each individual chooses . . .each one is queen in her realm. Wherefore let us no longer make the external qualities of things our excuse; it is up to us to reckon them as we will (220).

Montaigne recognized that the evaluative framework of the context in which we live inevitably influence us. But he denied that this is the end of the matter. We can often rely on our personal attitude to guide how we respond to these evaluations and how we resolve conflicts between them. We cannot be free of the evaluative framework that has influenced us, but we can impose on the evaluations that follow from it our own sense of importance that reflects our personal attitude to how we think we should live, given the context and the circumstances in which we find ourselves. In order to be able to do this

> we must reserve a back shop all our own, entirely free, in which we establish our real liberty and our principal retreat.... Here our ordinary conversation must be between us and ourselves... here we must talk and laugh. . . . We have a soul that can be turned upon itself... it can keep itself company (177).

He knew and did not mind that this is contrary to

> the common attitude and habit . . . of looking elsewhere than at ourselves . . . we are an object that fills us with discontent. . . . In order not to dishearten us Nature has very appropriately thrown our vision outward. We go forward with the current . . . to turn backward toward ourselves is a painful movement. . . . We are all steeped in it, one as much as another, but those who are aware of it are a little better off (766).

They are a little better off because they can realize that it is

> an absolute perfection and virtually divine to know how to enjoy our being rightfully. We seek other conditions because we do not understand the use of our own, and go outside of ourselves because we do not know what it is like inside. Yet there is no use our mounting on stilts, for on stilts we must still walk on our own legs. And on the loftiest throne in the world we are still sitting on our own rump (857).

But even if we manage the remarkable feat of approximating this ideal, we must still live in the world, if we live at all. And the question remains how best we can do that without violating the personal attitude we have formed in our back shop. Montaigne's answer is that

> the virtue assigned to the affairs of the world is a virtue with many bends, angles, and elbows, so as to join and adapt itself to human weakness; mixed and artificial, not straight, clean, constant, or purely innocent. . . .He who walks in the crowd must step aside, keep his elbows in, step back or advance, even leave the straight way, according to what he encounters. He must live not so much . . . what he proposes to himself but according to what others propose to him, according to the time, according to the men, according to the business (758).

Cato scorned this, and thereby he scorned realism and compromise, the indispensable requirements of stable and peaceful social life. Montaigne saw that we should participate in public life, perform appropriate services, and yet do so only as far as it does not prevent us from going against our personal attitude. The services we owe to our society are

> limited and conditional . . . I do not want to be considered either so affectionate or so loyal a servant as to be found fit to betray anyone. . . . There is no remedy. I frankly tell them my limits. This whole procedure of mine is just a bit dissonant from our ways. It would not be fit to produce great results. . . . And so public occupations are by no means my quarry; what my profession requires, I perform in the most private manner that I can (603).

But we can do this and be satisfied with our personal attitude only if we know how to enjoy our being rightfully, walk on our own legs, not on stilts, and sit on our own rump, not on committee chairs. Cato did not know it, Montaigne did. If our own Catos knew it, our public life would be less fraught with perfervid moralists who propose yet another ideal theory commitment to which makes them unwilling to seek a realistic compromise with those who doubt their certainties.

THE VALUE OF CONFLICTS

According to Iris Murdoch:[96]

Man is a creature who makes pictures of himself and then comes to resemble the picture. This is the process which moral philosophy must attempt to describe and analyse.

Years later, having followed her prescribed description and analysis, she concluded that the true picture we should try to resemble is of the

Good as absolute . . . the principle which creatively relates the virtues to each other in our moral lives. . . . The sovereign Good . . . [which] is clearly seen and indubitably discovered in our ordinary unmysterious experience . . . the positive experience of truth . . . which remains with us as a standard or vision, an *orientation, a proof* of what is possible.[97]

In words similar to those of the first passage I have just cited, Strawson writes:[98]

96. Iris Murdoch, "Metaphysics and Ethics" in *Existentialists and Mystics* (New York: Allen Lane, 1957/1998), 75.
97. Iris Murdoch, "Metaphysics: A summary" in *Metaphysics as a Guide to Morals* (London: Chatto & Windus, 1992), 507–508.
98. Peter Strawson, "Social Morality and Individual Ideal" in *Freedom and Resentment* (London: Methuen, 1974), 26.

Men make for themselves pictures of ideal forms of life. Such pictures are various and may be in sharp opposition to each other, and one and the same individual may be captivated by different and sharply conflicting pictures at different times.

He agrees that we should aim to understand the conflicting pictures we are captivated by, but he does not think that there is a picture of the sovereign and true Good:

the region of the ethical is the region where there truths but no truth (29).

By the ethical, he means all the various evaluations, which is what I mean by the evaluative framework. This is one of that crucially important disagreements about how we should live. I have argued in various ways throughout the book, in agreement with Murdoch and Strawson, for recognizing the importance of understanding the pictures we make—pictures that partly form our personal attitude. But I have also disagreed with Murdoch's view and agreed with Strawson's that we should not formulate a personal attitude that aims at an ideal picture of the one and only true Good. There is no such Good, although there are many goods. The pictures we make and the good we may aim at are many and conflicting.

However, I want to add to what Strawson says that it is not only the individual ideals of personal attitudes that may sharply conflict but also the various evaluations that comprise evaluative frameworks. And since personal attitudes and particular evaluations jointly form the evaluative framework of life in a particular context at a particular time, conflicts are unavoidable parts of it.

These conflicts are threefold: between various ideals of how we should live, given the persons we are and the possibilities available in our context; between moral, personal, political, religious, and other evaluations within the evaluative framework; and between personal attitudes and the evaluations that make the prevailing evaluative framework what it is. Struggling with such conflicts is an unavoidable part of life in a society that recognizes the plurality of personal attitudes and the evaluations of the evaluative framework.

Might these conflicts not be resolved by rejecting evaluations that fail to meet some requirements that all reasonable evaluations must either meet or be rightly overridden by other evaluations? There are such requirements, but they are so obvious as to be hardly worth mentioning. Evaluations should take into account the relevant facts, be logically consistent, remain open to criticism, explain why they should be accepted, and why the consequences of following them are in some sense better than the consequences of not following them.

In normal circumstances, in the absence of dire emergencies, all the long-standing and conflicting moral, personal, political, and religious evaluations of a stable society typically meet such basic requirements. The question is whether there are requirements beyond these obvious ones that could be appealed to resolve conflicts between evaluations.

It has been widely supposed that relying on what has been called the "all things considered" approach can resolve such conflicts.[99] The guiding idea of it is that when all the complexities of the conflicting evaluations and the context in which they occur are taken into account, we can rely on reason to evaluate the relative importance of the various conflicting considerations. If this were right, then the consideration of all things would be the long-sought universally applicable, context-independent evaluation on which we could rely to resolve conflicts between other evaluations. It is thought that this would be a

99. For surveys, discussions, and bibliography, see *The Oxford Handbook of Rationality*, eds. Alfred R. Mele and Piers Rawling (New York: Oxford University Press, 2004) and *Ethics and Practical Reason*, eds. Garrett Cullity and Beryl Gaut (Oxford: Clarendon Press, 1997).

purely formal approach that could be relied on to resolve all conflicts between all evaluations regardless of what they happen to be.

The problem is that such an approach is impossible. In the first place, all things cannot be considered because their number is infinite. The approach, therefore, must be to consider all relevant things. But what considerations are relevant depends on whether their relevance is evaluated from a moral, personal, political, religious, or some other point of view. And what is and is not relevant depends on the kind of evaluation from whose point of view we are considering things. Disputes about the relative importance of conflicting evaluations cannot be reasonably resolved by a formal and context-independent approach that by its very nature abstracts from what the facts, evaluations, and contexts are. It cannot be reasonable to ignore the changing circumstances that affect the relative importance of conflicting evaluations. There can be no formal and context-independent point of view from which it could be reasonably decided what the most important kind of evaluation is, say, of AIDS, immigration, pornography, public health, scarcity, terrorism, trade, or war. The "all things considered approach" cannot answer such questions because it is committed to be context-independent and formal.

If the great plurality of conflicting evaluations of what is and is not relevant is recognized, it becomes obvious that relevance depends on the context in which the conflicts occur. It makes a great difference whether it is peace or war, poverty or prosperity, revolution or reform, democracy or dictatorship, and so forth. The relevance of considerations depends on whether the evaluation is of the relative importance of works of art vs. improving living standards, space exploration vs. urban renewal, raising educational standards vs. crime prevention. And the same is true of the evaluation of bankruptcy, drug addiction, euthanasia, pedophilia, prostitution, and so on and on. The consideration of all that is relevant cannot depend on a formal approach that could be used in all contexts to resolve conflicts between all evaluations. The search for it is a persistent but unfulfill-able yearning that the human condition should be free from conflicts. As Stuart Hampshire rightly put it:[100]

> Neither in the social order, nor in the experience of an individual, is a state of conflict the sign of vice, or defect, or a malfunctioning. It is not a deviation from the normal state of a city or of a nation, and it is not a deviation from the normal course of a person's experience. To follow through the ethical implications of these propositions about the normality of conflict, these Heracleitean truths, a kind of moral conversion is needed.

The conversion involves abandoning the yearning for a context-independent formal approach to resolving conflicts between evaluations that do meet elementary requirements of all ideals of the human good. And it involves also recognizing that if we accept the plurality of evaluations, then we will not think of conflicts between them as obstacles to living as we think we should, but as catalysts that make us think about what our relative priorities are, what possibilities we have available, and what limits we should not transgress. If we do this reasonably and honestly, we eventually arrive at a personal attitude we think we should be guided by, given our experiences, preferences, commitments, personal relationships, and the context in which we live.

Deliberating about this need not be a conscious articulate pro-cess. It may be no more than a tacit decision to continue an inherited or a long-ago acquired way of living. Or it may be to resolve to change in piecemeal or radical ways some aspect of the not wholly satisfying life we presently have. Or it may be no more than the result of having found a way of living that we believe and feel is right for us, a way that

100. Stuart Hampshire, *Justice Is Conflict* (Princeton, NJ: Princeton University Press, 2000), 33–34.

satisfies our most important desires, and one that we hope will continue in the future.

The personal attitude we arrive at may be mistaken for various reasons. Our beliefs, emotions, and desires that motivate us may be internally inconsistent, impractical, or unsuitable given our capacities or incapacities. Or it may be injurious to those we love and to whom we should be loyal. Or the ubiquity of conflicts may unsettle the context in which we live and the resulting turmoil will unavoidably affect us. We are always at risk because both we and the circumstances of life in our context are always changing in great or small ways, and both the prevailing evaluations and our own evaluations may be mistaken. But there is no reasonable alternative to doing the best we can in our context to come as close as we can to living as we think we should.

THE ANSWER

I have been arguing that a reasonable approach to coping with conflicts must be context-dependent and particular. It may warrant us in concluding that one of the conflicting evaluations should be overriding, but it remains an open question of whether the same evaluation should be overriding in another context. Facts, reasons, evaluations, and consequences vary and change, as contexts change. As a result, no particular evaluation should *always* override other evaluations, not even if the evaluation is moral. No doubt, moral evaluations are *sometimes* overriding, especially when the minimum requirements of the human good are affected by the consequences of the conflict-resolution. But other, non-moral, evaluations may also be concerned with the minimum requirements. Civil unrest, emergencies, disasters, epidemics, scarcity of much needed resources, war, and serious dissatisfaction with the status quo may make it reasonable to override moral evaluations even if it involves the violation of the minimum requirements of the good of some people, among whom we may be one. Reason does not require that when a moral evaluation conflicts with a non-moral evaluation, then the moral evaluation should always override the non-moral one, regardless of the relative importance of the conflicting evaluations.

The answer, then, to the hard question "Should moral evaluations be overriding?" is that they should sometimes in some contexts be overriding, but they should not be always overriding. And conflicts between evaluations will persist even after the facts, the evaluations, the consequences, and the context have been considered. At that point, we cannot do better than evaluate the reasons for and against the conflicting evaluations and resolve their conflict as it seems most reasonable in the context. Certainty will elude us. We can do no better than to do the best we can in the circumstances in which we find ourselves.

I shall conclude this subject with observing, that, although virtue be undoubtedly the best choice, when it is attainable; yet such is the disorder and confusion of human affairs, that no perfect or regular distribution of happiness and misery is ever, in this life, to be expected. Not only the goods of fortune, and the endowments of the body (both of which are important), not only these advantages, I say, are unequally divided between the virtuous and the vicious, but even the mind itself partakes, in some degree, of this disorder, and the most worthy character, by the very constitution of the passions, enjoys not the highest felicity. . . . In a word, human life is more governed by fortune than by reason . . . and is more influenced by particular humour, than by general principles. . . . To reduce life to exact rule and method, is commonly a painful and fruitless occupation.[101]

101. David Hume, "The Sceptic" in Essays, Moral, Political, and Literary, ed. Eugene F. Miller (Indianapolis: LibertyClassics, 1777/1985), 178 and 180.

Chapter 12

Conclusion

I have been explaining and defending a particular approach to finding reasonable answers to hard questions. I cannot prove that it is the best approach, but I hope to have shown that it is better than the alternatives I have discussed. According to it, the hard questions are hard because reasonable answers to them conflict, and their conflicts are evaluative, context-dependent, particular, unavoidable, and recurrent parts of our condition. They make us uncertain about how to resolve conflicts between reasonable answers to the hard questions we face. But the conflicts are not only obstacles. They are also catalysts that prompt us to become critical and examine our reasons for or against the conflicting answers.

The preceding chapters show that we can resolve these conflicts by comparing the answers available in our context with others drawn from anthropological, historical, and literary contexts. The comparisons allow us to reject the mistaken assumption that we must either seek the one and only reasonable answer that aims at *the good* or accept that our answers are ultimately arbitrary. It is not true that either we are guided by

the reality of goodness . . . which everyone, whatever their temperament, is after, and which is the goal of their activities[102]

102. Plato, *Republic*, trans. Robin Waterfield (Oxford: Oxford University Press, c.380/ 1993) 505e.

or we end up with no reasonable answer because

> If I have exhausted the justifications I have reached bedrock, and my spade is turned. Then I am inclined to say: "This is simply what I do."[103]

The alternative is to recognize that reasonable answers vary with contexts and depend on our personal attitude, the prevailing evaluative framework, and social and personal circumstances. Nevertheless, in most contexts and conditions there are reasonable answers. Some among them are more, others less reasonable, and we can often tell which is which. Reasonable ones are context-dependent and particular but are none the worse for that. They may aim at *a* good, but not at *the good*. And they need not be arbitrary, because we often have good reasons to be critical of what we have been doing even after we have exhausted our justifications for it.

One advantage of the approach I have followed throughout the book is that we can rely on it to compare our context-dependent answers with the answers others gave in other contexts. By understanding why their answers were better or worse, we can understand how we might give better answers in our context. Ours are better or worse depending on whether they enable us to form a reasonable attitude to absolute value, conformity, civic obligation, justice, evil, forgiveness, shame, being true to ourselves, good intentions, and morality that helps rather than hinders our efforts to live as we think we should.

Another advantage of the comparative approach is that it enlarges our view of the possibilities of life. It shows us that our

---

103. Ludwig Wittgenstein, *Philosophical Investigations*, trans. G.E.M. Anscombe (Oxford: Blackwell, 1986), 217.

moral, personal, political, religious, and other evaluations do not exhaust our possibilities. We can broaden and deepen our evaluations by understanding how others in other contexts have evaluated their possibilities. And that provides us with an external vantage point from which we can examine and perhaps become critical of the range of possible answers we have been, or might have been, giving to hard questions. We do not have to choose between continuing the futile search for *the good* and accepting that our answers are ultimately arbitrary. We can accept instead that there often are several reasonable answers and that they are context dependent and may be individually variable.

In the preceding chapters I have shown again and again how we can find them. We can learn from the better and worse ways in which the older and younger Eleazar, Bartleby and Sarpi, the Kamikaze and the Draftee, Creon, Antigone, and the Sherpa, Anna and the Priest, Vere and Speer, the Queen and Hester, the Colonel and Peter, Mochulsky and Gerstein, and Cato and Montaigne answered the hard questions that they faced. And we can learn also why the reasons of one in each pair were better, often much better, than the reasons of the other.

I borrow the template for this approach from the redolent French word "terroir." It stands for a central feature of wine making. It originally referred to the soil, but its meaning has been gradually extended to include the complex combination of the condition of the grapes, microclimates, the quantity and frequency of precipitation, irrigation, and intensity of days of sunshine, the chemicals used, the insects that harm or improve the grapes, the timing of harvest, the barreling and maturing of the wine, and the evaluations by the vintner of the relative importance of these interdependent conditions. Of course these conditions vary from year to year. The art of wine making—the art (!) not the science—is to assign the right degree of importance in any given year to these various conditions. The aim, of course, is to end up with an excellent vintage. But that depends on the conditions and on the experience and practical know-how of the vintner.

And so it is with what we may call the art of life, which is not a science either. It also depends on attributing the right degree of importance to the manifold conditions that have formed us, made our personal and social circumstances what they are, and in terms of which we have to give, if we can, reasonable answers to the hard questions we face. The aim, of course, is to end up with as good a life as we can have, given the conditions, the context, and our experience and practical know-how.

The result is that some lives, like vintages, are good, some are bad, and many are middling. If we know what the conditions and the context are, we can tell what would make lives better or worse. And even if it is formidably difficult to evaluate what makes a life in its entirety good or bad, it is not hard to evaluate what makes it better or worse in particular respects. Loving relationships, interesting work, wholehearted and valued activities, good health, a sense of humor, adequate comfort, being glad of the outcome of the major decisions we have made, living without lasting depression, envy, grief, guilt, jealousy, or rage are among some of the conditions that make lives better and their lack make them worse. If these favorable conditions persist in a life, then they indicate that at least some of the hard questions have been reasonably answered.

Hankering after *the good* beyond such conditions is based on a mistaken expectation that reasonable adults should have left behind with adolescence. And it is mistaken as well to persevere in doing what we have been doing after we run out of reasons for it. If *the good* exists at all, it has yet to be found. And some of what we have been habitually doing without reasons are bad, and we should not be doing them.

I have stressed that if we follow this approach to finding reasonable answers to hard questions, we must rely on our personal attitude.

Even if we accept the guidance of a person, an ideal, a principle, or a theory, *we* have to decide whether to accept and follow it. It is true that what we decide depends on the conditions that have formed us. But we are still guided by our personal attitude to evaluate the relative importance we attribute to the great variety of these conditions. And for those evaluations we should have reasons, even if we know that both the evaluations and the reasons may be mistaken.

Relying on our personal attitude does not mean that anything we happen to believe, feel, or desire may be part of it. There are some basic and some formal requirements that must be met by all reasonable personal attitudes. The basic ones are the satisfaction of inescapable physical, psychological, and social needs. We may on occasion have reasons not to satisfy even them, but the unavoidable consequence of that is death or serious damage. Adverse social conditions or personal misfortune may have this effect, but the resulting death or damage cannot be part of a reasonable personal attitude.

The basic reasons set limits to what evaluations can be reasonable. The limits follow from human nature, and they are not arbitrary. We have many other needs we want to satisfy, but they are not basic. They are up to us and depend on the personal attitude we have. But the ones that concern the satisfaction of inescapable needs are not up to us. There also are some formal requirements that must be met by any reasonable personal attitude. They include logical consistency, the consideration of relevant facts, the explanation of why the reasons we accept are better than reasons we reject, and openness to serious criticisms.

Beyond these basic and formal requirements, however, we have many other substantive reasons for and against the particular moral, personal, political, religious, and other evaluations of the answers we might give to hard questions. But the reasons, evaluations, and answers we rightly or wrongly accept ultimately depend on our often faulty personal attitude formed of possibly false beliefs, misguided emotions, and dubious desires. Certainty will always elude our answers to hard questions.

The centrality of our personal attitude has two significant consequences. One is that there is a reasonable presumption in favor of living as the evaluations that follow from our personal attitude prompt us to do. By this I mean that we have good reasons to live that way unless there are better reasons against it. We may find such better reasons if our own criticisms, or those of others we respect, lead us to question the beliefs, emotions, and desires on which our personal attitude are partly based. And that attitude is reasonable only if our critical examination does not call into question the beliefs, emotions, and desires that make it what it is.

Another consequence is that, although our personal attitude may meet the basic and formal requirements, it may nevertheless conflict in several ways. Our beliefs, emotions, and desires may lead to conflicting evaluations; our evaluations may conflict with the evaluations that follow from the evaluative framework of our context; and the moral, personal, political, religious, and other evaluations that follow from the prevailing evaluative framework may also conflict with each other.

It is common in our everyday experiences that we have to cope with conflicting evaluations of each of these kinds. Their conflicts account for the hardness of the questions I have been discussing. The conflicts are between our own evaluations of how we think we should answer the hard questions we face. And however we resolve their conflicts, we must act contrary to some part of our own personal attitude, some of our own beliefs, emotions, and desires, or some of our moral, personal, political, religious, or other evaluations. This is why we find it hard to give reasonable answers to the hard questions to which such conflicting evaluations give rise. I tried to show throughout the book that the approach I have followed is a better way of finding reasonable answers than the alternatives to it.

Understanding why the hard questions are hard does not make it easier to resolve conflicts between the answers we might give to them. Some answers are more reasonable than others because they rely on a personal attitude and evaluative framework less encumbered by mistakes than others. The aim of the comparisons drawn in each chapter was to show why the answers of one in each of the compared pairs was more reasonable than of the other. By understanding why some of their reasons were better and the others worse, we can improve our answers. But we can do that only by the particular and context-dependent evaluation of their and our reasons for the answers. The reason for preferring the comparative approach to alternatives to it is that it enables us to explain how we can reasonably distinguish between better and worse reasons for our answers, why some of our reasons are better than the others, and what makes the reasonable resolution of conflicts between evaluations unavoidably particular and context-dependent.

If we follow this comparative approach, it becomes obvious why we should not think that final answers to hard questions have been found that reason requires everyone to accept. Nor should we think that all of our evaluations are ultimately arbitrary just because they are particular and context-dependent. It is not arbitrary to think that we can have reasons for and against the answers we give. We can derive these reasons from the critical examination of our personal attitude and evaluative framework. Both can be mistaken, and so can be our derivations. When it comes to hard questions, all answers, reasons, and evaluations are defeasible. That is why we should see our condition as an adventure in personal self-enactment. The self we enact may be defective, but, for better or worse, it is the only self we have. We have the best of reasons for trying to make it as little defective as we can.

WORKS CITED

Anscombe, G. E. M. *Intention*. Oxford: Blackwell, 1957.

Applebaum, Anne. *The Gulag: A History*. New York: Doubleday, 2003.

Aristotle. *Nicomachean Ethics*. In *The Complete Works of Aristotle*. Edited by Jonathan Barnes. Translated by W. D. Ross. Princeton, NJ: Princeton University Press, 1984.

Aron, Raymond. *The Opium of the Intellectuals*. Translated by Terence Kilmartin. New York: Norton, 1955/1962.

Berlin, Isaiah. "Two Concepts of Liberty." In *Four Essays on Liberty*. Oxford: Clarendon Press, 1969, 118–172.

Butler, Joseph. *Fifteen Sermons*. London: Bell & Sons, 1726/1953.

Cassinelli, C. W., and Robert B. Ekvall. *A Tibetan Principality*. Ithaca, NY: Cornell University Press, 1969.

Cavafy, C. P. *Collected Poems*. Translated by Edmund Keeley. Princeton, NJ: Princeton University Press, 1975.

Conquest, Robert. *The Great Terror: A Reassessment*. New York: Oxford University Press, 1990.

Cottingham, John. *Why Believe?* New York: Continuum, 2009.

Courtois, Stephanie, et al. *The Black Book of Communism*. Cambridge, MA: Harvard University Press, 1999.

Cullity, Garrett, and Beryl Gaut, eds. *Ethics and Practical Reason*. Oxford: Clarendon Press, 1997.

Deigh, John. "Shame and Self-Esteem." In *Ethics and Personality*. Edited by John Deigh. Chicago: University of Chicago Press, 1983/1992, 133–153.

Eliot, T. S. "Burnt Norton." In *The Complete Poems and Plays*. New York: Harcourt, 1971, 117–122.

Fest, Joachim C. *The Face of the Third Reich*. Translated by Michael Bullock. New York: Pantheon, 1963/1970.

Fest, Joachim. *Speer*. Translated by Ewald Osers and Alexandra Dring. New York: Harcourt, 1999/2001.

Frankfurt, H. G. *The Importance of What We Care About*. New York: Cambridge University Press, 1988.

Freud, Sigmund. *Civilization and Its Discontents*. Translated by James Strachey. New York: Norton, 1930/1961.

Friedlander, Saul. *Kurt Gerstein: The Ambiguity of Good*. Translated by Charles Fullman. New York: Knopf, 1967/1969.

Furer-Haimendorf, Christoph von. *The Sherpas of Nepal*. Berkeley: University of California Press, 1964.

Gilbert, Martin. *The Holocaust*. New York: Henry Holt, 1985.

Glover, Jonathan. *Humanity: A Moral History of the Twentieth Century*. New Haven, CT: Yale University Press, 1999.

Hampshire, Stuart. "Morality and Pessimism." In *Morality and Conflict*. Cambridge, MA: Harvard University Press, 1983, 82–100.

Hampshire, Stuart. *Justice Is Conflict*. Princeton, NJ: Princeton University Press, 2000.

Hampton, Jean, and Jeffrie G. Murphy. *Forgiveness and Mercy*. New York: Cambridge University Press, 1988.

Hawthorne, Nathaniel. *The Scarlet Letter*. New York: Dover, 1840/1994.

Hegel, G. F. W. *Reason in History*. Translated by R. S. Hartman. New York: Liberal Arts, 1840/1953.

Hegel, G. F. W. *The Phenomenology of Mind*. Translated by J. B. Baillie. New York: Harper, 1807/1967.

Herodotus. *The Histories*. Translated by Robin Waterfield. Oxford: Oxford University Press, 440 BC/1999.

Hobbes, Thomas. *Leviathan*. Edited by Richard Tuck. Cambridge, UK: Cambridge University Press, 1651/1991.

Hollander, Paul, ed. *From the Gulag to the Killing Fields*. Wilmington, DE: ISI, 2006.

Hughes, Paul M. "Forgiveness." In *Stanford Encyclopedia of Philosophy*. Edited by Edward N. Zalta. Stanford, CA: Stanford University Press. http://Plato.stanford.edu/entires/forgiveness/.

Hume, David. "Of the Protestant Succession." In *Essays, Moral, Political and Literary*. Edited by Eugene F. Miller. Indianapolis: Liberty Press, 1741/1985, 502–511.

Hume, David. "The Sceptic." In *Essays, Moral, Political, and Literary*. Edited by Eugene F. Miller. Indianapolis: Liberty Press, 1741/1985, 159–180.

Hume, David. *An Enquiry Concerning the Principles of Morals*. Edited by Tom L. Beauchamp. Oxford: Oxford University Press, 1751/1998.

Hume, David. *Dialogues Concerning Natural Religion*. Indianapolis: Hackett, 1779/1980.

Isenberg, Arnold. "Natural Pride and Natural Shame." In *Explaining Emotions*. Edited by Amelie Rorty. Berkeley, CA: University of California Press, 1980, 355–383.

James, William. "The Moral Philosopher and the Moral Life." In *William James: Writings 1878–1899*, Edited by Bruce Kuklick. New York: Library of America, 1992, 595–617.

Kant, Immanuel. *Groundwork of the Metaphysics of Moral.* Translated by Mary J. Gregor. In *Immanuel Kant: Practical Philosophy.* Cambridge, UK: Cambridge University Press, 1785/1966, 37–108.

Kant, Immanuel. *Religion Within the Bounds of Reason Alone.* Translated by Theodore M. Greene and Hoyt H. Hudson. New York: Harper & Row, 1794/1960.

Kant, Immanuel. *The Metaphysical Elements of Justice.* Translated by John Ladd. Indianapolis: Bobbs-Merrill, 1797/1965.

Kant, Immanuel. *The Metaphysics of Morals.* Translated by Mary Gregor. Cambridge, UK: Cambridge University Press, 1797/1996.

Keene, Donald. *Appreciations of Japanese Culture.* Tokyo: Kodansha International, 1971/1981.

Kekes, John. *Facing Evil.* Princeton, NJ: Princeton University Press, 1990.

Kekes, John. *The Roots of Evil.* Ithaca, NY: Cornell University Press, 2005.

Kekes, John. *How Should We Live?* Chicago: University of Chicago Press, 2014.

Kershaw, Ian. *Fateful Choices.* New York: Penguin, 2007.

Kitto, H. D. F. *Greek Tragedy.* London: Methuen, 1939.

Knox, Bernard M. *The Heroic Temper.* Berkeley: University of California Press, 1964.

Koestler, Arthur. *Arrival and Departure.* London: Hutchinson, 1943.

Korsgaard, Christine M. *Self-Constitution.* Oxford: Oxford University Press, 2009.

Lustig, Arnost. *Lovely Green Eyes.* Translated by Ewald Osers. New York: Arcade, 2000.

Lynd, Helen Merrell. *On Shame and the Search for Identity.* New York: Harcourt Brace, 1958.

Mele, Alfred R. and Piers Rawling, eds. *The Oxford Handbook of Rationality.* Oxford: Oxford University Press, 2004.

Melville, Herman. "Bartleby, The Scrivener." In *Herman Melville.* Edited by Harrison Hayford. New York: Library of America, 1853/2000, 639–678.

Melville, Herman. *Billy Budd, Sailor.* In *Herman Melville.* Edited by Harrison Hayford. New York: Library of America, 1843/2000, 1353–1435.

Mill, John Stuart. *A System of Logic. Collected Works of John Stuart Mill.* Edited by J. M. Robson. Indianapolis: Liberty Fund, 1843/2006, Vol. 7–8.

Mill, John Stuart. *On Liberty.* Indianapolis: Hackett, 1859/1978.

Mill, John Stuart. *Utilitarianism.* In *Collected Works of John Stuart Mill.* Edited by J. M. Robson. Indianapolis: Liberty Fund, 1843/2006, 203–259.

Mishima, Yukio. *The Way of the Samurai.* Translated by Kathryn Sparling. New York: Basic Books, 1967/1977.

Mochulsky, Fyodor Vasilevich. *Gulag Boss: A Soviet Memoir.* Translated by Deborah Kaple. New York: Oxford University Press, 1990/2012.

Montaigne, Michel. *The Complete Works of Montaigne.* Translated by Donald M. Frame. Stanford, CA: Stanford University Press, 1588/1943.

Morris, Herbert. "Guilt and Shame." In *On Guilt and Innocence*. Berkeley: University of California Press, 1976, 59–63.

Morris, Herbert. "Persons and Punishment." In *On Guilt and Innocence*. Berkeley: University of California Press, 1976, 31–88.

Morris, Ivan. *The Nobility of Failure*. New York: Farrar, Straus and Giroux, 1975.

Murdoch, Iris. "Metaphysics and Ethics." In *Existentialists and Mystics*. New York: Allen Lane, 1957/1998, 59–75.

Murdoch, Iris. "Metaphysics: A Summary." In *Metaphysics as a Guide to Morals*. London: Chatto & Windus, 1992, 504–512.

Murphy, Jeffrie G. "Forgiveness." In *Encyclopedia of Ethics*. Edited by Lawrence C. Becker and Charlotte B. Becker. New York: Routledge, 2001, Vol. 1, 561–562.

Murphy, Jeffrie G. *Getting Even*. Oxford: Oxford University Press, 2003.

Nietzsche, Friedrich. *Beyond Good and Evil*. In *Basic Writings of Nietzsche*. Translated by Walter Kaufmann. New York: Modern Library, 1885/1966, 191–435.

Nietzsche, Friedrich. *The Gay Science*. Translated by Walter Kaufmann. New York: Vintage, 1882/1974.

Nietzsche, Friedrich. *Twilight of the Idols*. In *The Portable Nietzsche*. Translated by Walter Kaufmann, New York: Penguin Press, 1959, 463–563.

Oakeshott, Michael. *On Human Conduct*. Oxford: Clarendon Press, 1975.

O'Hagan, Timothy. *Rousseau*. London: Routledge, 1999.

Oakeshott, Michael. *The Voice of Liberal Learning*. Edited by Timothy Fuller. New Haven, CT: Yale University Press, 1989.

Ohnuki-Tierney, Emiko. *Kamikaze Diaries*. Chicago: University of Chicago Press, 2006.

Oman, Charles. *Seven Roman Statesmen*. New York: Longmans, 1902.

Paul, Robert A. "Act and Intention in Sherpa Culture and Society." In *Other Intentions: Cultural Context and the Attribution of Inner States*. Edited by Lawrence Rosen. Santa Fe, NM: School of American Research Press, 1995, 15–45.

Paul, Robert A. "The Place of the Truth in Sherpa Law and Religion." *Journal of Anthropological Research* 33:2 (1977): 167–184.

Plantinga, Alvin, and Michael Tooley. *Knowledge of God*. Oxford: Blackwell, 2008.

Plato. *Republic*. Translated by Robin Waterfield. Oxford: Oxford University Press, 1993.

Plutarch. "Cato the Younger." In *The Lives of the Noble Grecians and Romans*. Translated by John Dryden, rev. Arthur Hugh Clough. New York: Random House, c.100 AD/1932.

Rawls, John. *A Theory of Justice*. Cambridge: Harvard University Press, 1971.

Reid, Thomas. *Essays on the Active Powers of the Human Mind*. Cambridge: MIT Press, 1813/1969.

Rousseau, Jean-Jacques. *Discourses on the Origin and Foundation of Inequality Among Man*. Translated by Donald A. Cress. Indianapolis: Hackett, 1754/1988.

Rousseau, Jean-Jacques, *Letter to Beaumont* in *Oeuvres completes*, 5 vols. Paris: Gallimard, 1959–95.

Schneewind, J.M., *The Invention of Autonomy*. New York: Cambridge University Press, 1998.

Sereny, Gitta, *Albert Speer: His Battle with Truth*. New York: Knopf, 1995.

Sophocles, *Antigone*. In *Three Theban Plays*. Translated by Robert Fagles. New York: Viking, c.441 BC/1982, 41–110.

Speer, Albert, *Inside the Third Reich*. London: Weidenfeld and Nicolson, 1970.

Stocker, Michael, *Valuing Emotions*. New York: Cambridge University Press, 1996.

Strawson, P.F. "Social Morality and Individual Ideal." In *Freedom and Resentment*. London: Methuen, 1974, 26–43.

Taylor, Charles, *The Ethics of Authenticity*. Cambridge: Harvard University Press, 1992.

Taylor, Gabrielle, *Pride, Shame and Guilt*. Oxford: Oxford University Press, 1985.

Velleman, J. David, "The Genesis of Shame." *Philosophy and Public Affairs* 30 (2001): 27–52.

Velleman, J. David, *Foundations of Moral Relativism*. OpenBook Publishers, 2015.

Williams, Bernard, "Introduction" *Concepts and Categories*, ed. Henry Hardy. London: Hogarth, 1978, xi–xviii.

Williams, Bernard, *Shame and Necessity*. Berkeley: University of California Press, 1993.

Williams, Bernard, *Truth and Truthfulness*. Princeton: Princeton University Press, 2002.

Williams, Bernard, "The Women of Trachis." In *The Sense of the Past*. Princeton: Princeton University Press, 2006, 49–59.

Wittgenstein, Ludwig, *Philosophical Investigations*. Translated by G.E.M. Anscombe. Oxford: Blackwell, 1958.

Wootton, David, *Paolo Sarpi*. Cambridge: Cambridge University Press, 1983.

INDEX